DAUGHTER OF T

DAUGHTER OF THE RIVER

AN AUTOBIOGRAPHY

HONG YING

BLOOMSBURY

First published as *Je'er de Nil'er* in 1997 by
Eyra Publishing House, Talpel, Taiwan
First published in Great Britain 1998
This paperback edition published 1999

Bloomsbury Publishing Plc,
38 Soho Square,
London W1V 5DF

A CIP catalogue record for this book is
available from the British Library

ISBN 0 7475 4405 0

10 9 8 7 6 5 4 3 2 1

Typeset by Hewer Text Ltd, Edinburgh
Printed in Great Britain by Clays Ltd, St Ives plc

For Shuhui Tang, my mother

ONE

1

I never bring up the subject of my birthday, not with my family and not with my closest friends. At first an intentional omission, eventually I truly forgot. No one remembered my birthday for my first eighteen years, and after that I simply avoided the issue. No mistake about it, it all happened in my eighteenth year.

The potholed street outside the school gate sloped to one side. As I crossed the street a shiver ran down my spine; someone was staring at me again, I could feel it.

Not daring to turn around, I glanced to the left and right, but saw nothing out of the ordinary. I forced myself to keep walking until I was standing next to an old lady who sold ice lollies, then took a quick look behind me, just as a Liberation-model truck whizzed past, splattering mud in its wake. A couple of youngsters buying ice lollies stamped their feet and hurled curses at the speeding truck for muddying their shorts and bare legs. The old lady dragged her box of ice lollies over to the base of the wall. Who the hell drives like that? she grumbled. Scurvy people like you would be turned away by the Four-Mile Crematorium.

Once the disturbance was past, quiet returned, and I stood in the middle of the muddy, rutted street wondering if I was imagining things because I'd talked so much today.

At some point as I was growing up, these shivers became a regular occurrence in my life, always caused by a pair of staring eyes. More than once I nearly spotted whoever was behind those eyes, but only for a fleeting moment. The man with nondescript features and messy hair never came close enough for me to get a good look at him, which was probably how he planned it. He only appeared near the schoolyard before and after school, and never actually followed me, as if he knew where I'd be from one minute to the next. All he had to do was wait.

We heard all sorts of frightening rumours about rapes, but I was never afraid that was what the man had in mind.

I never told my father or mother. What was there to tell? They might think I'd done something shameful and give me hell. So I kept this a secret for years, until eventually my fears vanished and there was no more mystery. Perhaps being stared at is a normal part of life that everyone experiences at some time or other, and shouldn't be seen as frightening or loathsome. It would be difficult to get through life without ever suffering irksome looks, and I could easily have pretended I wasn't bothered by them, particularly since so few people back then were willing even to look my way.

Every time I tried to capture that stare, it escaped somehow, and so, to prove to myself I wasn't imagining things, I moved as cautiously as if I were stalking a bright green dragonfly. But sometimes, when one strains to bring something hazy into focus, success only invites disaster.

But I tried not to think about this, since that was the year my world turned upside-down. So much happened to me that I felt tied up in knots, like the green moss hanging from the stone wall beside the street, which resembled tangled locks of devil's hair.

2

My house was on the southern bank of the Yangtze.

The South Bank District of Chongqing consists of low rolling hills that form a series of gullies. In the event of a thousand-year flood, should the entire city be swallowed up, our hillside would stand stubbornly, the last island to go under. From early childhood, this was a strangely comforting thought for me.

If you ferried over from the Dock on the opposite bank, Heaven's Gate, you could reach either of the two landings nearest my house: Alley Cat Stream and Slingshot Pellet. Both required a climb up the bank and a twenty-minute walk along a rutted street to reach my house halfway up the hill.

By standing on the ridge in front of my house, I could see where the Yangtze and Jialing Rivers merge at Heaven's Gate, the gateway to the city. The peninsula created by the two rivers is the heart of Chongqing. A motley assortment of buildings on the surrounding hills looks like a jumble of children's building blocks. Pontoon quays dot the riverbanks, steamships tie up beside the quays, and cable cars, dripping rust, crawl slowly up and down the slopes. Dark clouds blanket the rivers at dawn, raising scaly red ripples; at dusk, when the sun's rays slant down on the water before settling behind the hills to the north, a few bursts of sunlight emerge from the dark mist. That is when lamps lighting up the hills are reflected on the surface of the water, pushing the darkness along. And when sheets of fine rain cover the rivers, you can hear riverboat horns wail like grieving widows; the city, caught day and night between two fast-flowing rivers, with its myriad scenic changes, is always sad and enigmatic.

The hills in South Bank teem with simple wooden thatched sheds made of asphalt felt and asbestos board. Rickety and darkened by weather, they have something sinister about them. When you enter the dark, misshapen courtyards off twisting little lanes, it is all but impossible to find your way back out; these are home to millions of people engaged in coolie labour. Along the meandering lanes of South Bank there are hardly any sewers or garbage-collecting facilities, so the accumulated filth spills out into roadside ditches and runs down the hills. The ground is invariably littered with refuse, to be carried into the Yangtze by the next rainfall or turned into rotting mud under the blazing sun.

The garbage piles up, with fresh layers covering their fetid predecessors to produce an astonishing mixture of strange odours. A ten-minute walk on any mountain path in South Bank treats you to hundreds of different smells, a universe of olfactory creations. I've walked the streets of many cities with garbage heaps, but I've never been surrounded by so many smells. I sometimes wonder why the people of South Bank, living amid all that stench and walking among such filth, are punished by having noses on their faces.

People said that unexploded Japanese bombs from World War II lay buried in gullies on the hills, and that before the Kuomintang forces abandoned the city by the end of 1949, they buried thousands of tons of explosives. They also left behind, it was reported, over a hundred thousand underground agents – that is to say, every adult in the city was a potential spy, and even after the grand suppression movements and the mass executions of the Communist purges of the early 1950s, plenty of spies could have slipped through the net. That could even have included people who joined the Party after Liberation, but were plants who came out at night to do their dirty work – murder, arson, rape, you name it. You wouldn't find them among the tall buildings or wide avenues on the opposite bank, for they preferred to operate secretly amid the eternal foul odours of South Bank. A spot like this, so alien to the socialist image, is a perfect place for anti-socialist elements to come and go in secret.

If you walk out the compound gate, hugging the damp wall and listening carefully, you can hear the echoes of former night watchmen in the darkness. That cobweb-covered doorway might reveal quite mysteriously an old-style red-velvet embroidered shoe; that man disappearing around the corner, with a felt hat pulled down over his forehead, might have a knife hidden in his trouserleg. On dark, rainy days, every person walking on the narrow slope, where filthy water flows, looks like a secret agent. And on any given sliver of land, by digging down a couple of feet, you can unearth an unexploded bomb or some hidden explosives, or a secret code book with all sorts of strange symbols, or 'restoration accounts' of items confiscated from landlords and recorded by them with writing brushes.

The other side of the river is as different as night from day. The centre of the city might as well be in another world, with red flags everywhere you look and rousing political songs filling the air. The people's lives are 'getting better every day', with youngsters reading revolutionary books to prepare themselves for the life of a revolutionary cadre. South Bank, on the other hand, is the city's garbage dump, an unsalvageable slum; a curtain of mist above the river hides this dark corner, this rotting urban appendix, from sight.

After negotiating the wobbly gangplank of the river ferry and walking for ten or twenty minutes across cobblestones and garbage, you looked up and saw tiers of crumbling houses on stilts, wooden shacks and mud huts, a mind-boggling maze of indescribably ugly buildings. I alone could pick out one particular grey brick house with black roof tiles on a crag midway up the hill, stretching out over the river. The locals referred to this spot, located in one of Alley Cat Stream's side lanes, as Compound Eight Beak. Alley Cat Stream Street was a steep, hilly path paved roughly with stones and bordered on both sides by chinaberry trees, malus trees, some bushes that sometimes stank and sometimes smelled sweet, and some teetering, rickety shacks that should have crumbled long ago. The walls and gate of Compound Eight Beak were pitch black, with some random red and green bricks that added a bit of colour, which owed its existence to a lightning strike that had knocked half of the bricks to the ground; during repairs, the broken bricks were insufficient to complete the job, so red bricks gleaned from somewhere were added.

But this wasn't my house. To find that, you had to look further up, past an expanse of identical grey rooftops. I lived in Compound Six, uphill from the other two relatively decent, parallel compounds, a spot where moss and mildew stained the walls and rooftops. It had a small courtyard in the centre, a communal kitchen on each side – one large, one small – and four attics. A tiny passageway connected the larger kitchen to the back yard. There was also a dark, dank staircase that led to three rooms and two rear doors on the down slope.

I know it sounds like a landlord's home, and to tell the truth, I can't say what sort of family once lived there. But when the Communists came in the winter of 1949, the owners were smart enough to take off and cover their tracks. Their furniture and some locally made looms were confiscated. The families of sailors living in South Bank wooden shacks quickly moved in, some with a formal permit, others without. Terms like hall, corridor, back yard, side room, and attic were retained only for the sake of convenience. The hall led to six small rooms belonging to four families, and thus was shared by them all.

Thirteen families moved into a compound that had once been home to only one; each one or two rooms housed a separate family, most comprising three generations. With relatives or neighbours from back home visiting on a regular basis, I never did work out just how many people lived there – I would get lost in my counting after one hundred.

3

Our family room occupied about a hundred square feet of space, equipped with a small wood-framed southern window with six bars, like a prison cell. But of course burglars would never honour a family like mine with a visit. We only closed the window when it was raining or on cold winter nights. Besides, our neighbour's mud wall, which was only a foot away, was a very tall and very imposing barrier. Since opening the window didn't brighten up the room at all, we had to keep a light on even in the daytime. If I stuck my head out the window and looked up over the wall, I could see the forked branches of a malus tree. A creek that flowed down from the playground on High School Avenue veered downhill at a precipice in front of the tree and emptied into the river. The gurgle turned into a roar in the night stillness, more like a heated argument or mortal combat than the screech of an alley cat.

Fortunately for us, we also had an attic, much less than a hundred feet square and barely waist-high at the lowest point. A skylight facing south opened on to a grey sky. If I got up in the middle of the night and wasn't careful, I'd bump my head on the ceiling and jangle the roof tiles.

My parents, three sisters, two brothers and I crowded into those two rooms. Our quarters were so small and the occupants so numerous that all six kids had to sleep on two slat beds my father had made for the attic. He and my mother slept downstairs on a coir-frame bed. The remaining space of the main room was filled by a five-drawer bureau, an old wicker chair, plus a dining table and stools.

Once we kids had grown out of childhood, we had to take down the table in my parents' room at night to put up a cot for my brothers. In the daytime it was taken down and the table restored to its proper place so we could eat. Then when it was bathtime, down came the table and the stools. I know it sounds complicated, but it was easy once we got used to it.

By 1980, my family had lived in this compound for twenty-nine years. On the 1st of February 1951, my parents moved here from north of the river with my two older sisters. In the 1950s Mao Zedong was urging everyone to have more and more children. With more people the country was more powerful, things got done more easily, and if a nuclear war wiped out half the world's population, China would dom-inate the planet. So in the space of a few years, China's population increased by 150 per cent, reaching a billion in the 1980s.

With my birth, our family numbered eight people. At first it didn't feel all that crowded, since my brothers and sisters, who had been sent down to the countryside, seldom came home. But once the Cultural Revolution ended and the young urbanites started returning to town, my brothers and sisters came home to stay. By 1980, our little two-room place, more crowded than a pigsty, was bursting at the seams; there was hardly room to stand. Needless to say, in the summer of that year, with family members stepping all over each other, tempers flared.

Mother said there was a letter from Big Sister, who would be home in a couple of days.

Big Sister was in the first group of youngsters sent down to the countryside, which meant she'd have the hardest time returning to the city. She had divorced twice, and had three kids, the oldest a mere six years younger than me. Her children were no sooner born than she sent them to my parents to care for, so she could head back to her next divorce or next marriage. 'Damned trouble-maker!' The mere mention of Big Sister drew curses from Mother. 'How could I have given birth to a viper like her?'

Whenever Big Sister came home, in no time she and Mother were at each other's throats, screaming and banging furniture. The things they said made my head swim. Sooner or later, Big Sister would reduce Mother to tears, then walk off triumphantly.

So why, I wondered, did Mother speak so fondly of her when she wasn't around? As soon as she heard that her eldest daughter was coming home, she got so fidgety she could hardly contain herself as she waited in eager anticipation. I could never shake off the feeling that they shared something the rest of us children could not fathom, and even if we could, it would have been some arcane confidence that had nothing to do with us.

A number of things happened that summer that got me thinking that this confidence involved me, somehow. And since Big Sister was the only member of the family out of whom I could pry anything I, like Mother, eagerly anticipated her return.

I knew I was special to Mother. Of her eight pregnancies, two of the children had died. I was number six. I always felt I occupied a special place in her heart, and not just because I was the baby. I can't find the words to describe her attitude towards me. She never spoiled me or winked at my short-comings, always keeping a tight and cautious rein on me. It was as if I were someone else's child under her care, and she didn't want to do anything that would make her appear negligent.

Father treated me differently, too, but not the same way as Mother. A man of few words, he had, if anything, even less to say to me. His reticence was intimidating: if he was angry, he picked up a stick or a bamboo switch and lashed out furiously at the disobedient child. While Mother was quick to overlook my brothers' and sisters' faults, Father was less forgiving. But he never lost his temper with me, and never scolded me.

Sometimes I could feel the anxiety that filled Father's eyes when he looked at me; Mother stared daggers at me. I sensed that I was their great disappointment, something that should not have appeared in this world, a puzzle they couldn't solve.

4

Father was sitting on a stool in the hall rolling tobacco spread atop another, slightly taller stool, whose red paint had peeled away until only a few flecks remained here and there. Four inlaid tiles around a red flower decorated the seat, and I had no idea where such a fancy stool could have come from. He skilfully rolled the tobacco leaves despite the faint light, since he didn't need to see what he was doing. His eyebrows, while not particularly dark, were long; his cheekbones were prominent, and his eyes bright in spite of his failing vision. After the sun went down he couldn't see a thing. He seldom smiled, and I don't recall ever hearing him laugh, or cry. Not until I was grown-up did I understand that his temperament was formed by countless life experiences. Great at keeping secrets, he was the member of my family I understood least.

I had come home from school to find our door latched. I heard sounds of bathing inside.

'Your mother's home,' Father said, his Zhejiang accent thick as always. 'Are you hungry?' he turned to ask.

'No,' I said.

I hung my schoolbag on a peg on the wall.

'Eat a little something now if you are.'

'I'll wait till Fourth Sister and Fifth Brother come home,' I said. The sounds of bathing inside suddenly put me ill at ease.

Mother spent her days as an hourly labourer, struggling with a carrying pole and two lengths of rope to earn enough to help support the family. Oxygen tanks that required the effort of four porters had to be carried down a gangplank by only two. She had fought to get this job, and once, when her foot slipped and she tumbled into the river, she held on to the metal tank for dear life. The first thing she said after she was dragged out of the water was, 'I can keep carrying them.'

It's not that she had hopes of becoming a 'model worker', but that she was afraid of losing her job – labourers like her could be let go at any time. She carried baskets of sand, tiles, and cement. Before I was born, right after the local pharmaceutical factory was built, Mother volunteered to carry fire bricks for the furnace. This was at the start of the famine, and she was already skin and bones. Four bulky fire bricks were loaded into the baskets at each end of the carrying pole, then carried from the riverbank up the hill, a trip that required fifty minutes even without a load. The wages were less than two yuan a day. Two other female labourers carried only two bricks in each basket, yet were still so exhausted and hungry that the job was too much for them. Thinking no one was looking, they simply dumped their bricks into a pond alongside the path. But someone saw them, and they were fired on the spot.

Somewhere along the line, Mother offended the head of the Residents' Committee and lost her work permit. Her only option was to look for work in another neighbourhood district.

The head of the second Residents' Committee, a kindly soul, said to her: I've got a porters' group made up of 'elements'. Would that be a problem? Mother quickly said it wouldn't. And so she began working alongside a group of individuals under 'surveillance by the masses', people who had historical or current political problems, workers who took the jobs other people refused.

Mother followed the porters' group to a far-off shipyard in White Sand Bay, where she laboured hard, sweated hard, and chanted hard, just like the men; she matched them step for step, carrying stone blocks for the foundation and steel plate for the ships. Once again she fell into the river, and this time it nearly killed her; they performed resuscitation until a stomachful of filthy river water came spewing out of her mouth.

Decades of coolie labour had left Mother with heart problems, anaemia that eventually developed into high blood pressure, rheumatism, a damaged hip, and aches and pains all over. It wasn't until I entered middle school that she managed to find different work: stoking a boiler in the shipyard. This new job − keeping the boiler going all day long − was considered light work. The fire was secured in the middle of the night, and opened at four in the morning, when the ashes were removed and new coal added so that, by five o'clock, when the morning shift arrived, boiling water would be ready.

She lived in the factory-women's dormitory, coming home only at the weekends, where she normally went to bed right after dinner. Even if I tried to boost her spirits by bringing water for her to wash with, all I got were scowls and growls.

I wiped down her back after rolling up her shirt; her shoulders, calloused from all those heavy loads, looked like a camel's back – a hump where the heavy carrying pole rested. Then I wiped the front, where her shrivelled breasts hung like empty sacks, useless, superfluous skin that lay against her belly. By the time I'd wrung out the cloth and turned back to wipe her down again, she was fast asleep, her arm hanging over the side of the bed, her legs spread inelegantly. Snores – piglike grunts – reverberated throughout the house and slobber dribbled from her mouth. When I put her arm back on to the bed, I looked away in disgust.

While Mother was working, all the household duties fell to my father, who was on disability retirement. After the sun went down, even though he couldn't see a thing, he could still manage the laundry and cooking by groping his way along. He raised me virtually single-handedly from the time I was a baby.

On Saturdays, Fourth Sister and I rose at the crack of dawn to queue up at the butcher stall, where, by combining all our coupons, we could buy about half a catty's worth of pork. We'd cook a fragrant pot of meat, then stare at it greedily, waiting for night to fall and for Mother to come home. But instead of showing her appreciation, she'd wield her chopsticks dismissively, managing to pick all around the meat. One night Father had had enough; he pounded the table and threw down his ricebowl and chopsticks. Then they chased us kids outside and had one hell of an argument; the more it heated up, the softer their voices grew, to keep us from hearing what they were saying. I figured Mother was using Father to vent some spleen, which made me angry with her.

Mother hardly ever took us out, either to shop or to visit relatives. And her moods got more bizarre as the years passed, as we could tell from the vile language that emerged from her mouth. I got used to hearing people in the compound or in the streets hurling at each other filthy words, gutter talk, and genital-laden epithets aimed at their ancestors. But she was my mother, after all, and all those curses and dirty words made me very uncomfortable.

I found fault with nearly everything she did: she banged things too loudly when she did housework, she made a habit of spilling pickling-vat liquid on the floor, she slammed the downstairs door so hard that the attic rattled, and whenever she spoke she yelled. It was more than I could take. I hated calling her Mother, to her face or behind her back, and we hardly ever smiled at each other.

I couldn't help but wonder: eighteen years earlier, when she began raising me – nineteen, actually, when she got pregnant – what kind of mother was she then?

I don't remember ever seeing my mother when she was good-looking, even presentable, for that matter.

Or might I have conveniently erased any memory of her that was at all attractive? I watched as, little by little, she turned into a sickly woman with rotting and repaired teeth, that is, what few teeth she had left. Her eyelids were puffy, dull and lifeless; squinting till her eyes were mere slits, she could hardly recognize a soul. Even if she'd tried, she couldn't have made her strawlike hair look good; it kept falling out and turning whiter by the day. The tattered straw hat she wore most of the time helped a little. And she kept getting shorter, as if being pressed down by a heavy weight; her bent back made her look even shorter and puffier than she really was, slightly top-heavy. She shuffled when she walked, as if the soles of her shoes were made of lead; her legs grew thicker and stumpier from all that back-breaking labour, and her toes were splayed. Her feet didn't bleed even when she stepped on a sharp stone. Since they were steeped in mud the year round, athlete's foot caused her a great deal of suffering.

Once, and only once, I woke up early to the sound of Mother's wooden sandals banging against the stone steps, a surprisingly pleasant sound. Carrying a paper umbrella, she was walking out of the compound in the drizzling rain, and I was struck by the thought that she once had, she must have had, silky-smooth skin and a young, supple face.

Gradually I came to realize why Mother didn't like mirrors. She complained once to my sisters that there wasn't a decent mirror in the house. They held their tongues, apparently knowing instinctively that it was her way of saying she hated the things.

Age created a wall between Mother and me, above which grass and shrubs grew, taller and taller, until neither of us knew what to do about it. Actually, it was a slight, brittle wall that we could have toppled if we'd wanted to, except that it never occurred to us, at least not to me, to try. I saw warmth in Mother's eyes no more than once or twice, occasions when I felt that maybe I wasn't superfluous after all. It seemed to me then that all I had to do was reach out to touch her heart; sadly, the look vanished before I had a chance.

Not until my eighteenth year was I finally able to look back and get a clear picture of the past.

5

The door opened and Mother emerged, fresh from her bath. 'Bring the pail, Little Six,' she said. She was wearing a homemade sleeveless, collarless shirt, knee-length shorts, and a pair of worn wooden sandals.

Together we picked up the tub to dump the dirty water into the pail. Mother said Big Sister would be home tonight, tomorrow at the latest.

'You can wait as long as you want,' I said with studied cruelty. 'She's just setting you up for a fall.'

'No, she isn't,' Mother said decisively. 'If she wrote to say she's coming home, then she is.'

Her face softened with the mere mention of my eldest sister, and as I looked up, I lost track of what I was doing, spilling water on the cement floor. 'Pay attention,' she growled. 'Can't you do anything right?'

I picked up the full pail and carried it over the threshold. 'Don't dump that. Save it to mop the attic floor,' Mother said, louder than she needed to.

Water was a valued commodity, not just because it was so expensive, but because it could be cut off at any time. Several hundred families shared a single tap behind High School Avenue. Queuing up was only part of the problem, for once the water came, it was usually a dirty yellow; but if we went down to the river to fetch water, a hard, sweaty job at best, we had to treat it with alum or bleach to make it fit for drinking or cooking, and it left a metallic taste. Except for times when the running water was off, we fetched water from the river only for laundry or to mop the floors.

Each family had so little living space that the water had to be stored in small vats in the communal kitchen, and that was never enough for anyone. The men and boys normally bathed in the river, unless they were too lazy to go down the mountain; then they'd wash on the courtyard steps, using a basin of water, dressed only in underpants. Why not, since they went around in the summer wearing nothing more than that anyway? Some of the more bashful men bathed at night, but they were in short supply, so open-air bathing was the norm. They'd use a basin of water to wash down, top and bottom, and with their underpants soaked, you could see everything they had. Even as a little girl, I knew exactly what men had hanging between their legs – that ugly, shameful thing – and when I went to the kitchen for something or out into the courtyard to dump dirty water in the ditch, I'd confront a line of men in the courtyard, young and old, standing shoulder to shoulder, virtually naked, all but blocking my way. They thought nothing even of pissing into the drain hole in public.

Over the long, drawn-out summers, a month could go by without a drop of rain. Then when the Yangtze began to rise, the water flowed slowly and inexorably from the upper reaches, and hundreds of metres of riverbank would be swallowed up overnight when the flood season arrived.

Anyone who has never suffered through the heat of this city cannot possibly understand how it burns its way out from your heart and clogs up every pore on your body, to lie there baking your skin. Normally there is no wind, but when there is, it's like adding coal to a fire, like being caged in a steamer until you think you're overcooked.

When we females bathed, the males had to hang around outside until we had finished and they could come home, sullen and grumbling. First we'd fill the wooden tub, adding a few drops of boiling water to warm it up a bit, then latch the door, strip naked, and take a fast bath, nervous as cats. We'd wet ourselves down, quickly rub a sliver of soap over our bodies, and rinse off; that was our bath.

With five females in the family, sometimes there wasn't enough time for us all to bath individually, so we sisters would crowd into the room together. Since I couldn't stand letting other people see me naked, even my mother and sisters, I normally waited around to be the last, taking a basin of cold water inside and latching the door behind me so I could take a quick sponge bath. Everyone thought I was being eccentric, keeping a family room all to myself, and they weren't happy about it.

That was in the summer. Once the weather cooled off, the inconvenience of bathing increased. Hot water was particularly scarce; but since we couldn't afford to go to the public baths, we simply took fewer baths or no baths at all. Labourers carried the stench of sweat with them wherever they went, adding yet another powerful odour to the pervasive medley of smells.

The winter cold was as oppressive as the summer heat. Our houses weren't heated, and heating materials were virtually non-existent, so we warmed our hands by wrapping them around a hot-water bottle, and huddled around the stove to keep the cold at bay. Sometimes we simply cocooned ourselves in quilts and lay in bed. At night we bundled up in as many clothes as we could wear and climbed into bed, suffering until morning with freezing hands and feet. I don't think there was a winter in my childhood when my hands weren't covered with chilblains that made my fingers look like carrots.

I jammed the mop into the bucket, holding it in my right hand and cradling the handle in the crook of my arm, then gingerly carried my load over to the foot of the stairs, listing to one side. Shifting the bucket to my left hand, I grabbed the creaky banister with my right hand and prepared myself for the climb to the attic.

'Don't worry about mopping the floor now,' Mother shouted crankily. 'There's still hot water in the kettle. Take your bath first. It'll be cold if you put it off.'

She was always ordering me about like that. So I put down the bucket and stood at the foot of the stairs, looking unhappy.

After mopping up the bath water that had splashed on to the floor, she carried the mop over to a dry corner, which quickly absorbed some of the dripping water.

Father looked up and gave me a sign to do as Mother said.

Not wanting to disobey him, I picked up the basin and went into the kitchen for some hot water. Then I closed the door and took off my clothes to wash. The sight of my own sweaty, naked body and the smell of underarm sweat sickened me.

TWO

1

There are a dozen or so universities and colleges in this city of four million, but no College Avenue. Yet in South Bank, owing to the hilltop presence of a secondary school, there is a High School Avenue. Many years ago, it seems, the appearance of the first high school in this slum area was an event of singular importance.

But for the local high-school students, colleges might as well have been on a different planet. You could count on your fingers the number of South Bank high-school graduates who had the good fortune of passing the college exams. Some secondary schools drew a blank in that regard for a decade or longer, and eventually closed their high-school section, an admission that students around here were undeserving of a decent education. On the other hand, you could easily have populated any number of school reunions with local pedlars, river boatmen, and shipyard workers.

I lived fairly close to High School Avenue, a wider, stone-paved street that wasn't terribly steep. Both slopes of the street were packed with squat, ramshackle wooden huts that housed families who made their living by selling odds and ends: soy sauce, vinegar and salt, or needles and thread, shoelaces and buttons. A comic-book stall occupied the top of the steps, where you could also buy snacks like candy and peanuts. On rainy days, the old lady moved the books back to her house, where she set out wooden stools inside the doorway.

Sometimes you could hardly make your way from one end of the street to the other, what with the mass of humanity crowding the steps, the ground under the eaves, the doorways and the open windows.

'You oily-tongued, sharp-beaked turtle spawn, you think you can dump your chamber pot on my head, do you? You don't know who you're fucking with. You thought you'd sink your claws into something nice, and now you can't get 'em out.'

'Why waste words on the son of a bitch? Kick the shit out of him!'

'Fuck your ancestors! Who the hell do you think you are?'

'Fuck everyone in your family – eight generations back – while you're at it.'

Bystanders, afraid a fight might not break out, did everything they could to ensure it would. 'Fuck off, balls-itch, if that's the best you can come up with!'

People from Chongqing have short tempers and sharp tongues. Like firecrackers, they're so loud you can hear them blocks away. And the tempers of people who live in South Bank are a lot shorter than those in the city centre. No empty threats for them – disputes aren't settled until knives flash. But they're very straightforward people. If they like you, they'll do anything for you. People in the city centre, on the other hand, like to see which way the wind is blowing; they prefer to size up their opponents, and won't fight unless they think they can win. But turn your back, and sooner or later they'll get you, until you don't know whether you're a man or a ghost.

As a child I saw plenty of street brawls. Later on, after I'd started reading martial-arts novels and watching kung fu movies on TV, I realized that the good guys, the heroes, were actually nothing but well-dressed bullies whose language lacked the punch of that used by their street-fighting counterparts.

When the actual fighting began, onlookers would back away to give the combatants room. Ah, the local bully's met his match today!

'Hey, break it up! This guy's cut!' Shouts like this never did any good.

'Here come the police!' That's what it took. Men would

then run up and pull the fighters apart. Most of the time, people despised the police. But when a fight broke out, people would start dragging each other over to the station house. Everyone, it seems, respects authority.

The biggest building in the area – once a teahouse – stood next to the corner store and could accommodate upwards of a hundred people. In the old days story-tellers mesmerized the patrons nightly with rhythmic tales from *Romance of the Three Kingdoms*, *The Marsh Outlaws*, and *Exploits of Yang Warriors*, and the place was always packed. But sometime before I was born, it was converted into the Dining Hall of the People's Commune; then when I was four or five it was renamed Sun Compound to pledge fealty to Chairman Mao. Eventually it was turned into the headquarters of 'Rebel' factions and the site where local 'ox-demons' and 'snake-spirits' were held up to mass criticism; the victims of this public humiliation would be taken out and paraded up and down the streets in dunce caps. Since I wasn't allowed to step foot in the place at the time, I had to stand on tiptoe on the steps outside, waiting anxiously to see what was going on inside. For years after-wards, a sign proclaiming 'Mao Zedong Thought Study Group' hung outside the door. The 'students' kept chan-ging, but the wilted looks on their faces were always the same, and their mouldy, foul-smelling bodies stank just as much. As the 1970s neared their end, and the last bunch of targeted people had disappeared from the scene, a black-and-white TV set flickered inside every evening in front of a packed house of noisy grown-ups and their rowdy kids, the ones up front sitting on stools, while those in the rear stood on theirs.

I was not permitted this luxury, since I had to prepare for the college entrance exams.

2

The sun retained its punishing heat even after school was over. So with my schoolbag over my shoulders, I sought out cool spots to walk in. Tender pink oleanders bloomed beside the road, the branches propped up by the mossy wall. At a spot between two wall newspapers, I turned and walked in among the trees. The moist ground where the sun was blotted out had a sickeningly sweet, mildewy smell, so no matter how hot the sun was, I would rather bake under the sun than walk in the shade. Go home, I commanded myself silently. I'm not going, today I'm not going, I'm not going this time. Next time? We'll see. But not this once, at least.

Yet as I passed by the School Office building, my feet carried me on to the stone path. I climbed the stairs, and stood in front of that familiar door.

'Come in.' Those same two words. He always knew it was me at the door. Once I was inside, the crazy thoughts I'd had on the road vanished. I sat in an old wicker chair across from the history teacher.

Originally a large classroom, the room had been divided into cubicles. Red paper for writing slogans was stacked on top of the bookcase, along with several broken, nearly bald writing brushes. Each teacher had a desk, a frayed wicker chair, and two or three stools. The curtainless window facing south let bright sunlight stream in. Green paint streaking the glass pane in the little window next to his desk kept out most of the sun's rays and the muffled shouts from the basketball court beyond.

Hidden amid the lush green hillsides surrounding the city stood the English- and French-styled summer houses of the rich and powerful; once occupied by Chiang Kai-shek's closest aides and his US advisers, they now accommodated high-ranking Communist Party officials. I'd never set eye on those houses, so I could only guess what they looked like: that part of the city was an alien world to me.

The two-storey School Office building, with its ridged roof and large windows, was the nicest place I'd visited so far. That in spite of the fact that the stairs creaked and groaned when someone stood on them. The doors and shutters were held together by cardboard that cracked and split whenever it was kicked or pushed a bit too hard, something that appeared to have happened often of late.

The first time I walked into the office I mentioned to the history teacher that everything about the place seemed familiar, somehow, including the window with its green paint, the cardboard-enhanced door, and the thick wall-bricks, and that, if I hadn't been here in a previous life, it must have appeared in my dreams. Actually, so had he, or someone like him, and there were times when I wondered if he was the man who was stalking me. But before I could get this last part out, he gave me a curious look, and an unconscious little smile appeared on his face. From that day on he stopped talking to me like a teacher.

He kept his hair cropped short, which made it impossible to tell if it was thick or thin, soft or bristly, and made his ears seem bigger than average. He wore a light blue-on-blue cotton shirt, not the fashionable Terylene fabric favoured by most of the other teachers. But his desk was neat and clean, not all chalked up like the others in the room. He didn't smoke, but was never without his glass of tea, which he regularly refilled with hot water from a plastic-covered thermos bottle on the floor next to his desk. He had bushy eyebrows and a long nose that seemed out of place on his face, giving it a sombre appearance.

Now that I think back, he was quite ordinary-looking. And he had a flat style of lecturing, unlike teachers who turned their history lessons into lively tales of the past. He was just a run-of-the-mill high-school history teacher.

Yet there are people in this world whom you meet on a narrow path and whose role in your life can be described only in emotions, not in words. Once you're on the same narrow path, whether you desire it or not, you are drawn together by a powerful force as you stumble along, driven by fear and excitement.

That was what happened to me on the eve of my eighteenth birthday: suddenly my emotions erupted, and I couldn't find the words to explain to myself what was going on. At first I hated him for not noticing me – oh, how I hated him. I was just one of several silly little girls in his class, and quite possibly the one least worthy of his attention. So I began reading novels in class, and made sure he saw me doing it.

Like most teachers, he dealt with this behaviour by having me stand as he asked a question, something so simple anyone could have answered it. I just stood there without saying a word. Then, when he walked up to me, I surprised him by staring him down. At that moment he knew I was no ordinary student, and he froze, forgetting that this was a classroom and that it was important to deal swiftly with any student who challenged his authority. Order in the classroom quickly broke down, as some of the rowdier kids began banging on their desks.

'Take your seat,' he said softly. 'See me after class.'

My heart was racing as I sat down excitedly. I'd achieved my goal of having him notice me. From then on, I went often to his office for being a 'disciplinary case'.

3

I approached my eighteenth birthday with a face as pale and wan as always; I was still skinny, and my lips were bloodless. My clothes had faded after countless washings, my dry, lustreless hair was combed into two anaemic plaits. Mao Zedong had died four years earlier, and styles of dress were changing rapidly, as fewer and fewer people were seen in the baggy green or blue attire that everyone had worn for so long. Thirties-style nightclub songs were on the lips of people in corners here and there. After forty years of no-nonsense revolution, the city was taking its first cautious steps towards reviving the graceful good old days. Some of the bolder women began wearing cheongsams that showed off their figures. After negotiating the hilly terrain since childhood, young women here had long, sturdy legs and slender curved torsos, which enhanced their appearance when they walked.

The special airs of olden times even settled upon the rundown lanes and byways of South Bank, and the more I watched the changes, the less I liked what I saw of myself, my own appearance; I looked like someone who had missed her ship and was abandoned at some lonely pier: I wore a green cotton skirt that fell below my knees and a short-sleeved white blouse, both hand-me-downs from my sisters. Too big and loose-fitting, they made me look even smaller than I was. Cream-coloured plastic sandals, which were about an inch too long, slapped against my bare heels when I walked.

That's how I looked when I walked up to the history teacher's desk. All the other teachers had gone home for the day, so we were alone. He studied my face across the desk. 'You've got me wrong,' he said gently, 'if you think I look down on students from poor families.'

My heart skipped a beat. He was right, I realized, for the most part, at least. That was the main reason I felt so uncomfortable at school, and why I'd never felt happy there.

'I come from a poor family myself,' he said with a self-deprecating smile. No longer the blank expression I was used to seeing in class. 'If anything, I'm even less well off now, a bona fide member of the proletariat.'

He told me his father had been branded a counter-revolutionary, which slammed the door on his own college aspirations. Even after he and his younger brother were grown men, they helped their father sell popcorn on the street or delivered coal to people's houses. He said he knew every street and lane in South Bank. 'Back then you were just a baby crawling on the floor and trailing snot behind you.' A disdainful laugh escaped.

'Oh, you think I'm too young, is that it?' I said with a note of anger as I stood up.

'I'm twenty years older than you.'

What did he mean by that? What did age have to do with anything? Was he saying we were a mismatch? So, he'd already thought about us in terms of a match – boy-girl. I blushed and looked away. My heart was pounding, as if I'd taken something that didn't belong to me. Tears came to my eyes.

'Hey,' he said, 'why are you crying?'

'You insulted me,' I said spitefully.

'Insulted you?' He rose, took a handkerchief from his pocket, and walked around the desk to hand it to me.

I didn't take it. By then my tears were in my nose and on the verge of spilling out. I felt miserable, but still refused the handkerchief. Let's see what he does now, I said to myself. I didn't look up, even when I sensed he was close enough to touch me.

I absolutely refused to take that handkerchief, a demonstration of courage that took even my breath away. One second more, I was thinking, one more second and he'll be touching me. I thought I'd faint.

He did it, he touched me, his hand pressing down on my head. As if I were a little puppy, he roughly dried my eyes and face, then pressed the handkerchief up to my nose. Instinctively, I blew my nose.

Quickly moving away from him, I stood a foot or so from the desk. That creep, what does he think I am, a baby?

He glanced at the handkerchief smugly and put it in his pocket. Back in his chair, he acknowledged my embarrassment and petulance with a justified smile, for he had triumphed in proving the gap in our ages and in refusing to let me get close to him. Once again we were a teacher and his student, and I was red in the face with anger.

Calmly he told me that, even though I still had time to prepare for the entrance exams, there was much memorization work to do. He made a show of flipping through the papers on his desk, as if they were samples of my schoolwork. My grades, he said, weren't as good as they might be, and it was time to buckle down. He repeated that he'd come from a disadvantaged background, and that had kept him from entertaining thoughts of college. For me, he said, this was the chance of a lifetime.

He was sincere, I knew that, and there was nothing wrong with his logic. He knew that memorizing lessons was my major weakness. We sat there gazing at each other. I liked looking at him, and I could sense that the feeling was mutual.

Before long I was in high spirits again.

4

Nearly every time we said our lighthearted goodbyes in the playground, all I could think was I'll see him tomorrow, at least in class.

The school wall stood proudly in places, and crumbled humbly in others; not much of a wall. Beyond the tiny vegetable garden and playground, winding paths spread out like spokes. Smoke spewed from the smokestack at the pharmaceutical plant, which dumped its waste water into the neighbouring fields. The sun was embraced by dark rain clouds in the muggy air; not until the rains came would the temperature drop a bit.

But the rains never helped us much, since our roof leaked so badly, to which all the pails and pots on the beds and on the floor bore witness. We huddled together wherever we could find a dry spot, and when a pot was full, I carried it carefully out into the courtyard.

Our compound ought to have been condemned years earlier: there were wide gaps in the floorboards, the walls were speckled and crumbling, the roof beams sagged, and the stone image of the Kitchen God above the stove was covered with so much soot that its features were indistinguishable; it took plenty of elbow grease to bring its happy countenance into view again.

Moss covered the base of the walls and stone corners of the

courtyard the year round, a blackish green in spring and summer, turning to yellow in the autumn with tinges of blue-green; the dry spots had a fuzzy appearance, while the damp places were sort of mushy.

Er-wa lived with his family of five in two rooms built with broken bricks on the opposite side of the courtyard. Er-wa's mother, a woman who was little more than skin and bones, would be outside sweeping the ground in front of their door and hurling curses at everyone in sight; she never needed much of a reason. Years earlier, my mother had offended her somehow, and instead of letting bygones be bygones, she did everything she could to make life miserable for us, which in itself was a sign of her political activism. A jumble of words usually spewed from her mouth, something to do with VD, though it didn't make any sense to me.

One day her husband came home from his boat and found her flirting with one of the male neighbours, using all the sexual innuendo in her repertoire. He gave her the beating of her life, cutting up her clothes with a pair of scissors and actually smashing bowls on her body with a hammer. She didn't speak for a month, she was so frightened, which spared my family from her verbal attacks for a while. But it didn't take long for her peculiar noises to return to the compound, as if she couldn't help herself. And my parents listened to her wild, shrewish talk without a word or change of expression.

At school, even the most mischievous boys in class showed little or no interest in me; it wasn't worth their time to pick on me. Girls, on the other hand, tended to take their frustrations out on me. One day I was squatting in the toilet when one of them nearly bumped me into the muck below. Before I could steady myself, a tall girl heading out of the toilet stopped in the doorway long enough to say, 'Go ahead, scream, why don't you? Don't tell me you can't even do that.' But instead of screaming, I pulled up my pants and squeezed past her. Once I was outside, I took off running; I didn't even feel humiliated.

I always found it hard to show my feelings, particularly

since no one cared what sort of mood I was in anyway. My family figured I never had anything important to say, and the only person in the world who was interested in my views was the history teacher, who earned my complete trust. Finally I'd found someone who understood me. He viewed the world from a higher plateau than the other people around me. His expression as he listened encouraged me to pour out all my troubles, big and small.

I truly enjoyed having him listen to me, needed it, in fact. He knew what all those seemingly inconsequential matters meant to me. I held back with everyone but him, and there were times when I felt like pushing his desk aside to shorten the distance between us.

One day he reached into a drawer and took out a clipboard and a piece of paper. 'Sit still,' he said. 'I'll draw your portrait.' I did as he said, but kept talking.

From time to time he glanced up, then continued drawing. At last he put down his pencil, looked up and said, 'Forget all that other stuff. You should be concentrating on the entrance exams instead of worrying about other things.'

I said I didn't know why I was doing that, except that I'd never told any of this to anyone before.

He handed me the piece of paper. A pencil sketch. It was my face, all right, and all it had taken was a few lines. But the eyes were too bright, and were filled with passion. My neck and shoulders were bare – no collar – and I guess that must have expressed his distaste for what I was wearing. He'd drawn it at the top, leaving most of the page blank.

'What do you think?' he asked.

'It looks like a kitten,' I said. 'Those aren't my eyes.'

He took it from me. 'What do you know? You're too young.' He sighed, a little too loudly, I thought, and shoved the sheet of paper back into the drawer. I begged him to give it to me, but he said no, not until it was finished.

THREE

1

When Mother was home, we added a dish at dinner: stir-fried mung beans, plus the usual bowl of pickled-cabbage soup.

I mopped the upstairs floor – actually, all I did was cool the tiny space a bit by making the floor wet. The attic was barely big enough to accommodate the two narrow slat beds and the squat little table that I put up to do my schoolwork under a lamp. When, as often happened, I forgot to put it away when I was finished, anyone trying to get by had to turn sideways to do it. The floorboards consisted of two layers of thin wood, the space between them a virtual playground for rats. I wrung out my mop so the water wouldn't drip through the floor and into the room below. Hardly a breath of wind came in through the open skylight, and I was sticky with sweat, even though I'd just taken a bath.

'Come and eat, Little Six,' Fourth Sister yelled up to me through the opening.

I walked out on to the landing carrying my mop and pail and looked down. The food in her bowl was green and had an inviting aroma. Her face had grown gaunt, maybe because she was doing construction work, outdoors all day in the blistering sun and pouring rain. She had the ruddy cheeks of a farmer's wife. She was a lot prettier than me, and had a nice slender figure; at nearly five foot four, she was a whole inch taller than me. But like the rest of the girls in the family, some of her teeth were bunched up. 'You kids wouldn't listen when I told you to stay away from pickled turnips when your permanent teeth were coming in,' Mother often scolded us.

I no sooner brought a bowl of rice up to the table to sit with my mother and father than Fifth Brother walked in quietly and washed his hands at the washstand by the door. He had the narrow sloping shoulders of a girl. His hair was on the thin side, and his features were delicate, except for a prominent scar on his upper lip. He had been born with a harelip, and it was frightful to watch him eat. Always saddened by the sight, Mother placed the blame on Father, saying it was all because he'd chopped kindling on the threshold when she was pregnant with Fifth Brother, and instead of stopping when she'd asked him to, he had attacked the wood with increased fervour, a definite taboo.

When he was six months old, Fifth Brother was operated on by a local doctor to repair the lip, but it was a botched job from start to finish: the doctor used too large a needle and very coarse thread, then removed the stitches carelessly, which led to an infection and left an ugly scar in the middle of his upper lip. He was twenty-two at the time, four years older than me, although at first glance he could have passed for my kid brother. He never spoke unless he had to, and in that respect he even outdid my father; he was probably afraid he'd draw attention to himself, and to his mouth, if he spoke up. Fifth Brother was a shipyard welder who hitched a ride on a boat whenever possible to avoid walking for two and a half hours home.

The five of us sat at the table eating in the murky lamplight. Most of our neighbours preferred to eat their meals outside the compound gate, on the ground or on the steps, like one big family, free to take food out of anyone else's bowl. But at the slightest provocation, out came the curses, with chopsticks pointed menacingly at the offending party's face, and if things really heated up, rice bowls came crashing down on someone's head, sending a mixture of soupy rice and sticky blood dripping down the person's face. In no time, a crowd would gather round to watch the show while they ate.

With the meagre fare served up at mealtime, there was no

reason for us to crowd around the table. But my parents wouldn't allow us to run around when we ate, not because we were a particularly fastidious family, but to keep us away from our neighbours as much as possible. We were looked down upon by our neighbours, and my parents preferred to stay close to home. As for us kids, at most we'd stand in the hall or in the courtyard, while the neighbours' kids took their meals outside, either hunkering down on the stone steps or strolling up and down the street; sometimes they'd wander down to the river's edge, bowls in hand.

Fifth Brother filled his bowl and sat on a rattan stool by the door. Mother looked straight at me – I could see she wasn't happy – before telling us that the factory personnel office wanted her to retire two years early, at fifty-three, since she was in such poor health. If she did as they asked and stayed home, she'd get a tiny monthly pension. Everyone's chopsticks froze in mid air. I asked how much.

'Less than twenty-eight yuan.'

Getting no response from any of us, she continued: 'There was a time when twenty-eight yuan might have been enough, but not any more. Though if I keep working till there's an increase in the pension, I might have to wait until my eyes drop out of their sockets. Just think, Little Six, that course you're taking for the college entrance exams costs twenty yuan a month. And what good will it do you? We've got no money and no connections. We can't afford to keep you in school.'

She had raised the subject of money and her retirement the Sunday before, and had said there was no need for college. But this time, I could tell, she meant it. She wanted me to get a job and bring some money into the house. A college education was like a bottomless pit, and there was no way they could support me for another four years. Besides, a college degree without any back-door connections meant I'd have to 'meet the needs of the Party', and could be sent away to the devil knows where. We were a family of labourers, and in a nation where the working class were supposedly the masters we somehow never shared in the 'power'. Even given the fact that the children in our family – except for me, that is – worked with their hands, but had not been reduced to digging up sand on the riverbank to sell for a few cents, we were still no better off than the day I was born. Some of the neighbouring families had done well enough to move out of the compound, leaving us to get by as best we could.

Mother said I had no idea how hard it was being parents, how they worked their fingers to the bone for their children, and that, if there'd been a little more income, my father wouldn't be half blind today. With some extra money, if the doctors in Chongqing couldn't help him, he could go to an eye clinic in Shanghai or Beijing for treatment.

I'd promised myself, even as a little girl, that I'd do anything, make any sacrifice, so long as I could help Father get back his eyesight. But now the words wouldn't come.

As Mother looked away, thoughts raced through my mind. The soup in the bowl in front of us was nearly gone, leaving only the pickled cabbage at the bottom. Mother put some into Father's bowl.

'No more for me, I'm full. If Little Six wants to go to school,' he said, 'let her. You're the one who said it'll be harder for people to take advantage of her if she's got an education.' Father wasn't much of a talker, but that one sentence went to the heart of the matter.

'Keep your opinions to yourself.' This time Mother wasn't giving in.

I got up from the table, angrily slammed down my ricebowl, and went upstairs.

2

I never could take insults, since I lacked the ability to strike back. The end result of always giving in was an even more

32

violent emotional response. I could go the longest time without saying a word, just sit and stare at the wall or go to some place where no one could find me and imagine that I'd been cut off from the world. My self-pity would turn to anger, fiery hot, and I'd dream up ways to get back at my enemies – murder, arson, all sorts of violence, whatever it took, even suicide. I wanted my family to spend the rest of their lives tortured by remorse and wouldn't give them a chance to lessen their agony. I could feel the depth of sadness that would rightfully come their way.

After a while, these thoughts led to feelings of what pain was really like, and my insides seemed about to explode, sending boiling blood into my stomach and from there up my oesophagus, until it nearly choked me; with its passage blocked, a few foamy bubbles, with the smell of blood, escaped. Sometimes I felt the excruciating pain of my guts twisting up into knots that no doctor in the world could ever uncoil, which would force everything inside them out one end or the other. A sour, foul odour would pour out of my stomach and up into my mouth. That would send me in a panic for the wonder pills that Father kept in a little medicine cabinet, things like cinnamon-bark golden elixir, bezoar antitoxins, and essence of forsythia.

Father would ask what was wrong, and I'd tell him I had an upset stomach. He'd look at me with a worried expression, then help me pick out the best medicine for the job, one that would extinguish my internal fires, dissipate the flow of heat, and detoxify the poisons. I'd walk off as soon as he handed me the pill, not wanting to discuss why my stomach was acting up again.

After a while, he'd climb back to the attic to see if I was feeling better.

It's nothing to worry about, he often said, something you were born with. You were lucky enough to come along at the tail end of the famine. But even that graze was hard enough. After going hungry in your mother's belly, your stomach is

33

now trying to get even. You'll never know what we had to put up with to keep your mother – that is to say, you – from starving.

By counting back from my birthday, I figured Mother got pregnant with me in the winter of 1961, the last dark winter in the three years of famine. Even in Sichuan – the richest agricultural province in the country, often called 'Heaven's Granary' – at least seven million people starved to death, one out of every four famine victims in the nation. Most died in the snowy winters of 1959, 1960 and 1961, and the spring of 1962, when the 'green failed to meet the yellow'.

I was always curious about this catastrophic famine, as if it were tied in some mysterious way to my life, and made me different from other people: my frail health and morose disposition seemed somehow to be linked to it, belonging neither to a past life nor to this one, but wedged on to the long narrow rope bridge between the two. As I set out on to that bridge, an evil wind turned me into something not quite human.

One day I asked my history teacher about the famine that ended with my birth. His face paled and he looked away. Panicked, I asked what was wrong. Instead of answering me, he jumped to his feet and walked to the window, where he grabbed his hair with both hands and stood there trying to compose himself. 'Don't trust your own flesh,' he said, 'and don't trust your own bones. Toss stones into your belly, and when the hot cinders begin to sizzle, we'll ward off the menacing powers of Paradise.'

I was dumbstruck, more rocked by his strange mutterings than by the staggering figure of the tens of millions who had died.

It took him a long time to compose himself, and then I learned it was during that time that he had become a public enemy of the Communist Party. It had started with a letter he sent to the Central Government spelling out the human costs of the growing famine in Sichuan. He was not yet twenty at the time, and I wasn't even born. The letter was sent back to the local security organs, who quickly labelled him a rightist-opportunist and put him under detention. All he'd written was that the famine was caused by cadres who were interested only in pleasing their superiors to advance their own careers, and to hell with the rest of the populace. For years they'd sent up glowing reports of record-breaking harvests, and none had ever accepted responsibility for a single death.

Fear and temporary amnesia kept most Chinese people from talking about such things. They were only too eager to be magnanimous and forgiving.

Only the thin layer of skin of my mother's belly separated me from hunger. She starved herself for the two years leading up to my birth in order to feed her five children. The monthly ration in our city was twenty-six catties of grain per adult, from which were deducted 'volunteer' contributions of two catties to the Central Government, two more to the province, two to municipal authorities, and two to the individual work unit, leaving a grand total of eighteen catties a person, only six of which were of rice – the remainder included a variety of lesser grains: corn, soya beans, and coarse wheat flour. Few Sichuanese had ever felt the pangs of hunger before this; famines were things that happened to people in the northern regions of the Yellow and Huai Rivers, where water had seriously eroded the loess soil. In the fertile regions of the Yangtze and Jialing Rivers, grains grow like the hair on young people: lush and vigorous.

All five children in the family were at the growing age when they could never get enough to eat. If you were hungry, no problem: you went out and bought an expensive flatcake, at two yuan apiece, two days' wages for a common labourer. Even with every penny left over from our monthly expenses going to buy these flatcakes, each child still got no more than half. On holidays, determined not to let them pass unobserved, they'd buy a flatcake and give each child a little piece.

Every couple of days, police would come to drag someone from the neighbourhood away in handcuffs for stealing from the state granaries. The sentence was often ten years or more. People could be starving right and left, but the granaries must be filled in preparation for the coming war with the Soviet Revisionists or American Imperialists.

In Alley Cat Lane alone, it is no exaggeration to say that someone in seventy or eighty per cent of the families was guilty of pilfering or other criminal acts. In the struggle to keep bellies full, it was a rare individual who could proudly beat his chest and crow: My family is pure as the driven snow. Of the four sons from one family in the compound, for instance, three had spent time in jail, in a virtual revolving door of criminal activity, all to keep the family from starving.

Greens were also rationed, a few ounces per person per day, and that included the tough skin of cabbage; this kept people from fighting over discarded skins. Even the chaff of soya beans left behind from making tofu was a rationed item. The refuse of peanuts used to make oil, pressed into a big flatcake, was a delicacy you could obtain only if you had connections. The sole edibles we common folk could gather with no restrictions were the leaves and fresh inner bark of elm trees ground into paste. Huge quantities of Sichuan trees were destroyed during those three years, left to die after their bark had been stripped bare. Wild grasses and mushrooms on the mountain slopes were picked clean by children carrying bamboo baskets or back packs, and more kids were poisoned by toadstools than the hospitals could take care of.

My eldest sister took the other kids to a nearby village to pick wild onions that were barely distinguishable from common weeds. She told them to search the tall grass while she went into the fields to steal cultivated vegetables. But the peasants guarded their pitifully undergrown crops jealously, and when they spotted her, they drove her away with clubs.

But once in a while, she'd return with a few stringy vegetable stalks.

Third Brother refused to forage for wild grasses, he avoided kids who frantically searched the hillsides or farmers' fields for food, and he never joined those people who tried their luck with fishing poles on the riverbank. The river itself was his source of food. Undaunted by even the coldest water, whenever he saw something that looked like food, he dived in after it: vegetable skins, leafy greens, even melon rinds, it was all there for the taking. He was a strong swimmer; nothing could keep him from reaching his objective. Once he had whatever it was in his grasp, he'd swim back to shore and take it home, where Mother would wash it, cut out the rotten parts, and throw it into the wok. From time to time he'd return with a worn-out plastic sandal, which he'd sell at the recycling station for a few pennies.

But he wasn't always that lucky. Most of the time all the river offered up was muddy water, and he'd return home empty-handed, to the smug delight of Big Sister. But he was luckier than those kids who never returned from their search for food. Water from the snowy peaks of Qinghai kept the river temperature icy cold most of the year, and if you cramped up while you were swimming, getting back to shore was nearly impossible; sooner or later you'd be swept into one of the swirling eddies. Youngsters weakened by hunger never had a chance.

Naturally, whoever managed to bring food home was rewarded with a larger portion at that meal. One day, when Third Brother returned with some turnip leaves, he strutted proudly around the house, and when it was time to eat, he was actually crowing.

We kids eyed the food like hawks, afraid we might get a bite less than was coming to us. Sometimes, when one of us tried sneaking a little extra, a loud argument, even a fight, broke out. My eldest sister, the biggest of the bunch, never came out second best.

Sometimes, Father would return home from the boat in time to break up a fight among his children with his bamboo pole. Eating less than anyone gave him that right.

3

The municipal zoo owned a very rare and extremely valuable South China tiger, one of the world's most endangered species; the zoo keeper was instructed to supply it with living prey. All around people were starving, but since this was the only tiger of its kind anywhere in the province, it came first and people came second, just as high-level cadres came before mid-level cadres, and so on down the line. The tiger's keeper was a squat little man who had developed a fondness for the ferocious animal and was the only person it would allow near it. If he was sick and had to be replaced temporarily, the newcomer would toss the tiger's food to it over a high fence to avoid being attacked. Sometimes, when the keeper approached the animal, it would startle people with what seemed to be strangely aggressive behaviour; but the man knew that his tiger was just showing off for him, being affectionate. He was a model zoo keeper.

Then came the famine, and the zoo keeper suffered from hunger like everyone else. Somehow he managed for the first year, but before he'd made it through the second, he began holding back one of the rabbits earmarked for the tiger each week, killing and cooking it for himself. People said it wasn't just gnawing hunger that caused the tiger to tear its keeper limb from limb one day, but the smell of rabbit that clung to him. But that doesn't explain why the animal ate everything but one of the man's feet. After an investigation that lasted several days, the police determined that the tiger was sending a warning to its next keeper to keep his hands off its food.

This story made the rounds for a while then died out, and my guess is that it was just a cautionary tale with a political message. Eventually, the tiger starved to death, and if its keeper hadn't already been eaten, he would likely have shared its fate.

People lacking a privileged position got by any way they could. On Father's boat, each deckhand was given an ounce of rice to make gruel for breakfast, and two ounces for lunch and two for dinner. They weighed out their allotment then boiled it over a fire, filling the bowl with water just before it was ready to eat, in order to swell the kernels and stretch their absorption-power to the limit, thus tricking the stomach into thinking it was getting more than it was. The sailors never strayed far from the galley while the rice was cooking, keeping a wary eye on each other to make sure no one got sticky fingers.

A job requiring men always to be on the move provided the sailors with strange but useful connections. Whenever they made port, they'd go in search of whatever meagre local products they could find, then sell them at their next stops and pocket the profits. Invariably, disputes broke out between the haves and the have-nots, with the latter blowing the whistle on the former. Retribution was swift and severe: the guilty party was fired on the spot, which meant more food in his mates' bowls at the meals that followed.

Father was too decent for his own good, and even barely edible plants like thorny cactus were beyond his reach. When palm trees bloomed, the large corn-shaped flowers were fair game; but even these were gone before he got to them. If he was lucky, he'd get his hands on some palm-leaf tree roots, which he'd boil to remove the bitter taste then slice them up. The taste was awful, but it was better than some of the things people filled their empty stomachs with. Thoughts of Mother dragging a brood of kids up the mountain to forage for edible weeds only increased his determination to pull his belt even tighter, to eat just enough to stay alive and bring the rest home with him.

Then one day he tripped and fell headlong to the main deck from the cabin, and when he tried to get up, he rolled overboard. Blood gushed from a deep cut in his head, but only after they'd sailed from Yibin all the way to Luzhou was he finally taken to a hospital, where an examination showed that his eyesight was seriously impaired.

During that winter of starvation, Mother had to work as a porter in the plastic-sandal factory even though she was pregnant; the hard work and the need to keep me alive inside her should have given her the right to eat more than the others. But no, not in the eyes of my brothers and sisters, especially not for the sake of someone who wasn't even born yet. During those terrible times, they were forced to make sacrifices for me they didn't think they should have had to make, and as the years passed, this thought may have disappeared from their minds but not from their hearts. I always felt they held a grudge against me, but never knew exactly why.

I was so undernourished in the womb that I refused to budge, which confused and frightened Mother. I was born in the Women and Children's Clinic in central Chongqing. Mother told me that when she was passing by the entrance to a moviehouse where the movie *Hong Lake Red Detachment*, a paean to a woman leader of Communist guerrillas, was showing, her waters burst. She tried to keep walking, but the contractions forced her to sit on the kerb. Some kind passers-by, seeing she was pregnant and in obvious discomfort, helped her to the clinic.

All those kids, and I was the first to be born in a hospital. For the others, she had managed on her own – cutting the umbilical cord, cleaning the infant, and bundling him or her up. But when she counted the days she knew I was late, and was afraid I'd be stillborn, so she decided to go into the city centre. For a long time after coming into this world, I didn't cry; finally, the doctor picked me up by my feet and swatted me on the backside, sending a mouthful of bitter liquid out of my throat, followed by my first feeble cries.

Everyone said I was lucky to have been born as summer turned to autumn in 1962. The good harvests that year brought an end to a famine that had lasted three years and claimed the lives of tens of millions of people, until the survivors were reduced to cannibalism. Unlike the rest of the Maoist era, during those three years the songs of glory to Communism were somewhat muted.

By the time I was beginning to understand what was going on around me, and the people had food on their tables again, Mao Zedong translated his fervour into a political experiment known as the Great Proletarian Cultural Revolution. Everyone said I was lucky, because the famine had taught Mao that there were no limits to what he could get away with, including throwing the nation into anarchy, just so long as he didn't mess with people's food. During the Cultural Revolution, factories stopped producing and schools were shut down, but the peasants generally still tended the fields. Admittedly there were food shortages, everything was rationed, and malnourishment among children and adults was common, but hardly to the extent of mass starvation. If people had to spend much of their time searching for food and eating whatever was available, edible or not, they would not have the energy to wreak havoc on their fellow citizens.

Hunger was my embryonic education. Mother and daughter survived the ordeal, but only after the spectre of hunger was indelibly stamped in my mind. I haven't the heart to think about the cruel sacrifices she made to keep me alive.

I had the outward appearance of youthful calmness, but that's all it was – an appearance. Deep down I was tormented by thoughts that I was somehow superfluous, and I didn't know why. Sometimes I didn't even want that stranger, the man who was always following me, to go away; in fact, I longed for him to be more menacing, to do something so heinously violent that people would shudder at the mere thought of it. At least I wouldn't be superfluous any more. That sort of ending would make people sit up and take notice of me. Such thoughts excited me.

Night in and night out, sleep took me roughly from one bad dream to the next, until I woke up screaming, covered with sweat, as if I were deathly ill. In my dreams I was always hungry and could never find my ricebowl, though I could smell food. Quietly I began to sob. Hoping no one would hear me, I was driven by the desire to fall to my knees before anyone holding a ricebowl. For the sake of getting my hands on a fragrant piece of braised pork, I would gladly prostrate myself at the feet of someone who had insulted or demeaned me. Then I'd wake up, and as I mulled over my dream, I'd berate myself, begin hating myself, as I wondered where such a powerful bodily need had come from.

You weren't born that way, I kept telling myself. You can't know what happened to you in the womb; how can you carry scars from abuse you never received? But then how was I supposed to explain my behaviour? I was, for instance, incredibly sensitive to the taste of food. I wasn't a child any longer, but I thought constantly about food and was always hungry. Yet no matter how much I ate, I remained thin as a rail. Just the smell of egg-fried rice drifting over from a neighbour's kitchen had me salivating in no time. Snacks never interested me, and I despised my 'spicy-mouthed' schoolmates who spent their pocket money on them. But fatty chunks of pork, that was a different matter. My persistent fantasy was to grow up independent enough to eat meat at every meal.

I was also incredibly sensitive to any sort of mistreatment. Little slights that didn't faze other people always had a powerful effect on me. And once my feelings were hurt, nothing seemed to help, no matter how hard I tried.

I knew I wasn't a strong, aggressive girl, and my tongue never served me well. Just being with people was nerve-racking. Wherever I was – at school, at home, or with a group

The riverside slums of Chongqing, today

The boat on which Hong Ying's father worked on the Yangtze River (foreground)

Mother and Father in the 1950s, after Liberation

Mother, with Hong Ying, aged two

Mother in 1961, aged thirty-four

Big Sister in 1962, aged sixteen

Big Sister and her
sent-down friends
in the village, 1964

Hong Ying in 1980, aged eighteen

Fourth Sister, 1980

Fourth Sister's
fiancé, 1980

of girls – I was the scrawniest person, with the gauntest face and the stringiest hair. So I invariably searched out a remote corner, as far removed from the eyes of others as possible to avoid the pressures they forced upon me; I knew that the best way for those people to feel good was at my expense.

Could the effects of the famine still linger on after eighteen years? People a few years older than me had gone hungry, while those who were my age had suffered from the famine in their mothers' bellies. How could they be so happy? How had they managed to put it all behind them and immerse themselves in the pleasures of youth? They enjoyed life, they loved it, while I was always melancholic and unhappy.

Had I experienced something different from all the others; was that it?

When I asked Mother about those times, all she said was, 'Oh that. Nothing much. Only Three Years of Poor Harvest, Soviet Revisionists and American Imperialists. Anti-China Chorus. What else? But we pulled you ungrateful bunch through it all, didn't we? Why dredge up accounts that have already been written off?'

But Mother's cold detachment only reinforced my curiosity. A female porter, one of Chongqing's so-called 'polers', how had she made it through those terrible times? Who'd given a damn about her? She had only herself. Maybe she'd won the favour of the person who ladled out portions in the Dining Hall of the People's Commune and, with a dip deep in the pot, got a slightly thicker porridge than the others; or maybe she'd flirted with the man in charge of doling out vegetables and, with a flick of the wrist, received a few sprigs more than she had coming to her. In the midst of a famine, everyone's eyes shone greedily, and fights could break out in an instant over pennies. The Dining Hall of the People's Commune was where deals were made, if you knew how you could find ways to stave off hunger, even for a child in the womb. There was only one problem: the person in charge of the Dining Hall was invariably a gruff, hundred-per-cent-reliable Party member, so what chance did a family like ours, with absolutely no connections, have to share in the spoils?

More than once my eldest sister complained that, when she went to the Dining Hall, she was always given the thinnest, weakest gruel there was – more like water than actual food – and it did no good to sit down and cry over it. So she'd bring it home, drinking half of it on the way, which forced her brothers and sisters to go over and cause such a scene, drawing a big crowd, that the Dining Hall worker had no choice but to add a little thickness to the pot.

'It's your fault people treat us this way! We're that close to becoming a bunch of hungry ghosts.' Big Sister never could keep a lid on that mouth of hers, but there was no call to treat Mother like that.

As her face reddened with anger, Mother could hardly breathe. But somehow she held her tongue and didn't argue back. Why was it that, when anyone brought up the years of famine, Mother never said a word, even when they took their frustrations out on her? Had she done something she couldn't talk about?

5

All the next morning at school, I couldn't think of anything but what Mother had said, how all she'd get was a pitifully small pension when she retired.

What about me? Should I do what she wanted? If I stopped studying for the entrance exams, there'd be no reason to keep going to school, and I wouldn't see the history teacher any more. That's what hurt the most. But if I stayed at school, what was I going to do about textbooks and exercise books for this semester, let alone the next? I couldn't ask Mother for the money. I could probably borrow the textbooks, but what about the exercise books? Then, while I was worrying about myself, I thought about the little bit of money Father got for his disability. His night blindness was a work-related injury, so he should be drawing full salary. If I could somehow pull this off, so Father would get several years of back pay, I should get something out of it, shouldn't I? So I plucked up the courage to take the ferry into the city centre.

'We can't reach up to heaven and can't keep our feet on the ground. The devil himself wouldn't show his face in a crummy place like this.' Our neighbour was always griping about having to live in South Bank. It was miles from everywhere – hospitals, coal shops, markets, theatres, the post office – and to get anywhere you had to climb up or down several hundred metres. Everything required planning for a long, arduous trip. So it was a big deal for me to cross the river and go into the city centre.

In 1980 the Chongqing Yangtze River Bridge was completed, a link from the city centre to South Bank, and the citizens celebrated joyously, calling it a great victory for socialism. From now on, they felt, they too could be considered genuine residents of the city. But it didn't take long to discover that for those of us fated to live in the hillside slums south of the river, a trip to the city centre meant walking to the top of the hill where there were roads, then taking a long, circuitous bus ride before actually crossing the bridge. It not only took a longer time, but was more expensive as well. That bridge didn't do us much good. The only times any of us ever squeezed on to a bus to cross the bridge was when the river was fogged in, or a floodtide kept the ferry from operating. It was faster and cheaper to go by boat, so in the end nothing changed.

It was about three in the afternoon when I found the office of the Provincial Steamboat Company, where several cadre types were sitting at their desks reading newspapers and drinking tea. One was talking on the telephone.

No one paid any attention to me or to my questions, so I walked in and said I was the child of a retired employee, and wanted to know why my father hadn't received his full disability. Still they ignored me. I repeated myself. The man on the telephone hung up, walked over, and sized me up.

'What do we have here?' he said officiously. 'A little girl who's come to ask for her dad's wages. Go home. We do our job in accordance with Party policies and under the authority of Central Government directives. There can be no mistakes.'

I could feel my teeth knocking against each other; keeping my eyes fixed on the desktop, not on the man, I poured out my prepared speech: not only shouldn't my father be receiving a partial medical pension, but his seniority was miscalculated. He was listed as starting the job in 1949, the year of Liberation, when in fact he had been with the company well before 1945, when the Anti-Japanese United Front between the Kuomintang and Communists was still in place. All this was documented.

But before I'd finished stating my case, a clean-shaven man who'd been sitting at his desk drinking tea stood up, looked down his nose at me, and said, 'You're still young, but you've got spunk. I'll let you have a look, but after you've seen what I have to show you, go home and stop pestering us.' He took out a key, with which he unlocked a cabinet and removed a file folder from a tall stack, flipping through it until he found what he was looking for – a small notebook. He opened it. 'Here, see for yourself.'

I looked down to where he was pointing. I was stunned! 'Following successful treatment for syphilis, patient's eyesight deteriorated.' My father, who wouldn't allow any of his children to say a dirty word – could he have been with other women? No, he had room in his heart only for my mother. How could he be associated with this disease?

'That's impossible!' I shouted. 'There isn't a person in the world more decent than my father.'

The cadres exchanged glances, then burst out laughing.

Now I was really puzzled. Father was on his boat, day and night, all those years. That's where his eyesight problems began, when he fell into the river. He nearly died, and ought to be getting full disability.

'He's not getting what's coming to him. Won't you please help us straighten this out?' I asked in a soft, pleading voice.

'Which one of his children is this rude little girl?' one of the men asked.

'Number six, I think.'

'Ah, number six.' Mixed with his laughter was a discernible note of derision, and his eyes seemed to be unpeeling me as they worked their way down from the top of my head. These people dealt with tens of thousands of cases, and still they knew more about my father's case than I did. Their dossier cabinet held the fates of countless labouring men and women.

I was crushed, and it took all the will-power I had not to cry. Fears accompanied me as I walked out of the office. How could people have so many secrets? Secrets that could shake me to the core if I accidentally bumped into them.

FOUR

1

After dinner I sat at the table deep in thought, watching my brothers and sisters come and go. 'Little Six,' Mother said, 'I don't like that look on your face. You should be glad you were allowed to go on living. Being alive is all that counts, especially for someone with your background. So just accept it.' She was sitting on the bed repairing a torn pillow.

I hadn't seen her for days, but the same old problem still preyed on her mind: taking the college entrance exams did not fit my background. 'Don't support me if you don't want to,' I said with a pout. 'But why all this life and death nonsense?'

'Because that's what this is all about,' she said. 'Your third aunt, a cousin who was closer to me than my own sister, she didn't survive, did she?'

Mother said the last time she took herbal medicine over to Third Aunt at Stony Slope to give her a bath, in the spring of 1961, her cousin was laid up with dropsy from severe malnutrition. Her skin was nearly translucent, her face swollen like an oil-paper lantern.

Her husband had owned a little butcher shop, which he ran with a hired helper, and life wasn't bad. But by the early 1950s, not only could he no longer engage hired help, the shop was even converted into joint state–private ownership. He was arrested in 1957 and sent to prison for having said in a teashop one day that everything was great now that the Communists were in power, except that life had been better for him before Liberation. Someone reported him, and during the ensuing investigation, it was discovered that he had once been a member of a religious society. For that, he was labelled a 'bad element' and sent to a labour-reform camp.

In order to survive and raise her two young sons, Third Aunt went to work as a porter. Both boys died anyway and eventually the work was too hard for her, so she began gleaning cast-off vegetables at the marketplace, and took in washing when she could.

Mother crossed the river and rushed over to see her the minute she heard she was ill. Her arrival was greeted with tears from Third Aunt, who struggled to sit up. Just look at me, cousin, she said, grabbing Mother's hand. I can't hold out until my husband returns.

The first thing Mother did was make some thick soya-bean soup, since everyone said soya beans were especially nutritious. Third Aunt wouldn't eat it. You have so many mouths to feed, she said. Take that home for them. But Mother left the soya-bean powder behind when she returned home, never dreaming that Third Aunt would die so soon thereafter.

Then one Sunday that winter, Mother was in the hall when a gaunt, sallow-faced man she didn't recognize dragged himself in the door. Not until he came up close and called out Second Cousin did she realize it was her cousin's husband. Four years earlier, he had been sentenced to seven years of labour-reform. In total shock, she asked how he had got out three years early.

Instead of using the stool Mother had moved over for him, he sat on the threshold. He had been a man who loved to laugh and tell stories, someone who could keep a straight face while everyone else was rolling with laughter. Obsessed with neatness and cleanliness, he had always kept his hair neatly combed. Now he was dressed in rags and could barely open his eyes. He looked like a scraggly weed, with scars all over his discoloured skin; and he'd never sat on the threshold before.

He told Mother there had been nothing to eat in the labour-reform camp, not even wild vegetables. All the sparrows and rats had vanished, most to nearby villagers, who were quicker on their feet than the inmates. The old and the sick were the first to go, and those left behind were too weakened by hunger to bury them. So the authorities let him out early and told him to return to Chongqing, where he was to submit to surveillance by local authorities.

She's gone, he said. Why couldn't she wait another few months? Mother had been agonizing over how to break the news that Third Aunt had starved to death. But he already knew.

He said he had nowhere to go. Since his house was vacant, the housing authority had reassigned the three rooms to another family and confiscated his furnishings. Naturally, the new tenants weren't willing to take him in as a boarder.

But before Third Uncle had finished his story, Mother was summoned into the kitchen, where she was confronted by a group of neighbours with advanced political consciousness. They came straight to the point: You may not house that labour-reform convict in this compound! Even if you tried, a class enemy wouldn't be able to register for his residence and rations here. How could you find food for someone who should be dead anyway? Send him on his way, the sooner the better. We don't want the likes of him around! They gave Mother no chance to come to his defence, since their shrill words were meant for his ears as he sat on the threshold in the adjoining room.

You could say our neighbours went easy on Third Uncle, since they could have forcibly driven him out themselves. So Mother walked out of the kitchen hesitantly, only to find that Third Uncle was already gone. She elbowed her way through the crowd that still surrounded her to run after him.

Third Uncle was so sickly, she easily caught up with him. The trees on the slope had not yet sprouted, bearing no edible young leaves. Mother handed him two yuan. When he refused to take it, she said she'd take him home with her if he didn't, and to hell with what other people said.

Finally he took the money. I'm a lost cause, he said, and still you find it in your heart to take pity on me. He started to cry, so did Mother. Hers were tears of frustration for not being able to let her kin stay at our house.

Two weeks passed and Mother, still worried, took the ferry to the house in Stony Slope where Third Uncle had lived. She asked around, but no one knew where he was. A family of six lived in the house now, just as Third Uncle had said.

Third Uncle had wandered for days, with nowhere to go and no one willing to give him the documents he needed to get food. Surviving by begging back then was next to impossible – there were beggars everywhere you looked. Who had food to give them? He spent the nights in the public toilet at the bottom of the slope, with nothing to eat or drink, and no rags to protect him from the cold winds. After growing bloated from dropsy, he finally starved to death, his eyes still open. The woman who now lived in Third Aunt's house gestured to show how wide they were.

His body? Mother was shaking so badly she nearly collapsed, and had to grab hold of the door frame.

Took it away, the woman remarked tersely. Who are you to him? Ah, well, it doesn't make any difference. Take my advice and forget him. A labour-reform convict can only bring trouble. With that, the woman closed the door, forcing Mother outside. She heard the bolt slam.

'Why did I only give him two yuan? I had five on me. He came to me for help. I was pregnant with you then, I did it for you. So he died, cold and hungry. And he'd been so generous with us when we needed it.' Mother bit off the thread, put her sewing kit away, and looked up at me. What she had said earlier rang in my ears: You should be glad you were allowed to go on living.

That public toilet where he died was like all others: filthy, smelly, putrid, a place where, if you weren't careful, you could fall into a pit of excrement. Dying in a place like that

51

was worse than dying at the side of a road. Mother's remorse struck me as being little more than an excuse to justify her own actions. She could have stood up to the pressure and let Third Uncle stay with us, at least for a few days. But withstanding the pressure would have made her a better person. She simply didn't have it in her; she was selfish and scared. There was no rice in the barrel and no oil in the pot, and she had 'political pigtails' that could be pulled at any time. So for the sake of my brothers and sisters, and for me, Mother became a coward.

Does this mean that I was born laden with guilt?

2

After clearing the table, I took the dishes into the kitchen, where a naked fifteen-watt bulb cast a dim light. The water was cold and the fire in the stove was out. I'd be wasting coal to make a fire just to wash dishes; luckily, there wasn't enough oil to make them greasy. We may be poor, Father would say, but that doesn't mean we can't be clean. So every two or three weeks, we'd scrub with baking soda the dishes, the wooden wok lid and the bamboo table in front of the stove.

Sounds of weeping emerged from the home of Mama Wang, directly opposite the kitchen. A moment later, her open door was slammed shut. 'All day long, all you ever do is fight! You'll drive me straight to the crematorium!' Mama Wang was trying to break up a fight, while actually contributing to it with her cursing. Her youngest son and his wife, who had three kids, put on a show for us every two or three days, and it had got so bad that when Mama Wang's two daughters came home, they never stayed more than a few hours. Her second son had joined the People's Liberation Army in 1956, when eastern Tibetans rose up in rebellion, and was sent to the border between Sichuan and Tibet. The herdsmen rode like the wind, attacking the camps at night and lopping off their captives' heads. Eventually, the government sent paratroopers with flame throwers to build a wall of fire before the frenzied horsemen could be stopped. Mobilizing raw recruits like Mama Wang's second son was like sending them into the jaws of death.

But overnight, Mama Wang gained the stature of martyr's kin, and every year, on Soldier's Day and New Year's, the Neighbourhood Committee marched into our compound, with gongs and drums, to paste a letter of honour with a red official seal on her door. One year she was even awarded a small wooden plaque with red letters proclaiming 'Glorious Family of a Martyr', which was hung above her door where everyone could see it. Mama Wang basked in the glory, her face wreathed in smiles. And any time a quarrel erupted over some trivial matter, she would utter the fateful words: 'I am a martyr's kin.'

'Your son is dead, but you've never shed a single tear over him,' her youngest daughter-in-law would berate her during an argument.

'Why should I be sad?' she'd answer self-righteously. 'He sacrificed himself for the Revolution, and I couldn't be happier.'

This son was the best-looking of Mama Wang's children, and the most obedient. He had excelled at school, and would have gone on to college if, at the tender age of nineteen, he hadn't felt that being a soldier in the PLA was the greater glory.

'When a boy is too good, the devils come looking for him,' Uncle Wang could be heard muttering to himself on his days off. The picture of aggravation whenever he was home, he invariably returned to his ship before his leave was up. A framed five-by-seven black-and-white photograph of his second son, a smiling middle-school student at the time, hung on the wall between the bed and the dresser, and every time I looked at that photograph, I shuddered to think of that head rolling to the ground.

When local children started kindergarten at the age of three or four, they were taken as a group to the local Class Struggle Museum. But since the kindergarten required tuition of several yuan, I had to stand on the other side of the wall and listen with envy to the singing of 'Never Forget Class Suffering', accompanied by an accordion. Only after I started school at the age of seven was I lucky enough finally to see this museum and its display of torture instruments used by the reactionaries against the revolutionary masses, plus an array of gory photographs of slain revolutionaries. There were also hideous photos of counter-revolutionaries executed after the victory of the People's Revolution.

'Always be on guard against remnants of Kuomintang Rule, who have survived in a variety of disguises! Revolutionary novels show how whipped Kuomintang agents were ordered to destroy this city and bring an end to our happy lives in new China. Never forget class struggle, report to the police and Party branch office all saboteurs hiding in the dark corners of society!'

These interminable warnings and admonitions had us ten year olds looking over our shoulders, anxious and fearful, as if surrounded by secret agents. On rainy, gloomy days, when people wore conical hats to cover their faces, everyone looked evil.

I rarely went to Mama Wang's house, because her smug martyr's-kin grin reminded me of the Class Struggle Museum, and such daytime thoughts normally led to nightmares later on.

After dumping the dirty water out of the wok, I hung it on a wall peg, then picked up the spatula, chopsticks, and a stack of bowls, and quickly left the kitchen. Knowing that Mama Wang was actually afraid of her youngest son, and that her blustery curses were just an excuse to vent her anger, I was sure she'd soon find a new target. And sure enough, as I was passing the stairs on the left side of the hall on my way into our room, her curses assailed my ears.

'What's that bulb doing on at this hour? It's still lights out! Are you blind? The government has called on us to save electricity – every kilowatt-hour and every drop of water counts. Our blessings were paid for in blood! This month's kitchen electricity bill is going to make my heart bleed!' She sounded so distressed, yet so self-assured.

I wanted to review my maths lessons, but her endless harping upset me so much I got up and walked outside. It was so dark that the sky seemed about to crash down on my head. Daytime, my eye! You're not the only one who pays the electricity bill, everybody pays their share, I grumbled inwardly. Then I thought about the pictures of the executed revolutionaries and counter-revolutionaries, a whole wall full of them. I wondered why all the executed counter-revolutionaries had their pants down around their knees. Bloody, grey muck on top and something sticky and black down below. Someone said they didn't want the condemned to kill themselves or run away on their way to the execution ground, so they took away their sashes, which were the only things holding up the old-fashioned baggy pants. But those things between their legs, why were they so ugly? And was it only bad men whose ugly thing was exposed when they were shot?

3

People cooling off outside or gossiping with friends had all gone home, so I sat under the streetlight quietly going over my lessons. My eyelids were battling to stay open, and the words on the pages began to get blurry and all twisted. Afraid of being locked out, I kept checking the door, since I'd have to yell for ever before anyone opened it for me. Finally, unable to stand it any longer, I picked up my book and my stool and headed back, closing the gate behind me and sliding the heavy latch into place. The compound was deathly still, the sound and fury of that day seemingly belonging to a previous life. The silence created a sense of unreality.

The attic door was ajar, so I went in and closed it behind me. With Indian summer behind us, the nights were quite a bit cooler than the days. Breezes entered through the skylight, and, while the room wasn't as stuffy, it was still too warm for a blanket. I changed into my cotton nightgown, lay down on the grass mat, and covered myself with a sheet. All of a sudden, I heard Fourth Sister and her boyfriend, Dehua, turning over in bed on the other side of the curtain, and my sleepiness vanished into thin air.

Fourth Sister was sleeping in the bed that all us girls had once crowded into, directly opposite the attic door. I was in the other bed, the narrow one next to the door, where my two brothers had slept. The ceiling sloped from left to right; it was lowest right above my head. The curtain, added after we grew up, had been washed so many times it was pasty-coloured. Connecting the two walls with the curtain was a small piece of linen, behind which was hidden a covered chamber pot.

More rustling from behind the curtain: Dehua pulled back a corner and went over to piss in the chamber pot. Fourth Sister got out of bed and went in after he came out.

Lying there with my eyes closed, I listened to the splashing sounds coming from the other side. The pungent odour filled my nostrils, but I remained motionless until they finished their business, went back to bed, and fell asleep. Then I rolled over and stared at the skylight.

Ever since I was a child, my family had lived together, male and female, with no self-consciousness. Shame and civility were things we could preserve in an abstract sense. We were all used to it. But now Fourth Sister had a boyfriend, bringing a non-blood resident into an already crowded room, and his presence made me very uncomfortable.

The moonlight filtering in through the skylight had a blue tinge, enshrouding the pitch-black attic in eeriness. Alley cats prowled the broken tiles of the eaves, their heavy footsteps sounding like an intruder walking across our roof in the darkness to spy on the movements in the house below. All sorts of disturbing sounds could be heard in this rundown compound late at night. Suddenly I recalled the shadowy figure who dogged me during the day. Why was he following me, and not some other girl? For the very first time, I shivered at the thought. Why, I wondered, was I born into a world where happiness did not exist? Why did I have to experience so many slights, so much negligence and sorrow?

I pulled up my nightgown, as my breathing grew heavy. My body had developed into the wicked figure of a woman. Some places protruded gracelessly, showing pasty white in the darkness of night. I was nearly eighteen, and it was time to start seeing some of life's exciting colours. But so far not the slightest hint of brightness had emerged. I needed dreams, I thought forlornly. But I had nothing, and the years to come wouldn't be any better. My schoolwork seemed to have hit a dead end. The more I studied, the harder it was to retain all those formulas and socialist theories. No one from Alley Cat Stream had ever been admitted to college, so what made me think a girl like me, to whom no one had ever paid any attention, would be the exception? My grades were no better than anyone else's, and I was sure I was fated to end up like everyone else on this hillside: carrying sand, emptying chamber pots, and raising kids.

I told myself that, no matter what, I had to have dreams; even an impossible dream was better than no dream at all. Without them I was lost, doomed to live out my life as a South Bank woman toiling for the rest of my life.

4

When I got up early in the morning, Father was still sitting on his stool by the stairs in the hall, smoking his bamboo pipe filled with cheap tobacco that had a stinging bite. I turned away to avoid the irritating cloud. I never saw Father eat anything in the morning. He just smoked his pipe. As a little girl I believed him when he said he wasn't hungry. But after I grew up I realized that he had got out of the habit of eating breakfast during the famine; the less he ate, the more there was for us kids. Then by the time there was enough food to go around, it was too late to break the habit. Food in the morning upset his stomach.

Father put down his pipe and took a crisp new banknote out of his pocket — it was a neatly folded half-yuan note. He looked quickly around the room before stuffing it into my hand, which caught me by surprise. Why be so furtive about giving me money? I took the money up to the attic, which looked strange in the bright sunlight. The curtain between the two beds was pulled halfway open; Fourth Sister and Dehua were nowhere in sight. The bedding was a mess, revealing loose bamboo strips. I sat on the edge of my bed and let my textbooks slip to the floor. Once the shadow of clouds glided over the hillside, the attic would sink into semi-darkness.

Mother's voice came rolling up the stairs. I have to go down to the river again, she was saying to Father. I did the laundry a few days ago, and the basket's already full of dirty clothes.

I stared at the crisp new half-yuan note in my hand as I heard her walk to the gate. Then it dawned on me: It's 21 September, isn't it? My eighteenth birthday. No wonder Father slipped me the money.

Mother hadn't mentioned my birthday the day before, and it was obviously the last thing on her mind today as she headed down to the river to do the laundry. This was my eighteenth birthday, and she knew better than I what that meant to a girl. Was she avoiding me? No, she'd just forgotten, it was as simple as that. But what difference would it have made if she had remembered? Nothing about me ever troubled her mind.

I went downstairs and walked outside, pointedly saying nothing to Father.

On my way up the hill to High School Avenue I passed the elementary-school dormitory, where some retired teachers holding their grandchildren sat or stood watching people pass by. A white-haired old woman called out to say she'd seen my elder sister. She wasn't alone, the old woman said. She had a travel bag over her shoulder and was walking with a short, chubby woman. There were too many people around for her to get her attention.

After all this waiting, Big Sister was finally back. But I hadn't walked much further when it occurred to me that she'd returned to Chongqing, but hadn't come home. Why? She wasn't one to hide things from people, so the old woman must have been wrong.

I headed towards Stonebridge, where there were crowds of people. It was Sunday, and a nice day – no rain, not too hot – and people from all over had come to the market. In addition to produce carried in from the countryside by peasants, just about anything you might want was arrayed up and down the two streets approved by the district government for selling. The cacophony of sounds included shouts, bartering, and the persistent buzzing of flies. To ensure that the meat they bought was fresh, customers demanded to watch the animals being slaughtered. A vendor seated on a long bench took a live frog out of his bamboo basket and slit its throat, then deftly skinned and gutted it, revealing four pale limbs that were still twitching. His hands and rubber apron were splattered with blood; piles of red and black intestines, livers, stomachs and lungs cluttered the area around his feet; and green skins were thrown everywhere. Slaughtered frogs lay in his basin, legs intertwined; bloody water ran at the base of the rough stone wall.

I walked down a row of steps and skirted the most crowded section of road. But there were still lots of people, including adults dragging their children along, talking and laughing, tightly knit, happy families. There were people everywhere – the post office, the moviehouse, teahouses. What to buy for my birthday? As I threaded my way through the crowds I passed a photographer's studio. For Father and me, half a yuan was a lot of money, but not enough for even the cheapest portrait. Men and women with Chairman Mao badges and 'little red books' that had once decorated the show window had been replaced by smiling women posing in their perms and skirts. Across the street was a pharmacy, next to it a department store. A few steps, and I was inside.

I moved from showcase to showcase without seeing anything I wanted and could afford. There were plenty of cosmetics – lipsticks, rouge, eyebrow pencils – but all too expensive for me. Besides, they were associated with 'beauty', a word whose significance escaped me.

I went up to the top floor, where a spectacular view spread out below me: there, to the north, were the Yangtze and Green Grass Flatland on its north bank, the shipyards, and an ancient tower. Off to the east I saw Stonebridge Square, which didn't seem so big from this distance. It was bordered on one side by an open-air market, on a second by criss-crossed patches of farmland, and on the other two by dirty, nondescript buildings, including a steel-processing plant and Provincial Prison Number Two, where political prisoners and hardened criminals served long sentences.

Originally, Stonebridge Square was just a tract of ground that could not be farmed because of all the garbage and broken bricks that had accumulated on it. During my final two years of middle school, classes were let out two days a week for us to perform voluntary labour, carrying sand from the riverbank to fill in potholes and turn the place into a respectable public square. We schoolkids laboured alongside grown-ups to help them fill their work quotas. It was hard work, but I completed my assigned tasks every time.

The most glorious moment in Stonebridge Square's history occurred when it was chosen as the site for huge open-air trials. Ear-shattering loudspeakers were erected on a temporary wooden platform; banners and scrolls were flapping all over the place. After the trials, armed guards herded the bound criminals on to trucks, where they stood with their shaved heads pushed down low. Around their necks hung wooden plaques listing their crimes: 'murderer', 'rapist', 'counter-revolutionary', 'grafter', 'robber', and one I didn't understand, 'sodomite'. Their names, crossed with red ink, were written below. The trucks then drove slowly up and down the main streets of South Bank as a warning to the populace. A few years earlier, executions had taken place in front of a mound on the edge of the square. But that caused such excitement and chaos that things went wrong sometimes with the firing squads or their prisoners: shots that went wide of their mark or prisoners shouting and yelling what were considered insults to the Great Leader and the Great Party. Once a prisoner with a shattered head took off running in the direction of the onlookers, scaring some of them half to death. And there were even cases of prisoners breaking free and running for their lives. After that, the final act in the drama – the executions – took place in a mountain gully from which there was no escape.

I nearly died in that square. The year I graduated from middle school, there was a public trial for Rebels who took too much pleasure in the Cultural Revolution, young men accused of 'beating, smashing, and looting'. In the factional battles their bullets had killed their opponents, and blood debts must be paid in blood. Teachers took their students to the trial for educational purposes. At least ten thousand people crowded into the public square that day, until even the tops of the walls were fully occupied. The sun was out, until thunder and lightning split the sky, and a deluge followed within seconds, just as the executions were to be carried out. The police would not let the crowd disperse, and no one dared move, though they were soaked to the skin. All of a sudden, one of the walls collapsed, sending a dozen or so people crashing to the ground. This threw the crowd into a frenzy, and people whose nerves were already jangled leaped to flee the square, running over the collapsed wall and trampling the people who had fallen with it. Trembling with fear, I crouched to the side and didn't move. But panic-stricken people surged past, stepping all over each other. The loud-speakers failed to calm down the people, and the police cars and ambulances careering all over the place only added to the confusion.

'Innocent heads have been lopped off, skull pots have been shattered. Heaven won't allow that, and demands sacrifice.' The person who said that was a beggar who lived in ash heaps behind restaurants. He was reported and taken away by the police.

On the way home, muddy and frightened, I saw small groups of people standing beside walls, winking and whispering furtively to each other.

5

Before work on the square was completed, news of Mao Zedong's death reached us. It was September 1976. 'Double nines, Emperor declines.' Only those who had participated in the construction of the square were given the honour of attending the solemn memorial service; all others had to settle for smaller ceremonies at their work units.

That day, Stonebridge Square was bedecked with white flowers and black armbands; a menacing atmosphere was created by the presence of armed police. The voice of Chairman Mao's chosen successor, Hua Guofeng, with its odd countrified accent, blared from the loudspeakers, adding to the grandeur. Sobs turned to wails, and all around me were tear-streaked faces; there's nothing quite so contagious as crying. I was fourteen, and fear gripped my heart as tears welled up in my eyes. Finally, I lost control and wept.

After the ceremony, as the teacher led us back to school, our eyes were checked as if we were cattle. Were they red enough? Puffy enough? Sad enough? That was how you showed undying loyalty to the Great Leader. My tears came fast and dried fast, and my eyes were neither red enough nor swollen enough. But I looked very sad, like most days. For once, a look of melancholy, which normally made people uncomfortable, worked to my advantage.

6

One year rains flooded Stonebridge Avenue for days, turning the roads and lanes into swamps. The storm and flooding swept all sorts of junk away and washed the stone steps so clean you could lie down and take a nap on them. But the river had changed: thatched huts, wooden tubs, entire trees, even corpses – impossible to tell if they were pigs or dogs or humans – were swept along on its surface. People went out in homemade rafts to scavenge for usable items. You had to envy those who took wristwatches from floating corpses, not just because watches were valuable but because it didn't count as theft – watches certainly weren't much use to the dead.

An overweight furniture painter who lived on Alley Cat Stream's major lane went out one day proudly wearing five watches that he had gleaned. He was quickly arrested and taken away by the police, shouting and complaining all the way that he was different from muggers, who toss their victims into the river after they've taken their valuables.

That storm washed away whole shaky houses, furniture and garbage included. But miraculously, Waterhouse, which was on stilts, stayed right where it was. Three days after the water receded, leaving mildew spots on its walls, it was open for business again. And now that the storm had passed, the captivating aroma of Waterhouse's meaty dumplings and pot-stickers filled nearby lanes. People said the owner owed his success to his father, who had studied Taoist magic on Mount Emei, and exerted his power on the filling of the buns. I only noticed how good the meat was, how much there was of it, and how deliciously fresh the garlic and onions were.

But after leaving the department store, I walked uphill to

the moviehouse. I'd always wanted to see a movie, and didn't care if it was in colour or had a good sound track, just so long as there were flickering images. Any movie would do, even a documentary of China's scenic wonders or of China's leaders welcoming foreign VIPs or of airborne crop-dusters in action. Sometimes Father slipped me five cents for a movie at school to satisfy my craving. But this would be the first time I picked out a movie all by myself, and I was thrilled by the idea. At that moment, a fierce battle raged between spiritual and material nourishment.

Food won out in the end. I walked back downhill, crossed the road, and went straight to the Waterhouse counter, where a dozen people were queued up waiting for a fresh batch of meat dumplings to come out of the oven.

The menu was written on a small blackboard: meat-filled buns, dumplings, baked flatcakes, noodles, steamed buns, triangular rice-cakes, and soya-bean milk. The prices for each and the number of required grain coupons were scribbled in varying shades of ink. I only had half a yuan, but I stood in the queue anyway, my attention caught by fluffy meat-and-vegetable-filled buns with thin white wrappings. Wooden stools around the shop's four tables were occupied by customers drinking soya-bean milk or slurping won-ton soup with pieces of onion floating on the top.

When it was my turn, the crewcut young ticket-seller waited impatiently for me to place my order. I handed over my half-yuan note and said coyly, 'Two meat buns.'

'Your grain coupons?' he asked, just as I'd feared.

'I forgot them,' I explained anxiously, adding under my breath, 'The buns are twenty cents apiece, two for forty cents. Forget the coupons and keep the change, what do you say?' I'm sure I was blushing from my cheeks all the way down to my neck. I hadn't thought about grain coupons, since I'd never bought snacks before. Besides, since they could be used for money, no one would ever give me any.

He turned and shouted into the storeroom, from which

emerged a wrinkled old woman wearing white sleeve-covers and a white apron, stained with flour and soy sauce. She asked what was wrong, then said it was OK. Turning to the steamers, she picked out two meat buns with a pair of tongs and put them on a plate.

'It's take-out,' I said.

She picked up a stack of yellowed paper from the showcase, removed one sheet, and put the buns on it. Then she put down her tongs, added two more pieces of paper under the buns. 'Be careful,' she cautioned me, 'they're very hot!'

Holding the steaming buns in both hands and soaking up the wonderful fragrance, for the first time in my life I knew what it meant to be happy. It's my birthday, and I'm celebrating!

Instead of taking the same route home, I walked down the narrow street that ran past Waterhouse. It was hilly, but a little closer. My stomach started to growl. Hurry up, eat them while they're hot, it was saying, but I just swallowed hard, wanting to get home to celebrate with my parents for having me. I ran up the steps beside the grain shop; they didn't seem particularly steep, but by the time I reached the top, I was out of breath.

Roads went off in three directions at the top of the hill. An old tea vendor had set up his stall under a malus tree, which was encircled by oddly shaped rocks. As I drew near him, a chill ran down my spine. I spun around. A neatly dressed man stood beneath the eaves of a locksmith shop; he couldn't see me, since he was talking to the locksmith.

Someone who was waiting for his key? I felt a little better, but when I turned back around, I couldn't shake the feeling that I was being watched; there was a rumble in my head. I was so rattled I dropped one of the buns. I knelt down to pick up the bun, which had rolled on to some dirty leaves under the stall. I blew on it, but the dirt stuck to the skin, so I carefully picked it off.

The man was gone by the time I stood up. Could it have

been the same man who used to follow me around? Maybe he'd been following me all day. But it was Sunday. In the past he'd only followed me to and from school, but now he'd changed his pattern.

Had I walked up the steps so fast a moment ago that I was dizzy? No, I trusted my feelings, and I was sure that was the man. Why had he hidden from me for more than ten years, only to surface today without warning? He nearly walked right up to me.

Rapes were fairly common in that area, since there were all sorts of hidden nooks and crannies on the hills or by the riverbank where it could be done without detection. Whenever a rapist was tried and sentenced, the details were publicized in minute detail. Most of the time the victim was murdered and left to rot, or was thrown into the river. Every girl was terrified of men.

Once, when the father of a girl in my class was arrested, she and her kid sister followed him for blocks, weeping the whole way. 'No wife, and no brothels, so what am I supposed to do?' the widowed dock worker roared. They said he'd seduced his neighbour's virgin daughter.

I didn't dare continue thinking along this line, I was too scared. So I turned and ran all the way to the playground on High School Avenue. Since it was Sunday, there were no shouts or squeals; no one playing ball, no kids out catching grasshoppers or butterflies. The sky extended far beyond the playground. I slowed my pace and walked down a small grassy path as I struggled to calm my nerves.

FIVE

1

I took a shallow earthenware bowl out of the cupboard and put the two stuffed buns into it after carefully removing the grease-soaked paper. A bowl of soupy rice was on the cupboard; hungry and thirsty, I slurped it down without coming up for air. Father came in, and I turned the light on. The room was still dark, but the outlines of the bed, the table and the cupboard were a little clearer.

I handed him the bowl. 'These are for you and Mother.'

'What about you?' He didn't take it.

'I've had one already. These two are yours.'

'You're not much of a liar,' he said. 'Where can you get three big meat-filled buns for fifty cents? You like them so much, you eat them.'

Mother walked in with washed ricebowls and chopsticks just then and stuck the chopsticks into a bamboo holder on the wall. 'Little Six,' she said, 'where were you off to so early this morning? I could have used some help putting up the laundry pole, but now you're all grown-up, and nothing I say means a thing to you. If you can't rely on a bamboo pole, how can you rely on bamboo shoots? Each one of you kids is worse than the next.' She was getting really worked up.

I told her to stop nagging, that I had one of her favourite treats. Sure enough, what she saw put a smile on her face. She even forgot to ask where the money had come from. 'What for? Where did these come from?'

I told her I'd gone to Stonebridge.

She asked which shop I'd gone to.

Waterhouse, of course, I said. They had the best reputation in town. Customers queued up to buy their stuffed buns and meat dumplings.

The words were barely out before Mother flung the bowl back into the cupboard, grabbed the head of the bed and was wracked with dry heaves. 'Stuffed buns from the Waterhouse!' She shook her head in disgust and took the damp towel I held out to her as she sat on the edge of the bed.

'You're overreacting,' Father said unhappily.

'Overreacting? Have you forgotten what those years were like?'

From the disjointed comments that followed, I got a vague idea of what was bothering her: during the famine, the filling in the Waterhouse stuffed buns reputedly came from children. Satisfied customers kept coming back, for the same reason that restaurants today sometimes add cannabis roots or poppy stalks to their hot-pots. Then one day someone bit into a fingernail and notified the authorities. The couple who ran the shop were arrested and the shop closed. It didn't reopen for several years, and then only as a co-operative.

'The women in our neighbourhood were a bunch of old gossips,' Father said.

'With meat being so scarce then, where did Waterhouse get theirs?' Mother asked. 'And such delicious meat, at that. Better than adding gourmet powder.' And there was evidence to prove it. Mother said that the three-year-old son of her carrying-pole partner for a year or two had disappeared mysteriously without a trace. For a time, the woman wept every time her son was mentioned, but after a while she stopped crying, and simply threw herself down an old well near the playground on High School Avenue. Her body wasn't discovered until someone noticed the stench coming from the well, which was later sealed. Mother said she was the best partner she'd ever had, a woman who never moved the rope so Mother would have to shoulder most of the weight.

'Lower your voice, why don't you?' Father said. 'Little Six

didn't buy these steamed buns for herself. If you don't want them, fine, but now even she's afraid to eat them, and all over some groundless rumours.' Father turned and walked into the hall.

'Lower my voice?' She raised it instead. 'You want me to lower my voice? Why? I'm too old to be scared.' But once Father was out of earshot, she lowered her voice.

I stared at the bun-filled bowl in the cupboard. All these rumoured incidents during the famine had happened before I was born, so there was nothing for me to be afraid of. But they'd certainly taken the joy out of my birthday. I brushed past Mother on my way to the bureau, where I opened the first drawer on the left.

'What are you looking for?' she asked as she watched me rummage carelessly through the drawers.

'The letter.' The drawer was filled with sewing kits, scissors, buttons, combs, and other things, and I was prepared to pull it out and dump it on the floor. 'Where's Big Sister's letter?' I asked.

'Not there,' she insisted as she felt around under her pillow. A little harmonica fell out of the pillowcase. When I reached out for it, she grabbed my hand, not roughly, but surprising me nonetheless. What was she doing with something like that? She acted as if it were her little treasure, something I wasn't to touch. I'd never owned a musical instrument, so I couldn't make music with anything, and the only toy I'd ever played with was a rag doll Mother had made for me.

'Oh, now I remember. It must have got mixed in with the wash.'

I was sure she was covering up something. She didn't want me to see my sister's letter, and I suspected she'd ripped it up in anger.

'I don't believe you,' I said.

'What's got into you today? Nothing but answering back.'

'Somebody saw Big Sister this morning. She's back.'

'So what? She can go where she pleases. As long as she

doesn't set foot in this house, I'll feel blessed.' But I saw how her face fell when she heard the news. The look of expectation was gone, and out came the same old grumblings: her eldest daughter was a trouble-maker, a bad seed, a ne'er-do-well who never listened to her. She drops out of school, she gets married, whatever she wants, without asking my opinion. Which is why things turned out so badly. 'Little Six.' Mother turned to me. 'You don't listen to me, even at your young age.'

'When have I ever disobeyed you? And I'm not a child. I'm old enough to vote and be elected to office.' She didn't take the hint that it was my birthday. In fact, my comment made her even unhappier.

'Oh, so you know all about voting, do you?' She sneered. 'I'd happily give my voting rights to anybody who wanted them. What's an election, anyway, but checking off only one box there? We're always told: You're asking for democracy? You don't even know how to read.'

Today's my birthday, Mama! I nearly shouted. How could you forget?

Instinctively I felt that this birthday was not just one of a series of numbers, but a special bead in a prayer bracelet that could only be counted forward; once that bead was counted, all sorts of unknowable taboos would be touched. I began to panic, and I desperately wanted my mother to hug me close. The thread that connected me to my fate was a time-bomb fuse that emitted blue sparks. It was time, I sensed, to take the next step, whether I was ready or not. Today, right this minute, I knew I had to get things out in the open with Mother.

I walked over and leaned up against the door, which creaked as it supported my weight. I quickly closed it, trying to control the anxiety inside me. Then I plunged ahead.

'You wouldn't shed a tear if somebody cut up my face or threw acid in it, even if I was raped and murdered.'

'What's that supposed to mean?'

'A man's been following me.'

She jumped up, walked over, and felt my sweaty forehead. 'Are you sure?' She glared at me.

I looked away. 'Don't believe me if you don't want to.'

'I know you only too well. If you can't make me squirm, you'll do it to yourself.' She kept her eyes on me a moment longer, then shoved me aside and ran out of the room.

Ten minutes or so later she returned, out of breath. 'I knew you were lying,' she said. 'There's no one out there.' She caught her breath before going on. 'What does he look like? How long has it been going on? How come you didn't tell me earlier?'

Seeing her so concerned frightened me. 'A long time . . . more than once.'

I said he wasn't a youngster, but he wasn't a drooling old man either. Middle-aged and probably more dangerous than the other two. 'I never got a good look at him, but if I had, I wouldn't have to be telling you.' That last comment was meant to upset her.

Mother snapped off the light. 'Go on, get out of here. Go up to the attic.'

I stormed out of the room, slamming the door behind me.

After standing in the hall for a moment, choked with resentment, I climbed the stairs to the attic.

2

I picked up a book, but couldn't read a word; wondering what was on Mother's mind as she sat alone in the dark downstairs was too great a distraction. So I turned on the tape recorder, an inexpensive old thing that looked like a washboard. Fourth Sister and Dehua had scrimped and saved for months to buy it, and we all trod lightly around the table so as not to break this family treasure.

How many times can you be drunk in life?
If we don't enjoy ourselves now, then when?

Come, come, come, finish this cup and then we'll see.
Good flowers bloom but once,
Good prospects rarely reappear.
After you leave tonight, when will you return?

This over-used tune, which was on the lips of everyone in the city half a century earlier, and then had been banned as 'obscene' for thirty years or more, had, over the past couple of years, broken through the siege of revolutionary songs and had me in its strange thrall. But on this early afternoon, instead of lightening my spirits, it made me increasingly restless. This was the first time in my young life I was actually worried about Mother. So I turned off the music and went downstairs.

Mother wasn't there. That's strange, where could she have gone?

Father was hunkering down out in the courtyard, his hands black and sticky from making briquettes out of coal dust. Unless he specifically asked for it, he peevishly refused all offers of help. Mother was the opposite: instead of asking for help, she'd wait for volunteers, to see who among her children desired to be her pet.

She was nowhere in the compound, or anywhere else in the vicinity, for that matter. Since I couldn't find her, I went back inside and stood in the doorway with a blank expression.

'Little Six,' someone said from behind me.

I spun around. Big Sister was leaning against the door to our room.

The old woman had been right that morning. Big Sister was back in Chongqing. My temporary absent-mindedness made her impatient.

'Have you gone deaf, Little Six?'

3

After washing, Big Sister asked, 'There isn't a soul at home. How come?' She opened a drawer in the bureau and took out a comb with several missing teeth and Fourth Sister's hand mirror. After blowing the dust off the mirror, she combed her recently permed, overdone hair.

In the six months or more since I'd last seen her, she hadn't changed much. Her face was a little rounder, her body fuller, and her eyes sharper and more vigilant than ever.

'Father's home, isn't he? And I'm home. So what do you mean, there isn't a soul at home?'

'Can't I ask a simple question?' She was smiling. 'You're too educated for me.'

I'd already forgotten the letter Mother didn't want me to read. My thoughts were elsewhere. 'Nothing ever goes the way I want it to,' Big Sister said, and I expected her to launch into a long monologue about another divorce.

'I knew you were back,' I said, to move the conversation in a new direction. 'Why all the mystery?'

She laughed and said she had no intention of coming straight home, wanting to see how frustrated that would make Mother. So her first stop had been at the home of a friend who'd been in the countryside with her. 'Oh,' she said, as if the thought had just occurred to her, 'how about Mother? Where is she?'

Exactly what I wanted to know. I said she'd been there at noon, but when I came downstairs, she'd gone off somewhere.

'Who cares about her, anyway,' Big Sister said sourly. 'She probably went to see Second Sister on the other side of the river. Second Sister's her pet, and we don't count.' Indeed, Second Sister had been luckier than the rest of us. She got out of being sent up the mountains or down to the countryside in 1969 by passing the entrance exam for a school training primary school teachers, so she didn't suffer the fate of the sent-down youth. Then, when it was time for work assignments, two well-connected individuals were fighting over the same job in an elementary school in the city centre, and she took advantage of the stalemate to get the assignment instead of the rural school she should have been sent to. Overnight she became an urbanite. Then she had a son, and a second son, and, of course, a doting husband.

'I'm famished, absolutely famished!' Big Sister said in an obvious fit of anger. She rummaged through the cupboard, a search that quickly turned up the meat-stuffed buns. Holding one in each hand, she dug in. 'Tasty, really delicious.' A minute later they were both gone and she was wiping her hands with her handkerchief.

'Little sister,' she said, changing her tone, 'how come your face is as pale as death? You look terrible.' Who wouldn't look terrible in that murky lamplight? But she was my sister, and even after not seeing me for so long, she could sense that something was wrong. 'Is it because I ate those buns? I thought they were leftovers.'

'You haven't lost your glib tongue,' I said. 'How could stuffed buns be leftovers in this house?' I could have said more, but didn't. Neither Father nor I could bring ourselves to eat them, and I'd had a big row with Mother over them. Big Sister might have been the eldest child in the family, but sometimes she acted like the youngest. Mother said she was the biggest trouble-maker in the family, not hesitating to make scenes in public.

Maybe she was right about Mother going to visit Second Sister, who was so easy to get along with and absolutely dependable and conscientious, both as a homemaker and a teacher. And she was a good daughter. Even when she was upset by Mother, she kept it bottled up inside and, unlike her three sisters, never openly quarrelled with her.

'Today's my birthday,' I blurted out. That was what I'd wanted to say to Mother. 'Mama forgot again. On purpose, as always.'

'My goodness, why didn't you say so?' Big Sister always knew how to put on an act. 'You should have told me earlier, Little Sister. Those buns must have been your birthday present.' She was no fool. She even tried to make up for Mother's lapse. 'Mother didn't forget, and don't you even think it. She probably got her dates mixed up. I wouldn't be surprised if she was counting on the old lunar calendar.'

'New calendar or old, I don't care. She forgot on purpose,' I insisted. They all treated me the same, whether they remembered my birthday or not. What difference did it make to them? Mother was always reminding me that I was lucky to be allowed to go on living.

'Let Big Sister make it up to you,' she said. 'Come here, let me give you a new hairdo. See my new perm? Not bad, hmm? Better than those kinky-headed girls on the street, wouldn't you say? Or those trendy yokels you see every-where. I did it myself, if you must know.'

Without waiting for my approval, she turned off the light and dragged me into the hall, where she sat me down on a stool. The light there was much better. Across the way, our neighbour Baldy Cheng's aged mother sat in her doorway, leaning against the wall, her eyes mere slits.

'You're a big girl now, so you need to look pretty. Put your head back. I'll give you a nice plait and pull the loose hair on the sides back to show off your neck and ears, especially the mole on your left cheek. A mole on the face means your lucky star shines bright and drives bad luck away. You won't suffer my miserable fate.'

She walked around in front of me, looked me over, and told me not to move.

A minute or so later, she returned with a pair of scissors to trim my fringe. Then she handed me the mirror. I stood up and looked at myself in the mirror. My two plaits were now one, quite a remarkable change. I took special note of how prominent my cheeks and neck appeared, and I liked the way I looked. That made me very happy, although I didn't want to show it and make Big Sister feel too good about herself.

'Well, what do you think? Like it? Why don't you say

something?' I'd never seen her like this, as if the more I ignored her, the more she wanted to please me.

'Just a gaunt, waxy face, ugly as ever, and nothing can change that. Anyone can tell it's all because you people bully me.' I gave her back the mirror.

'OK, Little Sister, today's your birthday. How old?'

'I was born in 1962, you tell me.'

'You're eighteen? My goodness! I thought you were only fifteen or sixteen. Your big sister didn't even know it was your birthday. If I had, I'd have bought you a present.'

I snorted contemptuously, although I felt warmth in my heart. She'd never buy me anything, but at least she said she would, and no one else had even done that.

'Your eighteenth birthday, that's a landmark. So tell me, what would you like me to do for you? Whatever you say.' She sounded sincere enough.

'Do you mean it?'

'Every word of it. There are all kinds of people I could trick, if that's what I wanted to do. Why trick a member of my own family?'

After a moment's thought, I said, 'I'd like you to walk along the riverbank with me.'

'Is that all?' She laughed. 'I expected something harder than that. Of course I will.'

4

So we walked out of the compound and down the stone steps, heading for the riverbank.

I had to clarify, or at least gain some understanding of, the riddles and shadows that had swirled in my life. Everybody knew something, but no one was willing to let me in on whatever it was. They had formed a conspiracy, boxing me into the tyranny of silence. Maybe they were imprisoned in the cage of non-speaking, and the truth I desperately wanted to learn lay in precisely what they would not say. But I decided to cast everything aside, even my studies for the college entrance exams, which were so important to me, so I could get to the bottom of things. If I didn't, all these years I'd have been living in a fog!

I congratulated myself for not having lost the ability to take the measure of people. Big Sister had come home on my birthday, just the person I needed, when I needed her. She was sixteen years older than me, which forced upon her an unshirkable responsibility towards me. I was confident that that figured in some of the things that bothered me. Fate had brought her home at this moment in order to answer some of my questions.

My brothers and sisters had closed ranks, all but Big Sister. She was forever quarrelling with Mother; resentment would fill her eyes at the height of their arguments, which might have been because she was the most favoured child in the family, and why she acted like a spoiled brat. In 1969, Mao Zedong disbanded his Red Guards, who had wreaked revolutionary havoc all over the country, and sent them to the 'vast lands of freedom' in the border regions. But my sister had answered the call to go down to the countryside way back in 1964; as a member of the first contingent of 'educated youth' to go into the villages, she had suffered through many more years than most. She spent nine years in a farming village before finally being reassigned as a coal miner in a mountainous area on the fringes of Sichuan Province.

When she was eighteen, just before graduating from a nursing school, she had been seen taking a stroll with a male student, for which she was criticized by her class's branch secretary of the Communist Youth League; school discipline did not permit such things. I've got a boyfriend, so what? she'd said stubbornly, and before long, fists were flying. She, and only she, was punished for the incident by being told she couldn't attend the New Year's festivities. She vowed to kill herself, and she tried, by jumping out of a second-storey window. She broke her leg, was sent to the hospital, and received a black mark on her record that would remain there for ever. When told to write a self-criticism, she went straight to the principal instead, and when the principal refused to intercede, she flung her student ID card in his face, left the school, and came home.

Cadres from the Neighbourhood Committee came to the house on a mobilization campaign. 'The Three Gorges are as beautiful as a myth,' they said. 'The fish in Mount Wu River are as plump as water buckets. The coal there can be wrapped in a handkerchief without smearing it. It's a wondrous place!' She believed them. She stole the family's household registration and cancelled her city residence, wanting to show the schoolmates and teachers who among them was most revolutionary.

Father said he'd sailed to Mount Wu, and it was nothing like the cadres had told her. It was wretchedly poor, and he forbade her to go, demanding that she go straight to the police station and get her city residence reinstated. She responded by accusing him of concocting counter-revolutionary rumours, which reduced him to tears. Mother cried too, but she went to the Neighbourhood Committee to plead her case, for which Mother was severely reprimanded. By trying to stop her daughter from going to a farming village, they said, she was sabotaging the 'up to the mountains and down to the countryside' movement. Do you know what sort of crime that is? You could go anywhere in China, and not a single person would dare help her reinstate her city residence. Shaken by the criticism, Mother could only watch as her daughter walked off, all smiles.

Her schoolmates laughed at her as an idiot, and Mother railed at her for being wild and disobedient. But I figured she couldn't wait to leave home, since she felt she didn't belong here.

She had always talked a lot to me, and there were hidden messages in what she said. Truths and half-truths, as if she were teasing me, from as far back as I can remember. Sometimes her expressions were very melodramatic, and if not for them, she'd have been quite a pretty woman, especially when she did laundry at the riverbank, with her lush black hair piled high up on her head. More than one person commented that her eyebrows and mouth looked like Mother's when she was young. Her face, her height and her full figure set her apart from her brothers and sisters. Chongqing women tend to have a particular kind of grace endowed by the city's misty terrain and rainy climate, and have a gentle melancholy about them. But Big Sister had the temperament of a man: tough and hot-tempered, quick to fight, with words or fists. She actually held a knife to her first husband's throat to get him to sign a divorce agreement.

She did things without thinking, and let the chips fall where they may. She'd make a mess, then leave it to others to clean it up. When she was in the countryside at Mount Wu, a local fortune-teller had told her that the smell of blood permeated her fate which had been in a maze, and if she could somehow make it past her fortieth birthday, she might be able to stabilize her *qi* and return it to its normal vessels.

'I believe what he said, even though I don't want to. Something bad will happen when I'm forty, I know it will. So I'll try to behave myself.' This had been Big Sister's mantra for years.

But there was something different about the way she was talking today. She was several steps behind me, and complaining loudly: 'I'm thirty-four this year, and if that damned fortune-teller was right, I only have a few years to live. Why should I go through life watching my step? I can't wait to see just what the hell's going to happen.'

I turned around and stared at her. 'You're all hiding something from me,' I blurted out. 'And you have to tell me what it is, sister!'

She continued walking down the steps, as if she hadn't heard me. I fell in behind her, staying as close as I could. With no houses or trees to block my view, I could see a couple of people swimming in the river. The Jialing River is clearer than the muddy Yangtze, and there is a visible zigzagging line where the two rivers merge at Heaven's Gate. Below the slope where we lived there was only the Yangtze, with its fast-moving, muddy waters. I repeated my demand.

'Tell you what?' Big Sister asked nonchalantly.

'You made me a promise a little while ago. You said that, since today's my birthday, you'd do anything I asked.'

She thumped me on the back. 'What's with you today?' She hit me pretty hard, but I shrugged off the pain and held my tongue, waiting for her to continue. At first she just laughed. 'A promise is a promise. But we'd have a better time if you lightened up a bit. Just you and me taking a walk, looking at the boats, and enjoying the scenery, what's wrong with that? If you want, we can go to the other side of the river and go to a movie or something.'

'I mean it, you have to tell me!' I ignored her little ploy, because I was getting desperate. Ships' horns were turning up the volume as they competed in the sky around me. My senses were always keen to those horns, and that afternoon they were especially so; to my ears, the sound of each horn was identifiably unique, as if invested with a soul crying out for its fate. I shivered.

'You know!' I shouted at Big Sister. 'Don't you? None of you want me to know anything. You want to deceive me, all of you, but you have to tell me today, sister, you just have to!'

Unflappable, she smiled, and my shouts were reduced to soft pleas that only she and I could hear.

'All right,' she said, her smile gone, 'what is it you want to know?'

'What happened to Father's eyesight and why was he forced to retire so early, before I was even born? I don't believe the story I heard.'

She asked me what story that was.

I told her that his file in the employment office at the

steamship company said the damage was caused by syphilis, and that people in the compound hinted angrily at something along those lines.

'What witch bastard, what rotten cunt said that?' Big Sister bellowed.

I clamped my hand over her mouth. We were close enough to riverside houses for people to hear her shouts. She turned and ran down the slippery stone steps, amid the reek of rotting piles of garbage, and into a dark cave under a ledge, where she fell to her knees and began kowtowing to the stone wall.

'Come in here and kowtow three times to the bodhisattva,' she commanded me.

'What bodhisattva are you talking about?' I asked as I walked hesitantly into the dark hollow.

'The Riverside Guanyin of Patched Clothing,' she said. 'She was destroyed during the Cultural Revolution, so you've never seen her. But local Buddhist devotees restored her recently. Come over here and ask her to protect the family.'

It was so rare to hear Big Sister speak about the family's well-being that I fell to my knees and kowtowed to the wall of stone, while she scooped up a handful of water from the base of the damp wall and drank it. Then she told me to do the same. I could picture the filthy run-off water that ran alongside the wall in our compound and told her I wouldn't do it. She bent down, scooped up another handful, and held it up to my mouth. 'It's Buddha water,' she said, as it dripped through her fingers. 'It's fresh, and it's a cure-all,' she said stubbornly.

So I opened my mouth obediently and drank it down. It tasted like pure spring water. 'OK, I did it,' I said. 'Come on, you've been dragging it out long enough, sister. Don't you think it's time you told me?'

'Told you what?' she asked me instead.

A good question. Just what did I want to know? Everything, of course, but how was I supposed to know what Big Sister knew and what she didn't?

After a brief silence, she said, 'All right, I'll tell you some things about my life. I don't know about other things, just my own life. And you have to promise me this will be our secret.'

We sat down beside a boulder and gazed out at the swirling eddies of the fast-moving river.

SIX

1

Mother came to Chongqing by boat, Big Sister told me, just another country girl escaping the fate of an arranged marriage. She slipped into this sprawling metropolis so her family could never find her. On the day she arrived, the city was fogged in, as if blanketed by cotton wadding. 'Chong – qing!' someone shouted from the ship's railing.

Mother squeezed her way out of the stinking, crowded below-decks cabin on to the main deck, and as she filled her lungs with the fresh river air, she caught a glimpse of strange-looking houses at the base of the surrounding hills and rows of stone steps leading up to the ancient city wall. As the ship drew up to the pontoon quay, she saw crowds of people waiting on the pier: men in Western suits and hats, women in cheongsams and high-heels, porters carrying poles over their shoulders, sedan-chair bearers, pedlars hawking their goods, and armed policemen. Everything was so new and strange that for a moment she forgot why she'd come to this place.

That was 1943, before the harsh winter had come to an end; the dense fog was a welcome sign of safety, since Japanese aeroplanes would have to wait until the visibility cleared in May before returning to scar the city with their bombs. As the provisional seat of the Kuomintang government, Chongqing was home to rear area hospitals, colleges, factories, and businesses, even herds of livestock. Served by the Yangtze and protected by the surrounding hills, this filthy, muggy city was thrust into the role of the nation's political and cultural centre.

Mother had escaped from home only a few days earlier, and despite the pain in her lower back suffered when she jumped out the window, she availed herself of the low-lying fog to start walking, not daring to stop for even a minute. But none of her relatives would take her in. At daybreak, as roosters crowed into the lightening sky, she fell in with a group of people going to the city centre to sell bamboo mats. She had only one possession, a white hempen mosquito net adorned with dark-blue birds, her sole dowry.

As night fell, Mother and a dozen or so girls from the small port town in Zhong County boarded a Yangtze steamship to take them to jobs in a textile mill. They slept in an open space below decks, just above the ship's hull. The two recruiters slept nearest to the door to ensure that nothing happened to the girls before they arrived at the mill. The girls were frightened by the slapping of water against the ship's hull, and the shrill blasts of the horn as the ship drew up to the dock. But Mother slept on as if drugged, curled into a ball, oblivious to all that was happening. It was a blissful sleep, maybe the first one for months.

2

Mother got her first good look at the city only after her shift at the mill, and what she saw wasn't lovely. With spring drawing to a close, a few days of safety remained before the foggy season ended. Mist drifting leisurely above the city formed dense clouds around hilltop ridges. The northern half of the city was enveloped in haze, while the southern half kept slipping in and out of view. Narrow streets zigzagged crazily through the city, rising and falling amid shanty towns where houses on stilts lining the roadways and hilly ground looked like swarms of grey, mountain-climbing lizards.

Big Sister was relating events that occurred thirty-seven years earlier, but there was a ring of familiarity about them. I doubt that there had been many changes in the city's slum neighbourhoods in half a century, except that they were more crowded now.

The city could make you shudder, with its unfathomable perplexities, hidden dangers and buried secrets. When Chongqing men walked down the streets, regardless of what they were wearing, their true identity was never apparent. They could be local riff-raff or real gentlemen; they could be secret agents or law-abiding citizens; they could be riot instigators or members of the secret police; or Triadmen or scholars or gamblers or officials or actors or drifters or pickpockets. The same held true for Chongqing women: you couldn't tell from their outward appearance whether they were housewives, homewreckers, or cheap whores. Every person, every type, was imbued with damp furtiveness and emitted an air of listless self-indulgence.

It was soon 1945. Gone were the all-too-familiar air-raid sirens and the chilling screams of people fleeing for their lives; residents soon lost the habit of looking warily into the sky, no longer fearful of the black spots that grew into Japanese bombers; air-raid shelters now stood deserted. Slowly but surely the city filled with the heady atmosphere of military victory. But the great turning point in history had little effect on one eighteen-year-old millworker. Fate had already determined that she would witness far more than her parents or siblings or any girls of her age still labouring in the fields could ever dream of.

I was sitting beside Big Sister on the pitted boulder, but the things she was talking about could hardly have been further away from me. A long-distance passenger liner sounded its horn as it approached Heaven's Gate Dock, like a funeral dirge played by a cheap street band. The sun was setting behind the hills on the northern bank of the river, draping them in a gentle red halo. The few bathers in the river were swimming back to shore, holding their dry clothes on their heads above the water.

This city had such a noisy history, and the words crashed into my ears with such chaos that I could hardly make sense of them without listening with my heart as well.

The man in the hat who walked into Textile Mill 601 in the Sandbar District had no intention of stopping at the apprentice workers' dormitory. But as he was passing by the entrance, he heard strange noises inside, and stuck his head in the door to see what was going on, the two odd-jobbers with him stopping in their tracks. The large tent-like structure, with straw bedding lining the walls, stank of stale sweat.

A young woman stood tied to a pillar, strands of undone plaits sticking to her cheeks; sunlight filtering into the tent seemed to fall only on her body, lending her skin a velvety sheen. Her eyelashes were dark and long, her lips pursed haughtily, moist and red with anger. The foreman's whip danced in the air as she strained defiantly against her ropes.

Big Sister was insistent that a turning point in our family's history occurred when the man stuck his head in the door, for he was bewitched by Mother's beauty and intrigued by her stubbornness that morning. He was amazed that a fetching little country girl like that put up such a resistance, refused to knuckle under even when she was being whipped, never begging for mercy, and causing the foreman a great loss of face. Beside himself with anger, the foreman turned and found himself face-to-face with the Triadman; he smiled humbly. Hierarchy was everything in Triad society, and the man in the hat was clearly the foreman's better. He asked what was going on, then stepped inside.

With the sun at her back, blurring the man's features, Mother noted only that he was wearing a hat, and that he was tall and held himself straight. Suddenly, she was frightened, for this could mean real trouble. In despair, she looked away, her face flushed with fear, her breathing laboured, her chest heaving.

When the handsome young man ordered her release,

Mother finally got a good look at him. The concern in his eyes moved her deeply.

A romantic by nature, Big Sister was always falling in love with one man or another. I was powerless to stop her narrative and don't have the talent to re-create it now. I can only paraphrase what she said and try to understand the logic behind this case of love at first sight: Mother was a country girl who had fought to preserve her chastity, and a pretty girl at that; maybe that was the Triadman's criterion for a wife, someone who would look after his home. As a petty chieftain in a secret society, one who had clawed his way up the ladder, he instinctively mistrusted the flirtatious women who swarmed to his bed.

He took a good look at Mother, exchanged a few hasty comments with the foreman, and hurried off.

Following Mother's brush with disaster, she returned to her normal work pattern, and over time she forgot the incident, as she had forgotten all the other dangers she'd faced in her youth. She led a frugal life, saving her money to send home. Then one day, two months later, when her shift was over, as she and the other girls lined up for a body search – to stop them walking off with balls of yarn or scraps of cloth – the foreman came up to Mother, all smiles, and asked her to go straight to the factory gate.

She walked out the door, and was stopped in her tracks by the sight of a new rickshaw, metal fixtures polished to a sheen, a liveried driver waiting for her respectfully.

3

Back in those days, the male diners at elegant restaurants always wore Western suits and leather shoes and kept their hair and beards neatly trimmed; the women wore high-heeled shoes and permed their hair in the style of their favourite Hollywood starlets; the addition of earrings, necklaces, brooches, and gloves added glamour and gentle sound to

87

their appearance. The side-slits of their satin cheongsams went as high as fashion dictated.

Big Sister was a born story-teller, always had been. The earlier generation revelled in tales of chivalric heroes, but by her time, movies and novels held sway. As a little girl, I'd curl up in a corner to listen quietly and avidly to stories from young people on their extended vacations home from the country. Crowded into the small space, where they sat on the two beds or on the floor cracking melon seeds, they talked about frightening ghosts in the mountains, or about Kuomintang 'Plum Flower' spies. Sometimes they related their own experiences: romances among their friends, gangfights with the peasants, knife-fights with local cadres who rode roughshod over them, and subsequent persecution by the police. One story after another, some causing gales of laughter, others met with tears and sobbing.

Mother, always complaining that I never helped out around the house, would shout, 'Little Six, come down here!' and Big Sister would chase me away with annoyance. But after I finished whatever it was, I'd squat down in the attic doorway to listen some more, ready for the next summons.

How much of this family history merely served Big Sister's itch to tell fanciful tales I don't know. To be honest, she's far more qualified to be a novelist than I. But she didn't even complete her education and she threw away the best years of her life in the service of the Revolution. They were gone for ever. During one of these story sessions she said that her fate had cruelly kept her from becoming a novelist; what she had experienced could have been turned into several wonderful novels. I was so sorry for her when I heard this, feeling she had been dealt a bad hand.

But now, as she talked, it was impossible to link the image of our mother as a pretty young woman to the thick-limbed, unfeminine woman with no figure but a terrible temper that I knew. I tried to imagine her in her favourite body-hugging indigo cheongsam and cloth slippers, no jewellery, her shiny black hair combed into two plaits and pulled back from her forehead – short hair would be nice too. Her dark eyes gleamed with a modesty that fitted her face perfectly, and when she smiled, she radiated gentle charm. Yes, she'd be beautiful. Big Sister was right, how could Mother not have enjoyed the spring of youth?

The man sitting across from Mother simply glowed. Dressed in a white linen suit, his hair recently trimmed, he was more dashing than movie stars in the posters; his fashionable haircut was enhanced by shiny hair tonic, his eyes and brows were neat and handsome. He definitely was not one of those fancy Dans of films of the 1930s and 1940s, or one of those effeminate stage actors of the time. An octagonal table lamp cast a soft light, the blue-edged dinner service was finely crafted ceramic that was nearly transparent. The moon and stars had climbed into the sky, the mountain city sparkled with lights in windows. Mother kept her head down, but didn't eat. Her hands rested in her lap.

What did they talk about? Forgetting the uneasiness of wearing smart clothes and eating in an elegant restaurant for the first time in her life, Mother listened attentively as he told the story of his life. Just when she had passed this story on to Big Sister, I don't know, but now I was hearing it.

He said he was from a place called Anyue in Sichuan Province. His family was so poor his mother had to take in laundry; his father was a sedan-chair bearer. Although his mother had given birth to eleven children, only two, the eighth and the last, had survived. She had given him the childhood name 'Longevity Boy', hoping he'd live a long and happy life. His younger brother was called 'Firewood Boy', to counter the evil-water element in his fate, as determined by a fortune-teller.

In 1938 an epidemic struck Anyue County, followed by drought, and within a week both his parents were carried away. He was fourteen, his brother five, and they were reduced to begging. One day, among a troop of soldiers on the lookout for recruits, he spotted an uncle who had left the tiny town years before. He tagged along as helper to his uncle, who was the mess cook. The warlord's army was short of men, so they let him stay, since he drew no pay. In 1942, by the time the army was camped in Chongqing, he had become a low-ranking officer. On the eve of the War of Resistance against Japan, Chongqing Triads could boast a membership of sixty or seventy thousand, including virtually all the troops in the warlord's army. He became a member of the fifth row in the Generation under the name 'Ritual', so it was no wonder the foreman was so obsequious before him. The 'Ritual' Generation was especially powerful in the lower section of society, with professional Triadmen operating in connection with the city's rich and powerful to profit from prostitution, gambling, opium trafficking, and opium dens.

Mother found it hard to believe that the suave, dignified man sitting across from her had once been a ragged, filthy beggar. Her heart was in chaos. In a life that had passed like flowing rapids, this was the first time she had actually been in the company of a man, except for a groom she had never met, but to whom she had been promised for a few bushels of rice.

Running away from an arranged marriage was preordained by her stubborn nature. As the young man talked about his life, tears filled her eyes, maybe because she began to understand her own, and faced the realization that her future children would likely be doomed to a life devoid of peace.

The sound of drums and gongs and firecrackers and the parading of armies kept the city awake for weeks on end, caught up in celebrations of victory after eight years of war. The Japanese had surrendered, and the Kuomintang government was preparing to move back to Nanjing. The ensuing power vacuum in Chongqing was filled by the secret societies, as they closed ranks with the government, which knew it must rely on local power bases to control the rear areas.

Mother and the man were married. Seventeen tables were

set up at the wedding banquet to entertain the guests, who toasted Mother until her head swam. Instead of the usual two red candles in the bridal chamber, there were two whole rows of them, all of which stayed lit till dawn.

Mother was soon pregnant, and the year after the war was won, a daughter was born. That child was her, Big Sister said, the offspring of a girl who had fled from an arranged marriage and a gangster; in other words, the daughter of a counter-revolutionary.

4

So Big Sister had a different father from the rest of us. She seemed pretty proud of that. A gangster was someone you could look up to, while our father was just a decent, hard-working labourer. I must admit I found Big Sister's vanity annoying.

Like all kids, I had to fill out endless forms when I started school. In the box where they asked for my Place of Family Origin – an identification concept the Communists took over from the previous regime for 'place of birth' – I wrote Tiantai County, Zhejiang Province, which is at the end of the Yangtze River where it flows into the sea. I'd never been there, and I couldn't speak the dialect.

Father was born on June the 1st, China's Children's Day, an easy date to remember. He had such a heavy Zhejiang accent that no one could understand him when he spoke, unless he slowed down a little, so I could guess enough to interpret for him. I sometimes twisted his words if I didn't like the person he was talking to, but he'd glare at me and explain that his youngest daughter had heard wrong and mistranslated, for which he was sorry.

In the cold, damp winters, Father's bronchitis flared up, since we had no kindling to warm the place, and he took large doses of medicine. But he refused to go to the hospital, no matter how bad he felt. A thin, short man to begin with, his illness reduced him to skin and bones, making him shorter than he was. But he'd stubbornly insist that he wasn't sick, and even if he had a high fever, all he'd ever say was, 'I want to go home.'

'Let him go back to Zhejiang!' we kids would say as a chorus.

'No,' Mother would insist. 'He doesn't just want to go home, he wants to go back to die.'

Like most people who migrated to Sichuan from down-river, Father came to Chongqing during the War of Resistance. At the age of fifteen, he signed on as an apprentice to empty and clean chamber pots and anything else he was told to do. A fast learner, he soon mastered the craft of fluffing cotton and repairing quilts. In 1938, when he was twenty-one, the Kuomintang came to Tiantai looking for conscripts. The village chief accepted a bribe and substituted Father's name for someone else, and he had no choice but to bid farewell to his family and travel to Chongqing as a soldier. The troops set up camp on the mountains south of the river, where his job was to send signals for air-raid warnings.

In the spring of 1943, not long before Mother fled her home in Zhong County and came to Chongqing, Father's unit was transferred to another city. Marching through the mountains at night, he was painfully betrayed by his intestines, and he slipped into a grove of trees to relieve himself. By the time he re-emerged on to the road, his comrades were mere dots on a distant mountain path, their torches signalling the distance. He decided then and there to head in the opposite direction, thus becoming a deserter, for which he could have been shot. Luckily, his absence went unnoticed, or he was thought to have died on the road. In wartime, who cared whether a common soldier lived or died? So he returned to Chongqing and signed on with a shipping company.

According to Big Sister, the only event in Father's life that showed his courage and wisdom was forming a family with Mother in the spring of 1947. For Mother to take the circuitous path to meet him, she had first to strike out alone a second time, to leave her family once again. In the four years that took, Father lived and worked as a sailor in a strange city that seemed intent on forcing him to spend the rest of his life there, fated to wait for a Sichuan girl who had, of her own volition, fallen on hard times.

Big Sister stood up, so did I. Pale moonlight improved the look of the riverbanks. The lights of a passing ship flashed atop dark waves; the reflections of lamplight from the hills on the opposite shore flickered like eyes blinking gently in the night. Someone was playing a harmonica, and for the first time in my life I was taken by its lovely sounds.

Big Sister sneered. 'What a foolish girl Mother was. She wanted to show how strong-willed she was, so she left. I guess I'm the same way. My real father, what a bastard!' she continued. 'Not only did that bastard start staying out all night, he even brought modish young women home with him. Then when Mother wept softly, he beat her. How dare a woman who can't even produce a son cry like that! he'd yell at her. I'll have to get a concubine!'

Finally, unable to put up with him any longer, Mother picked up her daughter and a bundle of belongings and ran back to her home town. But the ancestral customs there decreed that a woman who fled from a marriage was to be drowned. So after hiding out for three days, she returned to Chongqing, where her husband sent his henchmen to look for her. He never found her.

5

On the stone steps below a house on stilts, Father spotted a young woman with a newborn baby on her back; she was washing clothes in the Jialing River, the sweaty work clothes of sailors. She worked quickly and attentively, in order to bring in enough washing to eke out a living – unlike other washerwomen, who spent much of their time gabbing and laughing and cursing flirtatiously. When she stood up, not even the baby on her back hid her pretty figure from view.

She turned and looked up. He stared at her, spellbound. He thought she was looking at him, but he was wrong. She was only stretching a bit, before squatting down again to continue washing. The early spring water, crystal clear, but bone-chillingly cold, turned her hands bright red. She had rolled her sleeves up, and her hair was combed neatly into a bun, without a single strand hanging down over her face. She wore no earrings or necklaces or bracelets; a woman so pristine, so fresh-looking, that if it hadn't been for the quiet baby on her back, he might have thought she wasn't real, that she had come from another world, one that he had never known.

Most of the houses on stilts along the river were occupied by people who made their living on the river: sailors, porters, pedlars, prostitutes, plus some prison escapees; they came and they went like the river water itself. Rent in this slum area was much lower than in the city. She lived in one of those houses on stilts, making her living not only by taking in laundry but also from an occasional patching and sewing job. Even putting her appearance aside, the way she supported her little family, through hard work and frugality, should have had plenty of boatmen chasing after her. But they left her alone, and she seemed pleased about that, content to live a modest, cautious life.

Why would men who had girls in every port steer a wide path around her? He learned the answer from someone who knew something of her past: You're captivated by that woman, just like all the other men. But she's the runaway wife of a Triadman, so keep your distance. Don't lose your head over a woman.

The early spring of 1947 marked a turning point in Father's life. Intrigued by machinery, and aided by his natural curiosity and quick wits, he was soon well versed in the navigational characteristics of the river and was hired as a river pilot. But whether he was in the main channel or a tributary, upstream or down, the image of the woman with the baby on her back squatting beside the river single-mindedly washing clothes never left him. The next time he saw her stand and look his way as she worked the kinks out of her muscles, he saw everything: goodness, loneliness, strong will, it was all there right in front of him.

So he started bringing his clothes to her to wash, always paying more than others did. Then, without waiting for a sign that he could leave, he'd turn and walk away without so much as looking back. 'These clothes are clean, they don't need to be washed,' she said softly. Red-faced, he stopped in the doorway, too embarrassed to move. He realized that he was bringing her clothes too often. Her baby was sleeping on the bed. She nimbly fetched a stool and invited him to sit in the doorway.

6

The Triadman tried everything to find Mother, including placing missing-person ads and sending men to her home town, but to no avail. Furious, he went back to Anyue County, where he picked out a girl who was still in high school. After a quick wedding ceremony, he set her up in town and returned alone to Chongqing. Even as a local despot, with a network of connections, he had no luck finding Mother, and assumed that she had moved far away. He never suspected that the taxi-dancer he kept beside him had bribed his men not to reveal Mother's whereabouts. As she washed clothes in the river one day, Mother had spotted a woman in fancy clothes, but had thought nothing of it.

By the spring of 1947, the sounds of celebration were replaced by the clatter of a new war, a civil war between Kuomintang and Communist forces. Local warlords, secret societies and religious organizations took the opportunity to expand their areas of control, and rumours flew as the city's residents cowered. The Triadman had no time to concern himself with the wife who had run off with a daughter. Had it been a son, of course, things would have been different.

Father, a taciturn man, knew he could win Mother's heart only by his deeds. Unlike the other men who salivated over her, he was unafraid of the murderous Triadman. Maybe, as a stranger to the place, he underestimated the power of Sichuan's underworld. But however you looked at it, this was our family's beginning.

Big Sister glossed over this part of her story in a few sentences, and each time I tried to bring her back to it, she did the same thing. I knew she wasn't unhappy with our parents' union – since that is what allowed her to survive – but the marriage of a poor man and woman was too commonplace, not romantic enough for her tastes.

I once found a photograph of Mother dressed in a white-on-white satin cheongsam she'd bought in a sale, and her hair done up fashionably. After the Japanese surrender, the rich and powerful rushed back to Nanjing and Shanghai, selling off what they couldn't take with them for whatever it would bring. Several streets served as second-hand outlets. Father wasn't in the photograph, only Mother, seated beside a flowery terrace, and the baby she held in her arms. Years later, Big Sister had coloured the white flowers on the black-and-white photo pink to give it some life. The woman in the frame looked out calmly, even a little melancholically, masking whatever was in her heart – misery or joy. It was the prettiest image of Mother I ever remember seeing.

7

I tried to imagine from her face what the man Big Sister called her real father looked like. He couldn't be short and thin, like most Chongqing men. He was given to wearing a long Chinese gown and a hat, a playboy who had a somewhat jealous nature. Loyalty came first with him; he was prepared to share everything with his society brothers, good and bad.

This man, whose life was so intimately tied to Mother, yet whom I'd never seen, was but a shadow to me, no matter how real he may have been to her.

He was sent to an arsenal on the north bank of the river to seize some Communists who were manufacturing gunpowder and didn't care too much to make it a secret. He returned home battered and bloodied, scaring the wits out of Mother. This setback kept him from rising higher in the Triad, which sent him into a drunken rage. He smashed and trampled on all the inscribed tablets their wedding guests had given them, and pulled his hair in agony. That was when Mother realized that life wasn't all milk and honey. With the political situation growing more desperate by the day, the number of military patrols and secret police out on the street increased; late at night came a frequent knocking at doors to ferret out Communists. He seldom came home, and when he did appear unannounced, he was gone again in no time. I doubt that Mother ever missed this sort of life after she left.

Big Sister said the man never carried any money when he went out. If he wanted something, one of the minor hench-men who were always with him wherever he went would pay for it.

'A gangster chieftain, what's so great about that?' I said with a sneer. 'You're lucky Mother took you away. If she hadn't, what do you think your days would have been like after Liberation?' I wanted to take her down a peg or two, but now I knew why she was always complaining about our poverty.

'I know that.' She cleared her throat. 'Life would have been hard on me no matter which road spread out before me.'

Shortly before the Communists took Chongqing, a huge fire raged in the city, racing up slopes as it was fanned by summer winds off the river. Shanties went up in flames in the superheated air, and even wooden barges and pontoon quays caught fire. People fled for their lives with fire all around them.

Carrying year-old Second Sister in her arms, and dragging Big Sister, who was three, behind her, Mother frantically avoided the smouldering houses on her way down to the river to look for Father's ship. Injured, moaning victims of the fire and refugees were everywhere. Total strangers, dirty-faced, their hair singed and matted, their clothes in tatters, huddled together to lament their fate. Some people were digging out utensils that had survived the fire, others were dumping buckets of water on structures that were little more than charcoal, and still others were running madly up and down the streets calling out for their kin, adults trying to find children, children looking for their parents.

After the fire was out, one shipload of bodies after another was carried from the river or the riverbank to be buried in common graves on a sandbar downriver, while the corpses of those who died in the city centre were burned in a clearing near the Dock at Heaven's Gate. Petrol was poured on the wooden cremation pyre to keep the fire going, as black-uniformed police stood guard. The city was shrouded in the stench of decaying bodies and dense smoke for days.

Mother heard gunfire near the Chongqing Hotel. People said they'd caught an arsonist and summarily executed him. Rumours flew that the Kuomintang fire-fighters had actually sprayed petrol on the fire to keep it burning fiercely, or that the Communist underground had started the fire in order to turn the populace against the government. Who knew what was true and what was not? At a time when the winds of war could sweep away tens of thousands of people in a single day, the Chongqing fire was but a minor tragedy.

This almost unprecedented conflagration occurred on the 2nd of September 1949; two months later, towards the end of November, the city fell under a siege by Communist forces. Yangtze sailors had abandoned their boats, knowing that in battles raging around this vital water route all boats were sitting ducks.

But Father didn't have the heart to leave, even though he

didn't own the boat. A dozen Kuomintang soldiers loaded crates of explosives on to his boat and, with drawn bayonets, forced him to sail upstream. Wrapped in a quilt, with only his eyes and hands showing, he called upon all his skill to zigzag through the barrage of shells from both banks. An officer on deck took a bullet in the thigh and collapsed into the wheelhouse, his blood splattering the windows and staining Father's quilt. Knowing the explosives could go up at any moment, the soldiers screamed in fright; some dived into the water and others cowered behind the wheelhouse on their hands and knees. But miraculously, Father was able to deliver his cargo where it was intended to go, for which the officer in charge handed him two silver dollars for the use of the boat. He then pointed his pistol at Father and said, 'Scuttle the boat!' before jumping ashore.

Father had used up whatever courage he had by then, but he had sailed through all that danger in order to save the boat. So as if he hadn't heard the man, he turned around and sailed off. Less than a mile from Heaven's Gate, when the artillery fire became so heavy that he was afraid he'd take a hit, he headed towards the shallows at Yellow Sand Bank to keep the boat out of harm's way.

That day cold gripped this strange, disaster-prone city, whose residents were fighting over provisions or fleeing from the battles. Mother, who was pregnant again, climbed the stone steps with a sack of dried beans in one hand and cradling Second Sister in the other, letting Big Sister walk on her own. Gunfire continued non-stop, winds bent trees nearly to the ground and swept gunsmoke high up into the blue fog. By the time Mother walked in the door at home, chilled blood was streaming down her legs. She had miscarried.

The landlady told her that if the dead foetus was a single segment it was a boy, and if it was bifurcated, it was a girl. She bent down and poked at the lump of flesh with a toilet brush. 'A boy!' she shouted. 'It's a boy!'

Hearing the retreating footsteps of the landlady, Mother lay on the bed in despair, certain that Father had died while transporting the explosives and that his corpse had floated downriver along with the wreckage of his boat. But he managed to escape the carnage on the river and make it home. Only his eyes showed through the black soot covering his face, which frightened the wits out of his two daughters. But Mother threw her arms around this husband who had broken free from the Demon of Death.

Three days later, the troops who had forced Father to transport their explosives were surrounded and annihilated by the People's Liberation Army. Their commanding officer told his captors about the boat, since he had been so impressed by the captain who had defied death in following orders, but forgot to mention the two silver dollars.

Years later, during the Counter-revolutionary Suppression Movement, Father was forced to write a detailed account of the incident, and he too forgot about those two silver dollars. He had been saved by his navigational skills and familiarity with the Yangtze, skills and knowledge that the new Communist regime found useful. So he was dispatched upriver to the stretch of the Yangtze called Gold Sand River, where the rapids are the most dangerous and hidden rocks the most plentiful, and where, in the absence of light-buoys, a single careless mistake can doom a boat and its crew. Yet for someone with his thorny past, this assignment was a show of leniency. But too many exhausting night sailings had already begun to take their toll on his eyesight.

Even as a little girl I knew there were two silver dollars at the bottom of one of our trunks. When Father and Mother argued, they kept their voices down, not like other compound tenants, who raised the roof with their domestic quarrels. They didn't want anyone to hear them, but I was too small to be noticed in my dark corner.

'Take those silver dollars to the bank and exchange them,'

Mother said. 'Then borrow the rest so you can go to a decent hospital and have your eyes taken care of.'

'It's too late for that now,' Father sighed. 'Besides, taking those coins in will just raise suspicions.' At the time I had no idea what 'suspicions' they were worried about, but in retrospect, I can see that their caution was warranted.

8

Big Sister yawned and gazed up at the mountain, where the sparse lamplight shone especially bright in the darkness. She said it was time to go home and get some sleep.

'That's it? That's the end of your story? You haven't answered my questions,' I told her. 'What about the syphilis?'

'That's easy,' she said. 'The Triadman was always whoring around. He got syphilis, passed it on to Mother, and she passed it on to Father.'

'But what about all those years in between? When was it discovered? Did Father know about it before they were married? Wasn't his eyesight ruined by all that night sailing?'

'That was cured long ago.' Big Sister nearly shouted. 'What a pest you are!'

Maybe she was willing to tell me, but didn't think it was much of a story, and maybe she still harboured some resentment. This was a picture of the monstrous life of China's poorest city dwellers, nothing more, and there was no way to romanticize it. There were always posters proclaiming 'VD Treatment, Guaranteed Cure' on the filthy, moss-covered walls in our area:

尖 銳 濕 疣 龜 頭 爛 痛
滴 蟲 陰 癢 菜 花 肉 芽
尿 口 紅 腫 陰 道 流 膿

Genital Warts Leprous Glans
Yeast Infections Genital Herpes
Itching Vulva Suppurating Vagina

I never did work out how to read these advertisements – up and down, left and right, backwards or forwards. All those confusing and frightening symbols pointed unmistakably to things that were dreaded and shameful. Even when the Red Sun shone most brightly, when Chinese society was at its revolutionary peak, boasting that it was the only place in the world where venereal disease had been eradicated, these ads never completely disappeared; and in the early 1980s, they were again everywhere. I never dared to look at them closely, nor did I know who was curing what and for whom. So when Big Sister raised her voice to me, I was too scared to pursue the subject any further.

SEVEN

1

After leaving my evening class, I noticed a light in the window near the history teacher's desk, so I climbed the stairs of the ridge-roofed building. He was reading a book, but I felt as if he'd been waiting for me. He smiled and asked if I was thirsty. Pointing to his teaglass, he said I could drink what was in it, if I didn't mind. He swore to Chairman Mao that he was free of disease.

But I stood at his desk without reaching for the glass. A drizzle was falling outside; the light inside the room was soft and gentle, and I had the feeling I was home. He was in a better mood than I'd seen before; his eyes actually sparkled.

He lived in a bungalow that had belonged to his parents, a single room partitioned into two, with a small rear door. I never got a clear picture of his parents' history, except that a year after Liberation, during one of the countless political movements, his father was kept under surveillance as an 'anti-socialist element' and lost his job. Just what it was that made him an 'anti-socialist element' even the history teacher wasn't sure. His mother worked as a bank teller, but eventually lost her job, too, and was reduced to taking in sewing at home. By the time I met him, they were long dead. His house was built on a slope, with half a dozen stone steps leading to the rear door. A robust malus tree stretched its limbs into the yard of a neighbour whose building on stilts was supported by the tree trunk.

There was also a grapevine behind the history teacher's

house, but it had wilted from lack of care. He had a brother, who had died in factional fighting during the Cultural Revolution. Soon after his death, the grapevine had a sudden spurt of growth, reaching out in all directions to entwine itself around the malus tree and nestle up to the wall and roof tiles, its leaves dense and lush, its purple fruit juicy and sweet. Green caterpillars that fell from the vine sparkled like crystal as their plump bodies writhed on the ground. The grapevine attracted thieves with a sweet tooth.

The history teacher told me he and some friends got together sometimes. 'Join us,' he said. 'You can listen to us talk about literature, and you can borrow some books.' I could tell from his tone of voice that he wanted me to take him up on his invitation; it was the first time he'd ever treated me as an equal. This group of friends, who shared similar experiences and backgrounds, would get together to read and talk about books, and to discuss topics of mutual interest. And they listened to a radio they'd rebuilt. Unlike most of the residents in the area, who tuned in only Hong Kong pop-music stations, they preferred shortwave broadcasts in Chinese from the BBC and Voice of America, something I never dared even to imagine. For thirty years, 'listening to enemy broadcasts' was a crime punishable by long prison sentences. Although by 1980 enforcement had grown lax and jamming measures had decreased, still, the mere mention of the words 'enemy broadcasts' could make you tremble with fright.

Thunderstorms around Chongqing can be ferocious. From the hillside you watch as lightning bolts split dark rain clouds above the river. But the storms seldom last more than ten minutes, a bit like the temperament of the people, who change their mind about blowing off steam almost as soon as they begin. What wears you down is the constant drizzle, and the mildew that eats away at furniture and brings swarms of insects out of the woodwork to dine on whatever the tables have to offer.

Drizzling rain covers the cobblestone streets with gooey,

slippery mud, until you can't see a single stone. The effect of the rain is despair that you'll ever see the end of it. Winter is the worst. People who can't afford rainboots have to walk around in plastic sandals, shivering as icy water squishes up between their toes.

Sometimes the drizzle is so fine it's little more than a mist floating in the air, eating away at the visibility until you can't see the opposite bank. Ships' horns send out their shrill warnings.

On one of those drizzly days, I climbed the hill, taking care not to fall on the slippery, uneven stone steps. I was wearing a worn old conical hat whose broken bamboo strips stuck out. I had to lean forward to keep the water dripping off the brim from soaking my clothes.

The history teacher's door was unlatched, since none of the neighbours would dare set foot in his place, thinking his house haunted, he guessed. But that fear made the place even more tantalizing. I stood beneath the eaves, tempted as never before, and asked if anyone was home.

No one answered my shouts, so I opened the door and walked in. The framed photograph of a woman stood on the bookcase. Her hair, though cut short, like all women in China at the time, was combed straight back and was black with a glossy sheen. She had an oval face and was wearing a turtleneck sweater under a coarse wool overcoat. My heart was beating wildly, for this was a photo of his mother, I could tell that at first glance; the resemblance was uncanny. She looked as if she wished to say something to me.

A porcelain vase whose cracks had been patched with cement stood in the corner. I saw traces of ancient scenery painted on it. An old-fashioned gramophone sat on a pedestal table next to the bookcase. Outside the window a bamboo grove glistened emerald green in the rain. Fresh laundry was draped across bamboo poles that hung between posts on the veranda, patiently drying in the wet weather.

There were books all over the room: on chairs, on the bed,

and on the dresser. And newspapers. Books were the staff of life for him and his friends, who could sit up all evening without saying a word, all absorbed in books; or they could spend the whole night arguing over a book or the fate of a character in one of them.

In my dreams I'd gone many times to the history teacher's house, to sit in a corner with a book, as a friend of his, listening to them talk or read beautiful passages. Maybe I was too timid and didn't fare well with strangers, or maybe I didn't want his friends to see me, for some obscure reason, but I never actually went and knocked at his door. It was enough to go there in my dreams. It made the days pass quickly, made life endurable.

I was four when the Cultural Revolution began, fourteen when it ended. At least seven of those ten years should have been spent in a classroom, but most of our time was spent in some form of voluntary labour: building terraced fields in a village, scrounging for scrap metals in factory garbage heaps, even sneaking into factories at night to steal usable machine parts and turn them in to the recycling station.

At the end of each term, class monitors, those expert informants, always levelled charges against me, saying my performance was terrible. I was terrified of the black marks that appeared on my report card: Doesn't love hard labour; lack of concern for the collective; is passive about national construction; lacklustre attitude towards political activities. Father would stand in the brightest spot in the room to read the report, brooding and silent. Mother didn't read well enough to take it all in, and didn't believe Father's version, so she had someone else read it to her. But what a loss of face that caused her, and when she came home, she was angrier than ever.

My performance reports got worse every year, and one year it was simply spectacular: Bourgeois thoughts, reads thick, yellowing novels; picks roadside flowers and hides them in her schoolbag; low political consciousness, reluctant to apply for Communist Youth League membership, smugly saying she has no time for such nonsense; refuses to open her heart to her teachers or class monitors, and doesn't accept criticism from the masses; lacks solidarity with her classmates, and refuses to mingle with them during recess. These were the opinions of my group, the fourteen pupils who pointed out each other's strengths and failings. For some unknown reason, I was forever the target of their criticism. The opinion of the class teacher was always something like 'I agree with the conclusions of the group, and hope the student will acknowledge the criticism, admit mistakes, and correct them.'

That may have been the year I first saw the history teacher. If I remember correctly, he was a substitute teacher for a week or two at my middle school. But I wouldn't have paid him any special attention, just as he wouldn't have paid attention to me. Men didn't interest me at the time, and I'm sure he didn't see anything in me worth taking note of; even today he would likely not find me particularly attractive.

What if that had been his only appearance in my life? What if he had treated me as coldly as everyone else – teachers, classmates, neighbours? But no, he was different from the others, and I should be grateful he came into my life, a favour bestowed by heaven.

At the beginning of that summer, Third Brother, who was always tinkering with radios – other people's as well as his own – repaired a cast-off radio and gave it to Father, whose eyesight was so bad. I borrowed it and moved the dial from one end to the other late at night, until I found the station the history teacher had told me about. For the first time in my life I heard someone read passages from the Bible:

Yea, though I walk through the valley of the shadow of death, I will fear no evil: for thou art with me; thy rod and thy staff they comfort me . . .

107

Surely goodness and mercy shall follow me all the days of my life: and I will dwell in the house of the Lord for ever.

Those words could have been spoken directly to me; otherwise how could they have moved me so, how could they have brought tears to my eyes? I fell in love with the Psalms and the Song of Solomon by listening secretly to short-wave radio broadcasts. I didn't care where that particular god came from, so long as he entered my heart and protected me. I'd sometimes unknowingly make the sign of the cross in front of the Buddha at the temple, or put my palms together in front of the cross, to the merriment of anyone who saw me do it. Some accused me of blasphemy, but I didn't think I'd done anything wrong.

2

I heard over the radio that the Yangtze had risen to its highest level in twenty-six years, and that the flood tide was rushing downriver. There was something else in September 1980, which was broadcast on the same day as the flood: the new marriage law set the minimum age at twenty-two for men and twenty for women. But the Party urged couples to wait until their combined ages equalled fifty. If you married at the minimum age, you wouldn't be taken to court, but your work unit might punish you for following the letter, not the spirit, of the law.

Maybe because I grew up malnourished and was slow to develop, people still called me a 'little girl' at the age of eighteen, and even I didn't consider myself an adult, though in two years I could legally marry. This revision of the marriage law, which made so many people happy, had absolutely no effect on me. Things that happened between men and women seemed quite distant.

Newspapers then, a mere four pages of cheap newsprint, were printed with such inferior ink that my hands always came away filthy. But in the Stonebridge marketplace, major newspapers like *People's Daily* and *Chongqing Daily* were displayed in wooden frames or glass enclosures, although there weren't many of the latter, since the glass would be smashed, not by newspaper thieves, but by vandals. They were probably the same people who smashed streetlights, turning just about every area into total darkness at night; Alley Cat Stream was the only exception, an obvious sign that that was where the culprits lived. But even if every streetlight had remained lit, the lanes of South Bank would still have been dark, since they didn't have enough streetlights to begin with.

3

The history teacher followed newspaper stories more closely than what was going on around him. Shanghai's famous attics and Paris's renowned lofts, he said, have produced countless writers and artists. Hardship could be a treasure. But he also said: No matter how strong you may be, you are still powerless before the world, and will never be able to enjoy what is simply not in store for you. He also said, however: The waterfall has always been there, unknown to people, until the river causes it to appear.

I enjoyed hearing him talk like that. His words were so profound, I thought, and I couldn't help but admire him. These must have been the sorts of things he said in their gatherings. He was an entirely different person than when he was in the classroom. The thought occurred to me that he was treating me like a friend now, someone who could understand what he was saying.

And so my interest in newspapers increased, opening up a window on the world. I skipped nothing, not even the little side columns. The tables of contents of literary magazines often appeared as advertisements on the back pages, and one day I noticed an ad for a Beijing literary magazine called *Contemporary*, which carried a piece of reportage entitled 'A

Winter's Tale'. The author was Yu Luojin, younger sister of Yu Luoke, a courageous young man who had spoken out against political oppression, declaring, 'Everyone, regardless of class background, has the right to political equality.' For that he was tried, found guilty, and shot during the Cultural Revolution. His sister then wrote about him and the further persecution that the whole family had to endure after his execution.

After reading the advertisement, I borrowed that issue of the magazine from the history teacher, and as I read, I copied the most moving passages into my diary. When I returned the magazine, I tried to share my thoughts with him, noting that Yu Luoke was only twenty-seven when he was killed. He abruptly told me to stop, with such harshness that it was as if this involved him in some way. His unexpected outburst confused me, but he calmed down once I changed the subject, although he turned cold and somewhat distant.

After leaving his office that afternoon, I sat on the stone steps by the school wall and sulked for a long while. I figured I was the only girl in school who talked with him about things outside lessons. He was neither better-looking nor more talented than the other teachers, so what made him so high and mighty? He must have known I had special feelings for him, and thought he could treat me any way he pleased. I was angry and I was hurt. A coward, that's what he was! Who said I had to respect him? Or pay him any attention, for that matter?

The evening-class bell rang. It was time for his review class.

That night he gave us some mock-exam questions, and the two hours were up before we knew it. I slipped out of the classroom when everyone else was milling about and took a deserted path across campus. But he caught up with me.

'What's your hurry?' he asked.

'Don't want ghosts to catch me.'

'Is that for my benefit?'

'How could it be?'

'You little devil, you're angry with me,' he said with a sigh, a newspaper rolled tightly in his hand. 'But I never tire of talking with you.'

With that sigh my determination to ignore him vanished, my anger disappeared. But I didn't slow down. He suggested that we leave by the school gate.

'Fine with me.' It was late, and all the other students had gone home, so there was no need for me to take the long way around, through the collapsed wall.

That evening was the first time we walked so close together. The feeling of closeness must have been enhanced by the fact that there was no one else around. Moonlight lit up broken stones on the road, leaves rustled in the wind. We walked in silence until we reached the spot where we went off in different directions. I stopped and turned to say goodbye. But he was in such high spirits he said he'd walk me a bit further. He seemed to know I was frightened by something; my face was burning up. I looked at him without his noticing it. Night covered my shyness and fears, and that comforted me.

Just before we reached the pond at the seedling nursery, I stopped. That was as far as I wanted him to go.

'Don't you want me to see you home?' He was standing behind my right shoulder, and when I reached to adjust the schoolbag strap, my hand touched his. I looked up and our eyes met. Our bodies were so close that my heart was beating rapidly. I lowered my head and said softly, 'I'm almost home, so please go back now.'

He nodded. 'You still have a way to go, so keep to the main roads. There's no need to be afraid, everything is predetermined by fate. You can run but you can't hide.'

Hitching my schoolbag up on to my shoulder, I turned and walked down the hill without looking back. I didn't stop until I was sure he couldn't see me any longer. What had he meant by that? I wondered.

I knew that if I turned around he'd still be standing there

watching me walk down the hill. And if I'd then turned and walked back to him, I'd have seen that sad look that only I detected. He was incapable of expressing his feelings. If he'd been able to do so, or if I'd been more understanding, maybe our hearts could have drawn closer together.

I was tormented by my desires, wishing he'd take me into his arms and kiss me.

My mother never once kissed me on the face; my father neither. Or my brothers and sisters. Whenever I was kissed in a dream, I woke up screaming. It must have been some deep-seated yearning. If someone had taken me into his arms every time I felt mistreated, even a pat on the back or the top of my head would have driven away the humiliation. But not in my family. People around here weren't given to hugs or kisses or intimate touching, except in bed, perhaps. They seemed to get along just fine without that sort of contact; but not me. I secretly indulged in dream kisses, proving that I was abnormal.

Hardly ever did the history teacher touch any part of my body, and I wondered if he was as frightened as I was.

4

After the flood waters receded, and before they returned, the long, wide banks of the river were exposed, lowering the pontoon quays. Rusty steel cables pressed down into mud that was dotted with cobblestones. Huge pitted rocks battered by waves rose with their vile visage in the shallow water. Those hidden rocks that made sailors tremble were now transformed into small turtle-shaped islands.

Every summer, people came from far and near to bathe in the river where the rocky banks were level. We said bathe instead of swim. Bathers floated on their backs, keeping their flat or protruding bellies above the surface as they frolicked in the water. Skinny boys engaged in water fights were naked as the day they were born. Sailors on cargo ships tied up to piers stripped to their sunburned skin and dived into the brownish water. For people like us, who had never seen a private bathroom, having a river nearby, whatever its colour and however choppy it might be, was a true blessing.

The Yangtze slows considerably when it reaches Chongqing in the Sichuan basin from the plateaux of its upper reaches. And still it claims many lives every year: reckless bathers, victims of capsized boats or murder, and people who have given up on life. Whether they die a hero's death or an ignominious one, their fate is the same: there will always be room in the river.

'Hurry up, there's another water club!' The shouts up and down the street and in every compound were like a drumbeat. People in sandals, some with ricebowls in their hands, would pour out of the lanes in a headlong rush to the riverbank. Looking at dead bodies was rare entertainment in the drab daily lives of South Bank residents.

At a lumber mill near the bend in the river at Slingshot Pellet Dock, the water flows slowly past the rocky bank, where the sawdust turns the water into a strange lumpy soup. Corpses there are coated with sawdust and bloat until they look like strange-coloured logs. Impossible to determine what kind of people they might have been, with their clothes long since washed away or knotted around their bodies. And even naked it's hard to tell whether they're men or women. But belief has it that if a relative or an enemy of the victim is among the onlookers, fresh blood will ooze from the orifices of the purple, waterlogged face.

Most of these corpses had been swept dozens or even hundreds of miles down the river, and might have travelled hundreds or thousands of miles more to some other distant spot if not for this dirty bend in the river. And yet, if they'd been in the water less than a week when they reached the shore, they would maintain one peculiar distinction: the women would be belly up, the men face down. Once I knew a bit about what went on between men and women, my heart fluttered when I pondered those unfortunate individuals. As the river was eating away at their flesh and bones, wasn't it also embracing them, giving them their last tender touch, their final sexual caress?

In the second-floor office of the slanted-roofed building, I sensed a blue glow in the purple night; the heat of the day had not yet dissipated, and in nearby fields, croaking frogs sent fireflies scurrying out of the trees. Talking to the history teacher made me happy. He kept squinting as he sipped his tea and listened.

I could always pick my skinny, dark-skinned third brother out of the crowd of kids bathing in the river. Mother was forever lecturing him: 'You may not care if you live or die, but I do.' Her comments went in one ear and out the other. He treated his own life with disdain, yet I don't think I ever saw him with so much as a scratch. And there were always a couple of snot-nosed, barefoot kids hanging around him, for he was their hero.

Big Sister's eldest daughter was only two months old when Third Brother, captivated by her pink cheeks, decided to take her down to the river one day when her mother was napping. There he let her thrash around in the water on her own. Meanwhile, sensing that something was wrong, Big Sister woke up, jumped out of bed, and was searching frantically for her daughter when Third Brother strolled into the compound, carrying the drenched baby girl, who still had blades of grass stuck in her hair. 'She learned how to swim on her own,' Third Brother said, ignoring Big Sister's fuming rage.

Mother was so angry she turned white. But she didn't raise a hand at him, and even refilled his bowl at dinnertime.

'You'll be a water club sooner or later,' Big Sister railed at Third Brother. He glared at Big Sister, his nostrils flaring; he scooted out of the compound and out of sight, most likely down to the river for another bathe.

'Get back here, Number Three,' Mother shouted at his back. 'You don't care about anybody, you damned hermit!'

My feet, seemingly having a mind of their own, headed towards the hall. 'Little Six,' Mother called to me harshly, 'don't you dare follow him!' She was scooping up a hand-made cloth bag and stuffing it with clean clothes and pickled vegetables to take back to the factory. Though she came home only once a week, she never forgot to nag me about something: 'I forbid you to go bathing in the river, especially by yourself. I don't even want you playing on the riverbank. The river can reach out and grab you, throw a noose around you. It doesn't care if you're good or not, and it loves children.'

Mother started telling me about the horrors of the river when I was barely old enough to walk and talk, and she never stopped. And so a girl who grew up on the banks of a river, the daughter of a boatman, never learned how to swim. I can't think of another boy or girl who lived on the river who didn't swim like a fish. But me, a girl who prided herself on being disobedient, took Mother's warnings about the water to heart.

I was even afraid of taking a ferry across the river, although I couldn't say why. Especially on holidays, when they packed us in like cattle. The ferry had life vests, but when a boat capsized, who had time to grab a life vest? I went down to the river once, and got there just in time to see a ferry flip over. Dark skulls dotted the surface of the water, bobbing like balls. I sat down on the stone steps in a state of terror.

Instead of listening quietly to me, as he normally did, the history teacher laughed at my fear of the water. Swimming is simple, he said. Girls look wonderful when they do the breast stroke. He rose from his chair, walked over, and stood behind me. My skin burned when he took hold of my arms. His large hands were warm and powerful. He stretched my arms out in front of me and guided them in a swimming motion. His manner was so natural that, when he brushed up against my back, I didn't realize what he was up to.

Then, all of a sudden, I did, and my face reddened. I threw off his hands and stepped away.

'If you don't want to learn, that's fine with me,' he said with a long face.

Silence filled the room. I sensed that something was about to happen. Several seconds passed, but I waited in vain. Once again I'd made a fool of myself. I turned to leave.

'Why not stay a while longer?'

'No.' I walked to the door and grabbed the doorknob.

I picked up my bag by the strap and turned to force a smile. He didn't move. His eyes were fixed on me. 'Drop by any time. Shall I see you out?'

'No.' I sighed, as if to purge myself of the melancholy stored up inside.

I didn't start crying until I was far from the building. Either he didn't like me or he was toying with me, like those villains in novels who take advantage of women, then abandon them.

That's exactly the kind of man he is.

On the way home I began to hate him and swore I'd ignore him from now on. But in bed that night I couldn't help thinking about him. Why had I run away? It was all my fault. I began stroking my face, pretending it was his hand, touching my lips and then my neck, then letting my hand slip down my undershirt to my breasts; my hand shot back as if from an electric shock, but was drawn inexorably back, and from there it began touching me below, bringing a sensation I'd never felt before. I closed my eyes.

During the daytime I refused to think about being with him, not even for a second. But wrapped in the darkness of night, when everything was still, the image of the history teacher filled my head.

What would I have done if he'd thrown his arms around me then? Resist or consent?

My face reddened, and I could hear rats scurrying in the space between the floors. A baby was bawling somewhere out there beyond the skylight. Then someone in the hall coughed. I sat up quietly in bed, and the coughing

116

stopped. But when I lay back down, it started up again, as if to keep me from sleeping.

Our New Year's Eve meals were always special. Normally thrifty when it came to food, we poor people went all out at New Year's, with stewed lotus root and meaty soup bones, stir-fried peanuts, and, especially, cold shredded radishes smothered with the mouth-watering chilli sauce that we went without the rest of the year. No matter how badly we wanted to start eating, Mother would always chase us outside to stand in the freezing hall or in the windswept courtyard while she stayed inside, doing what, we didn't know, but mumbling something or other. She said that was the only way the ancestors would be pacified.

'Our ancestors aren't around, so who'd know?' Too young to realize what was good for me, I spoke up while my brothers and sisters held their tongues.

'Nonsense! Our ancestors are standing next to us as we speak,' Mother said, staring daggers at me.

When we finally sat down at the table, she'd point to the bowls and chopsticks and say, 'See there. The chopsticks were pointing out, but now they're pointing in. The ancestors have been here.'

'They certainly have,' Fourth Sister said.

'Little Six, when are you going to learn to hold your chopsticks properly?' Mother caught me holding my chopsticks in the air, and I froze. 'See there, you're not supposed to hold them near the top. If you do, you'll go far away from home one day, and won't come back. Hold them down lower. That way you'll always be near your father and mother.'

I slid my hand down to the halfway point.

'No, that's not right either. Do you have wings on your ears? Is that why you never listen to me? Don't cross them like that. If you do, you won't be able to hold on to money, and you'll be poor all your life. Do it like this, hold them tight with your thumb and index finger touching. I can't teach you anything. Go ahead and eat for now, but make sure you learn how to do it right tomorrow.'

My brothers and sisters sat there eating the whole time, as if they hadn't heard a thing.

When Pure Brightness Day, set aside for grave-sweeping, rolled around, Father would go up on the mountain to dig for Pure Brightness greens, sometimes alone and sometimes with Fifth Brother and me in tow. He'd always be careful to leave the roots in the ground. That way there'd be more for next year. During the famine, not even the roots were spared, and wild vegetables were still hard to find, even now.

This was a particularly strange type of wild green, since it was tender only in the days before Pure Brightness Day. After that, it was tough and stringy, even when the leaves were covered with clear dewdrops in the early morning. Something like a woman's life: the good days passed far too quickly. Its leaves weren't very big, nor particularly thick; covered with a pale-white fuzz, they grew in small clusters. After washing them in water, we chopped them up and rolled them into flour to make flatcakes, which we lined up next to the frying wok. As soon as the water in the wok had all steamed away, we removed the lid and heated the entire bottom by moving the wok around. Grave-sweeping greens had a clear, fresh odour when cooked, and the cakes had a sticky texture. I loved their name: Pure Brightness cakes.

Father told us not to talk when we ate Pure Brightness cakes, but his stern demeanour differed from the way Mother performed her ancestral sacrifices; with him, there was always something fearful about it. He was far from the place of his birth in Zhejiang, and he had only learned of the deaths of his father and mother from a fellow home-towner on a forced march during the war. The spirits of his dead parents were probably too far away to come to the side of their son, who was stranded up the river.

EIGHT

1

I awoke before dawn and couldn't get back to sleep. Big Sister was spread out all over the other side of the bed, with one leg draped over mine. I moved away lightly, pulled my thin quilt over me and curled up against the wall.

She had only drawn a rough hasty sketch of those by-gone days as we sat on the riverbank, and I knew she'd left out the most important details, including the answer to my most pressing question: why I seemed superfluous in this family.

As I lay in bed, my head swam as never before, and even my breathing was laboured. My doubts deepened with every passing minute. It wasn't until the late 1960s that the Communist Party finally realized the stupidity of promoting large families, and by then this over-cultivated land could not sustain the rapidly expanding population. A decision on what to do, however, was delayed until the 1970s, owing to the Cultural Revolution. Since every change of policy by the government was violent, Family Planning became a draconian policy. But by then it was too late. Given the huge population base, each family was now allowed only one child; after that, either of the couple had to be sterilized. Much later on, to ease widespread resistance, couples were allowed to try once more if the first child was female.

So, there were too many Chinese. What about me, was I part of that surplus?

As dawn broke, the pain in my gut told me I'd be constipated again, something that always happened when I was troubled, even in childhood. It was a common malady among South Bank women.

Since we had no toilet in the house, and none anywhere in the compound, chamber pots had to serve the purpose. They were little help in a big family. A ten-minute walk up the hill on a twisting, muddy path was required to get to the nearest public toilet, an unattended facility with three pits on the women's side. I never saw inside the men's, but I know it was twice as large as ours, and had three more pits. That was a source of pride among local men: 'Girls know their place the minute they're born: they only have half as many latrine pits as we have.'

People began queuing up at the public toilet early in the morning; our queue was always a lot longer. Women with loose bowels or slightly older women simply went around behind the toilet to the open cesspool, where they dropped their pants immodestly and squatted down on the edge. The men, free to go where they pleased, sometimes went down to the riverbank to relieve themselves, then kicked sand on top of the mess, like cats or dogs.

I often heard people talk about something called a red-clawed monster, which haunted the women's toilet. They said its bright-red claws reached up from the latrine pit and bloodied your exposed private parts. Talk like that kept timid women from going to the toilet alone. Eventually, the police solved the mystery, or so they said: a local hooligan had covered his hands with Mercurochrome and haunted the women's toilet. But there was another, more convincing explanation: since there weren't enough toilets to serve the residents, some women had devised this scheme to scare people off so they could shit in comfort.

The three pits were so filthy that I couldn't find a clean spot to stand. And the maggots, some with long yellow tails, squirmed right up next to my feet. But if I felt like relieving myself at home, I'd have to wait till I was alone, then bolt the door and squat behind the curtain. Even then there might be footsteps outside and a pounding on the door; if I had forgotten to bolt it before going about my business, someone might walk into the hall, and I'd hold my breath and wait in agonizing silence until whoever it was left. If that happened, the need to relieve myself might vanish.

2

Women often discharged parasites in the toilet, and sometimes so many roundworms emerged that they'd form a writhing, glistening, pinkish clump on the floor. De-worming medicine was cheap, but few people used it, since it wasn't very effective in the long run. Denied nutrition in anaemic intestines, what the Sichuanese call 'slim pickings', the worms would leave to try their luck in the next reincarnation.

She was about ten years old, moon-faced, with a long thin neck, about my age. She lived on the street where the grain store was located. I'm not sure what brought her to our public toilet, maybe she was just passing by, or maybe the queue at her toilet was too long. I'd made it inside, and was second in the queue for one of the pits.

Summer had just arrived, and the stench inside the toilet was overpowering. She was squatting over the left-hand pit, when her mouth snapped open, her eyes grew round, and her nostrils flared; her whole face underwent a terrifying change, as a roundworm emerged from her mouth. She screamed and collapsed amid the muck on the floor. The stumpy woman ahead of me walked over and dragged the girl out of the toilet, warning me on her way out: 'That pit's mine, don't you dare take it!'

Once the girl was out in the open air, people in the queue gawked at her from a distance, since she was covered with excrement. The stumpy woman slapped her a couple of times, snapping the unconscious girl back to life, then announced shrilly, 'What's to be afraid of? We've all got things like that in our bellies.'

Mother told us girls that although fresh fruit and vegetables weren't ours to enjoy, personal hygiene was still important, especially after delivering a child. She told us to wash before going to bed, with clean water, not what we used to wash our feet in. Nine out of ten women have piles, she said, but not you girls, because I've taken good care of you.

But she too suffered from constipation, like her four daughters. It was the rare South Bank woman who didn't. Though she was frugal in most respects, she did not economize where sanitary toilet paper was concerned. Other people used newspapers, exercise books, and wrapping paper from the market. Even as children we were trained to go into the fields to dig for couch grass or pick young bamboo leaves, which we'd boil and drink as a laxative. But the most effective remedy was bitter gourd seeds. The taste of the boiled extract was so bad we'd hold our noses when we drank it, then wash it down with cold water to get the bitter taste out of our mouths. The women here, like the place itself, had persistent drainage problems.

Taking a shit was no easy matter, with all those eyes fixed on your exposed private parts. People next in line held on to their pants, their faces beaded with sweat as they anxiously waited their turn to relieve themselves. Older women would squat contentedly over the pits, enjoying a rare moment of territorial autonomy. Others would stare at the occupied pits and make crude comments about the occupants: That sagging vulva has been visited by plenty of men. See that one over there, that's a case of herpes! She must be a whore who's sold it so often, it'll be a wonder if it doesn't rot off.

Standing in the queue made me nervous; so did the squatting itself. I'd bring something to hold in front of me, without being too obvious about it. A fan, sometimes, or a book or my schoolbag. Always careful not to get any muck on my underpants and shoes, and not let the white or red maggots crawl up on to my feet, I also had to make sure that whatever I was holding didn't brush up against the edge of the pit; at the same time I didn't want the people in the queue thinking I was intentionally shielding my private parts from view. The last thing I wanted was for those sharp-tongued gossipy women to start saying I had some kind of problem. What did I have that was so great that I wouldn't let them see it?

When I saw the girl spit out the roundworm that day, I suddenly didn't have to go any more. So when my turn came, I turned and walked out of the toilet, followed by the curious looks of women in the queue.

Then one day the same thing happened to me. Having seen it before, I wasn't as frightened as I might have been. But while I didn't faint, I didn't take it in my stride either. I was carrying a bowl of steaming rice with red beans boiled until they were starchy and filling, and had just walked into the courtyard with a mouthful of beans. But before I could start chewing, a worm shot out of my mouth and fell squirming to the ground; it was grey and about a foot in length. Instead of screaming, I flung the bowl up in the air with such force that it struck an eave and sent beans raining down on the mossy ground, speckling it with red dots. I clamped my eyes shut, squeezing out the pooling tears, and stamped on the worm with all my might.

I didn't want to tell anybody what had happened, since my reaction had turned a ghastly event into a circus act that was more comical than frightening.

Father took me to Stonebridge, where he bought three doses of herbal medicine. Chinese medicine is best, he'd say, because there are no side effects. The prescription included black plum, Sichuan chinaberry, sliced betel nut, Indian costus root, Sichuan peppers, dried ginger, rhubarb, and things with really strange names. When the concoction, simmered in a crock bowl, was ready, I drank bowlfuls of the stuff, until my stomach couldn't take another drop. If only Mother had been home that day. It hadn't seemed so bad seeing her only once a week before, but how I missed her now.

Air swirled around inside my bloated belly that evening, as if a demon had been set loose down there.

I took to my heels and ran outside.

'Don't go to the toilet.' Father called me back inside, bolted the door from the other side, and sat guard in the hall to keep my brothers and sisters and any neighbours from walking in on me.

3

Every evening, as the sun set behind the hills, peasants in straw hats came from nearby villages to collect nightsoil for fertilizer.

'Empty pails!' they'd shout as they set down their big wooden buckets and waited for people up and down the street to bring their waste-filled chamber pots and commodes out from behind doors or under beds or curtained corners, carrying them with the caution normally reserved for urns holding the tablets of their ancestors. I can't recall how old I was when the chore of emptying the chamber pot fell to me, but after dumping the contents into the buckets, I'd scrub the pot with a bamboo brush, using the water left over from washing vegetables and doing the laundry. Then I'd carry it home, dumping the mucky water into the ditch that ran alongside the stone steps. Trees lining the path were always thick and sturdy, their leaves lush and dense.

If, by chance, I missed the nightsoil collectors, I'd have to carry the chamber pot to the cesspool behind the public toilet. When it rained, the road was so muddy I often slipped and sometimes fell, splattering myself with the sticky muck and smashing the pot it was in. I'd scramble to my feet and run home for some coal ash, carrying it back in a dustpan to cover the muck spilled on the road, then sweep it up and dump the whole mess into the cesspool. Getting the stone steps really clean was hard, and I usually had to borrow ashes from the neighbours to finish the job. What worried me was that anyone walking by would probably curse my parents and their ancestors! No matter how far away they were, my parents were sure to hear, and sure to take it out on me.

Every time one of those disasters struck, I imagined that my brothers and sisters, along with my parents, were standing by the compound gate, watching me with the same cold detachment as our neighbours as I frantically cleaned up the mess, splattered with shit.

Who knows, maybe they just wanted me to know that any wrong-doing deserved some punishment – same for every-body. But it wasn't easy for me to be understanding. Couldn't they have reached out to me? Why keep reminding me I was superfluous?

I was dogged by this kind of feeling, possibly unfounded, even when I was very young. One rainy day when I was twelve, Mother wondered why I hadn't left for school, even after the morning bell had rung. Holding my school-bag by the strap, I told her timidly that my teacher said I hadn't paid the tuition yet, and had already kept me after school twice.

Mother was sitting on the bed. 'We've just paid your tuition,' she said. 'Why do they want more?' She should have been over her back sprain by then, and I didn't know why she was home that day.

'That was last semester,' I said softly. I'm sure my face was bright red. I never was good at begging for money, even from my parents.

She didn't say anything for a moment before blurting out, 'You're lucky you get food to eat. But no, you want to go to school! We're poor, and we've survived this long only with the protection of our ancestors. We don't have the money. Do you think it's easy to come up with three yuan for your tuition?'

The same thing happened every semester, and I knew she wouldn't take out the money until I started crying. It wasn't so much that she didn't want to spend the money as that she wanted to give me a hard time, so I'd be grateful. My brothers and sisters only had to ask two or three times before she'd come up with money for them. But not me. What she harboured towards me wasn't anger, it was loathing.

'You should never have let me be born,' I said, hugging my schoolbag tightly as I sat in the doorway on my haunches, clenching my teeth to stop myself crying.

'You're right, I shouldn't have!' She didn't actually say that, but that's what I saw in her eyes, those cold eyes. I threw down my schoolbag and ran into the darkened hall. I don't want to live any more, my heart cried out. No one in this family wants me around!

The steps creaked under my feet as I bounded up the stairs, two and three steps at a time, not even touching the banister.

I stood by the bed in front of the curtain and took Fourth Sister's hand mirror out from under the pillow to look at myself, as I did every morning when I combed my hair. But today I couldn't see my reflection, no matter how I held the thing.

When Fourth Sister came into the attic, I asked her why I couldn't see myself. Her eyes grew wide and she bounded downstairs, nearly scared to death as she screamed for Mother and Second Sister and Third Brother. Her shrill voice hung in the air for a long time, like a song. I took another look at the mirror – it was still a mirror, but I wasn't in it. It fell to the floor and flopped over without shattering, showing a pair of chubby infants embracing plump ears of wheat and corn.

I no longer belonged to myself, and I felt myself fall to the floor, where my legs jerked out in front of me.

An uproar of noise encircled me. A face drew up close. 'Her spirit has fled.'

My spirit, fled? Dead already, at the age of twelve? My life ended, just like that? I felt light as a feather and free to roam, unbound and uprooted. I never thought death could be so simple, so carefree and relaxing.

But a new feeling rose inside me: a mixture of profound regret and unspeakable dejection. Already I longed for new life, even if it were more miserable than the one just given up. I'd only begun to live, there was no need for me to die. I wanted desperately to live again, to grow up.

I searched for Mother among the people gathered around me, wanting to tell her to burn my diary, which was under the bed. But I couldn't find her. So, in language that only she and I understood, I told her not to hold on to my appearance, that she could burn any photographs of me she had, just so long as she'd let me go on living.

Someone seemed to be lifting up my head, heavily and painfully. The footsteps coming up the stairs didn't sound like Mother's.

4

On the evening when Big Sister related the family story, I caught cold sitting beside the river. I must have lain sick in bed for a day or more.

I struggled out of bed and draped my legs over the side to slip my feet into a pair of black cloth slippers. After a moment, the room stopped spinning; the wall was just a wall, the table still a table, and the curtain remained hanging between the two beds. I was alone. As I stepped down, my right foot landed on a fleshy object. Quickly pulling my foot back, I looked down and saw a huge rat lying there, bigger than my foot. It wasn't moving.

Using two pieces of firewood I took out from under the bed, I picked up the rat and carried it gingerly out into the landing in front of the attic door. But when I started downstairs, the rat seemed to spring to life; it fell to the floor and bounced down the steps into the hall. I screamed.

The courtyard was deserted except for an itinerant barber

who was brushing off a man's neck. A couple of kids were feeding mulberry leaves to silkworms just beyond the gate, and someone was dumping dirty water into the drainage ditch.

My scream was thin and weak, and the people out there never paused in what they were doing. When I screamed again, Father poked his head up at the foot of the stairs. 'What's the matter, Little Six?'

I pointed to where the half-dead rat was lying, the words sticking in my throat. With his bad eyes, Father couldn't see anything, but our neighbour, Baldy Cheng, ran in with a pair of fireplace tongs. 'It's all bloody,' he said as he picked the thing up. Baldy Cheng was a cook on a cargo ship. When the ship was being unloaded or serviced in Chongqing, he was on holiday at home.

'Bloody?' His ageing mother's ears pricked up at this word.

'Bloody!' he repeated.

'That's a good sign,' the old woman said.

'Did you step on it?' he yelled at me.

I nodded.

'She stepped on it and killed it.' I don't know how she could have seen me nod, since she was sitting on a stool in her own doorway. 'You have to kill them with one step. If one doesn't do it, you need to find another way to kill them,' she remarked slowly.

'How come?' Baldy Cheng seemed to be taking it more seriously than his mother.

'If you need more than one step, the rat will have a second spirit even if it's dead, and it'll raise hell in the compound.' The old lady seemed very sure of herself. I sucked in a chilled breath and ran back up into the attic.

Fourth Sister and Dehua didn't come home that night. Neither did Big Sister; I don't know where she went, but I was sure she was staying away because she'd had enough of my questions. She knew I'd never rest until I got to the bottom of things. That night I couldn't sleep because of a baby

128

crying somewhere. Physically, I was feeling better, and my forehead wasn't burning up as it had in the morning. I'd be strong enough to go to school the next day. I needed to talk, that much was certain.

5

The next morning I heard someone ask for me downstairs; it was a familiar voice. I ran out on to the landing. The history teacher was standing in the hall. Under the watchful gaze of my father, I invited him up to the attic.

'There's nowhere for you to sit,' I stammered. I was so nervous I didn't know what to do with my hands and feet, so I stood next to the desk. Illusions hardly ever match reality, so maybe I'd dreamed about his popping into my dark, mouldy attic so often that, to my astonishment, it had actually happened. I'd never pretended I was better off than I was, but now that he was here and had abruptly entered my personal life unannounced, I was overwhelmed by the shame of abject poverty.

'You can sit on the bed if you like,' I said after a moment, remaining standing.

'Are you sick?' He looked at me as he sat down. 'That's what I suspected when you didn't show up yesterday. It's not like you to miss my evening lectures.'

I didn't say anything. His voice sounded strong and vigorous in the attic space, and clearer than at school. 'Nothing serious, is it?'

I just tilted my head.

He reacted to my silence by looking around the room and admitting that my living conditions were worse than he'd expected. But he liked this attic, where I'd lived all my life. 'You said you like to look out the window at the clouds, since they drift in different directions than at the riverbank.'

He'd remembered, and so clearly. But what moved me the most was when he said he liked my little attic.

He took out a package wrapped in Kraft paper and handed it to me.

'This is for you,' he said.

'A book?' The package was sealed, and I wanted to know its contents. 'What book?'

'Don't open it till you're alone,' he said. There was a strange look in his eyes.

I didn't even thank him. There was so much I wanted to say, but the words stuck in my throat. So I just stood there looking at him like a fool. He stood up and said he was passing Alley Cat Stream on his way home from school and thought he'd stop by to see how I was doing.

So he hadn't made a special trip to see me, after all. But in the midst of my disappointment, I felt his hand on my shoulder, and clutched the envelope tightly with nervous excitement. I didn't want him to move his hand, but he did. He was going to leave.

'Want to get some fresh air?'

I jumped to my feet.

'We can walk up the hill,' he said by way of explanation.

I didn't say anything. If my neighbours saw me walk out with him, everyone in the compound would be talking.

He must have read my mind, because before I could say a word, he offered to leave first and meet me around two-thirty in front of People's Clinic Number Five.

I saw him out to the steps, then watched his back disappear beyond the gate.

'Who was that?' I heard Mama Shi's voice behind me.

My caution had served me well. This gossipy woman was probably under the stairs the whole time, watching to see how long he stayed. It was the first time an adult man had come to see me.

'You don't have to tell me, I already know. His father was an "ox-demon and snake-spirit" reactionary. He's the eldest son of that rotten old man who sold popcorn all over South Bank, isn't he? He's married and has a kid. I'd

130

like to know why he came looking for you.'

'None of your business,' I snapped coldly as I went into the hall.

The wall clock read 11.45. It was always two minutes slow or two minutes fast, no matter how often anyone reset or rewound it.

Back in my attic room I tore open the package and took out a thick book entitled *Human Anatomy*. The cover said it was a medical textbook. I was puzzled. I gave it a flip, and it opened to a set of illustrations: a naked man, front and back, and a naked woman, also front and back, all with arrows and identifying words: breast, vagina, pubic hair, testicles, and so on, words I'd never so much as uttered. My heart was racing as I buried my face in the pages of the book. A few seconds later, I raised my head and looked around to assure myself that I was alone. Then I returned to the book to study the genital illustrations. For the first time in my life I felt as if my labia were opening and a fire snake were squirming around in my vagina. It was unbearable.

'Damn it! My teacher's a sex-crazed rogue!'

NINE

1

Quotations from Chairman Mao have a beautiful lilt when recited in chorus in the Sichuan dialect, rhythmic and melodic; even when they're recited not all that smoothly, the sound is like waves rising and falling, a bit like opera. Listening to them for a long while can be hypnotic, somnolent even.

For several years in the early 1970s, 'reactionary slogans' showed up on the school's toilet walls, on the stone walls, even on the ground itself. Most were simple and direct: 'Down with Chairman Mao', things like that. But if he was to be knocked down, why the respectful 'Chairman'? No one ever asked, since the slogan was so reactionary that it was not to be 'repeated and spread', even during an investigation. The police and school authorities treated each case as extremely serious; without warning, our schoolbags would be confiscated and our handwriting analysed, until the little counter-revolutionary would be ferreted out and forced to reveal the name of the big counter-revolutionary who put him up to it. The pupil would be expelled and sent home, the adult might disappear for a decade or more. For the investigation, every unit was mobilized, the talk on the street about nothing else.

No city in China could boast cruder or more vivid toilet graffiti, nor, probably, was there anywhere that produced a larger contingent of young 'reactionary sloganeers'. There was no greater crime than that of 'counter-revolutionary', and nothing that invited more frightful consequences.

Scribbling a few words could turn you into an overnight sensation, and what a temptation that was, one that plenty of foolish kids could not resist. With a mixture of fear and excitement they tried their hand at writing those few fateful words.

Once, when I was 'on duty' cleaning out the school toilet, and no one else was around, I had a powerful urge to write something that would shock others as well as myself. But I didn't, and that probably saved me and my family from becoming 'current counter-revolutionaries'. I didn't do it because, as I was taking out my pencil, I noticed a strange picture, done in charcoal, the genitalia all out of proportion. My face turned bright red, and I could hardly breathe. They said it was done by a bunch of boys who sneaked into the girls' toilet at night.

And it was mostly boys who wrote the reactionary slogans, although the police treated boys and girls the same in their search for suspects.

I hid *Human Anatomy* under my pillow, but then put it in my schoolbag to keep it away from my family. I'd seen pictures of those parts before, but this time it was different. The genitalia in photographs of executed men, or those of men bathing in the courtyard, frightened and disgusted me, and so did dirty pictures on the toilet wall. But the genitalia in the medical textbook looked clean, beautiful even, and dangerously seductive. I pressed my hand against my chest; I was sweating.

The clock downstairs rang out – it was one o'clock. I'd agreed to meet him at two-thirty. If I walked along the river then took a short cut up the mountain to People's Clinic Number Five, I'd have plenty of time, even if I walked slowly. My legs were so rubbery I could barely stand. I'd ask him what was the big idea giving me a dirty book like that. What kind of teacher was he?

2

There was a long queue at the water tap, but no water. Buckets lined the road near where five or six people were standing. The sun had risen early that day, and by noon it was scorching. I was glad I'd grabbed a straw hat on the way out, both for the sun and the rain. In the shade of the eaves, people were complaining. 'If we don't get some water pretty soon, not only will we die of thirst, but the buckets will start cracking!'

I walked downhill to the Alley Cat Stream ferry landing.

An indescribably filthy woman was standing on the little stone bridge in front of the recycling station. I saw her every time I came here. The bridge connected two ridges separated by a stream in which the only water that flowed was run-off from local factories; it glistened oily red in the sunlight, sometimes gave off a greenish-blue light. The woman's clothes barely covered her. People said she was in her thirties, but she had a baby face and a girl's breasts. The rest of her body was full – big thighs and hips. Every year or two her belly bulged. It started swelling in the spring, rose to its peak in the summer, and shrank in the autumn. No one knew what she did with the children she bore, just as no one knew her name or her past. Spat upon and beaten, she survived on scraps from neighbourhood restaurants or crumbs dropped on the street. At night she slept wherever she happened to be.

People said she was a nymphomaniac.

The little stone bridge by the recycling station was her favourite haunt, and the only place where people didn't bother her. There were two old men at the station; one moved things like newspapers, plastic sandals, rags, broken shoes, broken glass, and scrap metal inside from the gate, while the other one made entries in an account book, using an abacus, then handed coins or crumpled banknotes out through a tiny window.

One of my earliest memories is of seeing this nympho-maniac. Her eyes were clouded, her fingers grimy black, and her body was coated with gummy filth. She wore smelly rubber boots in the winter and went barefoot in the summer, oblivious to all the broken glass on the ground around the station. She might drop her pants at any time, in front of men or women; but she was always smiling, unlike those hateful 'normal' people who spent their time attacking class enemies.

Four years earlier, the Neighbourhood Committee an-nounced at a meeting that the Gang of Four had been arrested. When the meeting was over, people rejoiced that another group of powerful individuals had been toppled and another group of attackers had themselves been attacked; using washbasins, cooking pots, and frying pans as makeshift gongs, they paraded noisily up and down the streets, which were scenes of joyous celebration amid red banners and firecrackers. Bare-chested men shouted slogans at the top of their lungs, and the crowd continued to swell, mainly with kids out to have some fun. As the numbers increased, the demonstration moved towards the square at Stonebridge.

I was right in the thick of things, walking up the steps of High School Avenue, and not quite sure what the world was coming to. But I knew that, like everyone else, I was expected to mourn the passing of Chairman Mao and celebrate the arrest of the Gang of Four, his assistants in waging the Cultural Revolution. Then I spotted the nymphomaniac coming towards me from the opposite direction. Her face didn't look quite so dirty in the bright autumn sunlight. She was sporting a ragged crew-cut and was soaked from head to toe, probably from being pushed into the river by some of the crueller celebrants. A tattered man's uniform clung to her body, her belly flat at the time. She threaded her way through the tide of people.

I stepped away from the procession and hid behind a telegraph pole to watch, fascinated by her single-minded progress against the tide; she was totally unconcerned about what was happening in the world around her, or might happen in the days to come.

Since then four years had passed, and she was still as happily filthy as ever, while frustrations and expectations were piling up in my life.

The Yangtze was still muddy, much darker than the Jialing. Although the water looked hot, it was cool to the touch when you stuck your foot in. We riverbank dwellers have a special attachment to the river. People who come only to visit the river enjoy it for a moment, then put it out of their minds as soon as they turn and walk off, laughing at how we 'foolishly' skim stones on the surface. A river, they say, is fine to look at, but that's all. Just think of the time you waste trying to cross it, and when a boat capsizes, the river becomes a killer.

But the river flows through our hearts, it's with us from the day we're born. If we stop to rest on a hill, we turn to look back at the river, which invigorates us and keeps us going.

Breathing heavily, I'd walked halfway up the hill. People's Clinic Number Five was at the end of the road. The history teacher wasn't there yet. I was too early.

3

Afraid to walk into the clinic compound, I stood beneath a tree outside the gate to avoid running into anyone I knew. It was my first 'date', and I was very nervous.

As a teacher, he should have been punctual. But he was already twenty or thirty minutes late. I took off my straw hat to fan myself, because I was agitated, not hot. Always a man of his word, he'd never said one thing to me when he meant the other, at least not till now. He must have been ashamed of what he'd done – giving a virgin a dirty book like that – and knew that I'd seen through his little game.

I waited, as emergency patients were carried into the clinic

136

on makeshift stretchers, followed by worried family members. 'Hot sticky rolls!' Farmers with bamboo baskets on their backs hawked their goods at the gate. 'Get your sweet delicious sticky rolls!'

If only he could have walked uphill with me, as he had promised, this would have been a perfect day. Standing on the mountain peak and listening to pine trees swaying in the wind, I looked down at China's greatest river. From that high up, it looked like a sash girding the city with tender intimacy before merging with the Jialing at Heaven's Gate and widening out to flow to another city. Boats sailing up and down the river raised waves on the surface, but I was so far away I could barely hear their horns. Gusts of wind rustled my clothes and mussed my hair.

In my imagination, this scene required only me, and that was fine.

Trees were dressed in the afternoon sunlight, as sweet-roll pedlars continued to hawk their goods on the street. My stomach began to growl; I was getting hungry. People going home from work streamed past. Could I have got the place wrong? Or misheard him altogether? Why had he kept me waiting like this? All afternoon I waited, bathed in the smell of disinfectant. I know what was on your mind, I wanted to tell him, but if you're too embarrassed, I'll say it for you.

Other people can take advantage of me, but not you. I'll expose my bleeding wound to you if you try. These thoughts grieved and saddened me, nearly had me in tears. Unlike other people, he could make me cry without even trying. He had the power to make me forget myself or to turn me into something so fragile I'd shatter under a single blow. All I'd wanted was to like someone, to fall in love with someone. Now it was clear to me that this emotion was tied to a certain part of my body, and that when my heart was touched a sticky fluid flowed from within me.

4

While I was foolishly waiting outside the gate of People's Clinic Number Five, pandemonium had broken out at home. Even Father, who seldom groped his way upstairs, was in the attic, along with Second Sister and Third Brother. They were forcing medicine and bean milk down Fourth Sister's throat, along with glass after glass of water.

She had swallowed DDT, but not enough to finish the job. After opening her eyes, she refused to go to the hospital, gripping the bedposts so tightly they nearly splintered, and not letting go until Third Brother promised not to take her there.

It was Father who had heard the bottle thud to the floor and smelled the pungent pesticide oozing through the floor-board cracks. It must have been sometime after I left that she'd taken the bottle from wherever she'd hidden it in the hall and carried it upstairs to bed and sat down to think. But when her thoughts didn't lead her anywhere else, she decided to drink the stuff down and end it all.

Fourth Sister was the prettiest girl in the family. Her brows were so nicely arched she didn't need to pencil them in, and her dark eyes and lashes were enchanting; her breasts arched proudly, and she kept her hair trimmed at ear's length. At the time, even gossipy old women who wouldn't set foot in our house said to Father: Your fourth daughter has become a real beauty overnight!

But Mother never tired of saying that Fourth Sister's good looks could not keep her from a life of suffering.

Mother, more than anyone, knew that beauty spelled misery for a girl from a poor family; but even she was shocked by how early her predictions came true. Fourth Sister and Dehua had been in love for years, after meeting in the farm village to which they'd been sent. But they'd put off getting married for fear that they'd never be able to return to the city. Urban girls and boys who married villagers or each other while they were in the countryside lost their hypothetical right to reclaim their city residence. So they swore solemnly to remain loyal to each other for ever, but not to marry until they had returned to the city. After the Cultural Revolution ended in 1976, those with connections managed to return home, and fewer and fewer of the young urbanites remained in the villages. Dehua made it back in 1978 and carefully analysed his situation: Fourth Sister might spend the rest of her life in the village, fated to be a farmer's wife; and if that farmer were him, a life of poverty and deprivation was on the cards for them both. So he turned his attention to one of his former classmates, the daughter of a Party secretary in a factory, since that union would change his life, and might even lead to a career as a political cadre rather than a worker.

Except for my family, everyone thought that Dehua had made the right choice. Compared to a residence permit, love was a joke. Fourth Sister wrote long letters home, begging Mother to do anything necessary to bring her home and save her from becoming a farmer's wife.

Naturally, Mother was helpless: no connections, no roads to success, and no money. So when Fourth Sister came home on leave and got wind that Dehua had had a change of heart, she panicked, refusing to leave Chongqing and return to the countryside until Dehua promised to stay away from the other woman. Just before she returned to the village to find a way out of her predicament, a friendly neighbour dropped by on a visit, and when Fourth Sister broke down while relating her tale of woes, the woman took pity on her. She asked Fourth Sister if she'd be willing to work as a porter for a collective construction company in the suburbs. Fourth Sister agreed without a moment's hesitation.

So Fourth Sister followed in Mother's footsteps: she became a carrier of sand and bricks, except that Mother was a 'temporary labourer' and she was called a 'contract labourer'. She left early in the morning and returned late at night, since she had to cross the river and take two buses each way. She came home every day reeking of sweat and pretty much kept to herself, and it didn't take long for us to run out of things to talk about.

Dehua's factory was near the ferry landing at Slingshot Pellet, not far from our house. He was a handsome, genteel young man, and the first time I saw him I thought he could be one of those young scholars straight out of a storybook.

Whenever he came to the house, he took over the family chores: carrying water, chopping and cooking the vegetables, and washing dishes. And he was polite to everyone. But Mother never forgave him for breaking it off with Fourth Sister. Father, taciturn as always, was cool to him as well; he was too effeminate for his tastes, and fated to suffer. When night fell, Father would shout up to the attic that the road home was dark and treacherous, an obvious ploy to get him to leave. But my parents' hints or strategies seldom worked, and Fourth Sister insisted that he move in with us. It was the only way she could force him to make good his promise to marry her.

So I shared the attic with Fourth Sister and Dehua. To avoid them, I'd go outside and read under a murky streetlight until late at night. That didn't help my myopia. The attic was so small that their love-making often woke me up, but I'd hold my breath and squeeze my eyes shut, pretending I was fast asleep. And sometimes I simply groped my way downstairs and sat quietly in the dark. I hated them for making love and for the disgusting noise.

The only thing separating our two beds was a cloth curtain, so they couldn't avoid me altogether. If there were other people in the house, and there was no room for them to do what they wanted, they'd head down to the river or up the hill. But since they had no marriage certificate, if they were caught by the police or militia, not only would they be humiliated, but their work units would be notified and they'd have to write self-criticisms. The only place in this sprawling city where they could be intimate for a couple of hours was in the rundown cinema on the mountain top when a movie was showing.

'Do you really have to shine your shoes for work?' Father asked Dehua.

'I change them at the factory,' Dehua told him.

'Isn't that a lot of trouble?'

'No, it isn't.' Dehua was out the door before breakfast.

Father said to Mother, who had just got home, that this was a sure sign he hadn't ended his relationship with his former classmate. He was concerned that Dehua and the other girl had worked it out so that he'd leave Fourth Sister soon. People have a need to climb higher, and he certainly couldn't be happy about living in our tiny attic.

5

Dehua was called home from the factory. When he saw Fourth Sister, her hair was a mess, her cheeks were ashen, her eyes lifeless. He nearly gagged from the smell of the filthy contents of the spittoon, which sat next to her bed. Everyone in the room, except for Fourth Sister, was at him. The whole family seemed to want to tear him limb from limb. Second Sister was screaming at him, Third Brother kept clenching and unclenching his fists, and Dehua knew he'd met his match.

Fourth Sister's attempted suicide earned her the marriage certificate.

Mother gave Fourth Sister a new quilt just before the couple moved in with Dehua's parents in White Sands Bend. Our neighbour Baldy Cheng was in the hall. 'Don't you two know anything?' he said. 'It's bad luck to show the white cover of a wedding quilt.'

No one said a word. If someone had said something like 'Bad luck for a quilt is good luck for people' or 'Wind blows, the sun shines, and bad luck departs', that would have helped. But the best way to counteract this unlucky utterance would have been to pick up any breakable item — a bowl, a water jug, a tile, a glass — and smash it on the floor. It was like saying when you drop a chopstick, 'Chopstick on the ground, land will come around,' before bending down to pick it up.

But they were in such a hurry they forgot what the old folks had taught them. They said nothing, they smashed nothing, and it was probably at that moment that an evil wind, undetected by the human eye, swept over them.

After his mother passed away, Baldy Cheng stopped practising T'ai Chi shadow boxing or playing the squeaking fiddle. He bought a *School Pupil's Dictionary*, and started to study the Eight Diagrams, Five Elements, Yin and Yang etc. He told Father that the sudden death of his mother was caused by the inadvisable position of their stove, which should not face south, since it conflicted with his mother's Heavenly Stem and Earthly Branch.

He went on to thrust acupuncture needles into the blood paths of his own body. Soon his neck, his arms and legs, especially the backs of his hands, were covered with traces of needle holes. He was trying to change the circulation of his vital energy that could give him longevity. If only he 'caught' the *qi*, he could go without eating anything for half a month. This ideal state of the body was called 'No-Need-for-Grain'. Since the government had made it a strict rule that nobody could be exempt from cremation, his mother failed to enjoy the magnificent coffin he had prepared for her a dozen years beforehand. He sawed it into small pieces, then arranged them into this or that Immortal's Battle Formation according to the rules stipulated by the Eight Diagrams. He spent most of his time sitting at its centre, to keep away evil spirits and to invite felicitous wind.

This mountain city is shrouded in ghostly atmosphere. Centuries ago the Upper and Middle Reaches of the Yangtze used to be the cradles of shamanism, and even today any kind of witchcraft had followers who practised it at least on themselves. I couldn't convince myself of the magic of *qi*, but I believe that Baldy Cheng had acquired some magic power. Otherwise how could he have withstood the half-a-month fast? But in the years of Famine, Father too had days without any food. Viewed in this way, to practise *qi* is useful.

TEN

1

Peace was re-established by the time I returned that evening. Dehua had gone home to make the wedding arrangements, while Second Sister stayed over, sharing my bed. Big Sister slept with Fourth Sister on the other bed.

Second Sister and Big Sister had no use for each other, and they were always at odds over one thing or another. With her volatile temper, Big Sister could not keep angry words inside; Second Sister, on the other hand, thought things out meticulously, never losing sight of what was best for her. But she was frail, and more than once nearly died from a dangerously high fever. Mother said she had two lives, that she was a 'returner'. Reserved in temperament, she'd walk several hours to the school she attended and back rather than ask Father or Mother for bus fare. Her trouser legs and shoes caked with mud, she'd wash without a word to anyone, then attack the blood blisters on her feet with scissors, her hand steady as a rock. She was about to graduate the year I started elementary school. One day she and a classmate – a boy – took me to a seedling nursery to take some pictures, my first such outing. The bespectacled youngster, who had a camera about half the size of a brick, told me to pose snapping off a twig. 'Look at the sky!' he said. Instead of 'Smile!' he said 'Look at the sky!'

When we got back home, Father took Second Sister inside, where he told her that her classmate was too much of a sweet-talker and had shifty eyes. Not the sort of person she could depend on for the rest of her life. A quarter of an hour later, she saw her classmate to the door. He never came back. And when the film was removed from the camera, it was accidentally exposed. 'Not one of them came out,' Second Sister said sadly. 'What a shame!'

Then a friend of Mother's liked what she saw of Second Sister and introduced her to her nephew, a glib, handsome Rebel faction leader at a military factory. When Second Sister went to see him, he was busy in the 'cow-pen' on the factory ground floor. The windows were blacked out so no light could get in, but couldn't keep out the horrible screams from inside. The members of the other faction being beaten and tortured were shouting quotations from Chairman Mao.

Too frightened to look, Second Sister turned on her heel and ran. And it was a good thing she did. If she'd chosen that Rebel leader for a husband, she'd have regretted it; even before the Cultural Revolution was on its last legs, he was sent to prison for twenty years.

Second Sister was the only child in the family who let our parents choose her spouse, and her life is the most stable, and the happiest. She is the envy of all.

The light inside was turned off early. 'Little Six,' Big Sister asked from the other bed, 'where did you go today? Father said you took off around noon.'

'School.' My eyes were wide open. You weren't home either, I was thinking. Trying to avoid me. I rolled over with my back to her.

'You didn't go to school. You can't fool me,' she said.

'Then why'd you ask?' I grumbled softly.

2

Third Brother was the eldest son, a real tyrant, spoiled by Father and Mother alike. When he was fifteen, he and the other neighbourhood kids of his age all put on Red Guard armbands, but only he squeezed on to a train for Beijing, where he saw Chairman Mao. The night he returned from the capital, he reached behind him and, like magic, produced a handful of hard candies wrapped in plastic, transfixing Fourth Sister, Fifth Brother and me, all of us still very young.

His troubles with Father and Mother had begun in the summer of 1980. Now he was downstairs in a heated argument with Mother over the incident with Fourth Sister. Mother complained that he didn't care about the family and that she'd wasted her time raising him.

In order to make his exit from the family and not have to sleep in the crowded downstairs with our parents and Fifth Brother, he had hastily married a local girl without a word to Father and Mother and had moved in with her family as a live-in son-in-law. 'Your wife,' Mother later complained, 'has never once called me Mother.'

'That's her business,' he said as he stepped into the hall. 'After all, we all grew up without any help from you, our parents.' He went outside.

Up in the attic, my sisters and I heard what he said, but kept quiet.

Third Brother never shared his experiences in the country-side with any member of the family, nor did he talk about his years as a stevedore for the Yibin Steamship Company after returning to the city. He had good reason to complain, as his wife later explained.

In the mid and late 1970s, when the migration of young urbanites back to the city began and job assignments were passed out, cadres at all levels, toughened in the Cultural Revolution, openly engaged in a variety of brazen under-handed dealings: returnees with connections got cushy office jobs, those who could come up with bribe money were assigned technical jobs aboard ship, while those who had neither became stevedores. Third Brother and his fellow stevedores soon orchestrated a work stoppage, a right per-mitted them under the Constitution of the People's Republic of China. But if workers constitute the nation's leading class, it is only under the 'leadership' of the Party. So whenever such a 'disturbance' began, one phone call was all it took to bring the police to arrest the 'counter-revolutionary ringleaders', who would receive severe punishment, including even the death penalty. It was the Party's tried and tested method of quelling unrest among the workers. But this time the strikers were in possession of damning evidence of corruption among the cadres. Leading individuals whose ruthless tactics had prevailed during the last years of the Cultural Revolution now saw it was their hindquarters on the line, and decided to adopt 'peaceful measures' to settle the strike. Every last stevedore received a new job assignment. Third Brother was sent to the uppermost reaches of the Yangtze as a boatman on a pontoon. It was the same place to which Father had once been exiled, and he recognized it for what it was: punishment by the Party. And there he stayed for six years, until he managed to swap with someone from Yibin who wanted to go home. It cost him everything he had saved during those six years, but in 1980 he finally found work on a pontoon belonging to a local steamship company.

One day Mother was sitting on the stool in the hall and I was on my haunches helping her take apart a wool sweater to wash and reknit. The neighbourhood policeman, so young he was just beginning to shave, walked into the compound dressed in a neatly pressed uniform. Mother stood up, nodded, and said hello. 'Reform yourself,' he said to her with a long stern face.

The smile froze on her face. 'Yes, yes, yes,' she replied as she lowered her head. I looked down, my cheeks burning. For years after that, I was haunted by the sight of this fellow, who was only a few years older than I, publicly humiliating my mother for no reason at all.

Big Sister, the first to be sent to the countryside, Third Brother, who followed in her footsteps, and Fourth Sister, who worked as a coolie labourer, all had good reason to stay clear of our parents, who had never come to their aid, and had been in fact the reason they'd suffered more than most. It didn't matter that Mother had cried her eyes out in anguish each time she saw one of them off. As we grew up, we came to understand that a bleak future was our lot, no matter how we tried to change it, that the fate that befell our parents would surely befall us as well.

3

Sichuan's spicy hot-pot, long one of China's most famous dishes, once again became the pride of Chongqing after the hard times of the 1960s and 1970s. Anything edible could go into the pot, and at any time of the year: steamy summer, drizzly spring, freezing winter, or cool and crisp autumn. Morning, noon, and night – at three in the morning, for that matter – hot-pots were everywhere, in dank and dreary eating houses in remote alleys and in fine restaurants.

But when people in the compound talked among themselves, they remarked that while hot-pots in local eating houses looked the same as before, the spicy tingle of old was gone.

One New Year's Eve – I forget which year – it was so cold I had to stamp my feet to keep warm, even with two pairs of socks. Big Sister was back from her village near Mount Wu, and we were all sitting around the little iron stove eating from a hot-pot; the little meat that had been added to the turnips and cabbage was long gone, leaving behind a few drops of oil floating atop the boiling water.

Father told Fourth Sister to wash some spinach leaves and throw them into the pot. She volunteered me for the job, and Mother seconded the idea, telling me to do a good job without wasting water. So I took the spinach out and washed it in the communal kitchen sink.

When Big Sister dipped a leaf of spinach in the scalding water and put it into her mouth, she spat it out and complained that it was sandy.

148

Third Brother stood up. 'Go and wash it again,' he said.

'Were you talking out there?' Big Sister asked me.

I shook my head.

'Don't deny it,' Fourth Sister said with her mouth full. 'She talks to the wall all the time.'

'No wonder the spinach is sandy,' Mother said.

I wasn't paying much attention, until they started laughing. 'I tell you, I wasn't talking,' I said finally. 'Not even to myself.' Angrily, I slammed down the bowl in my hand. 'I don't want any more!' I snarled at Mother.

That was OK with her, she said. She told me to leave the table so my brothers and sisters could have a little more room.

I got up and left the room.

'She's got an awfully big temper for such a little girl,' one of them said as I was walking away. The hall was dark, but no one followed me in there, so I went out into the cold, not dressed for it. The streetlight beyond the gate had been shot out by a slingshot, giving way to complete darkness. On top of the tall building at Heaven's Gate Dock a neon sign was flashing in the night, and I thought I heard firecrackers across the river. I set out for the public toilet, since that was the best place to keep out of the cold. It would be deserted on New Year's Eve. I went inside, stepping carefully to avoid the muck on the floor, and found a relatively clean spot behind the door; I kept my breathing shallow amid the stench of shit and stood there for hours, shivering but clear-headed.

They didn't find me till daybreak, after looking for me all night, up one street and down another, never dreaming I'd be hiding in the toilet. It was Big Sister, anxious to empty her bladder, who found me.

This time, I figured, Mother would say something nice to me for a change. But she just glanced at my frozen face and purple lips, took off her shoes, and went to bed without a word. With a little laugh, Big Sister told Mother she should start treating the baby of the family a little better from now on. She looks innocent, and she may not say much or do what she's told, but she might have a better future than the rest of us, and could be the one who takes care of you in your old age.

'Oh, is that what you think?' Mother said. 'Don't try that sweet talk on me. She won't take care of me. Or any of the rest of you, for that matter. When I'm old, I'll be on my own, I know that. I'll thank heaven if she grows up, finds a man to marry, and can feed herself.'

4

A tall woman was cleaning the grease off the Kitchen God in the communal kitchen. The niche for the statue, with its palm-sized ledge, was high up on the wall, the place where people put candles and kerosene lanterns when the power was off. The rest of the time, the ledge served as a shelf for vinegar and soy-sauce bottles.

It was Auntie Zhang, one of our neighbours. She lived in a room in the easternmost corner of the compound with a balcony that was the envy of all. Seven square metres in size, it housed potted cactus plants, orchids, Solomon's seal, and lady's slippers. Since it had a drainage hole, water never accumulated when it rained. There were also two water vats and a large pickle jar. Word had it that she'd been bought out of a brothel by a dockworker in Wuhan. Another version had it that, after Liberation, when the brothels were closed and the prostitutes rounded up for 're-education', her man took her with him without spending a cent. She had an oval face, fair skin and fly-away eyes behind single-fold lids. Unlike most other women, she always earned a second look.

'Fly-away eyes? Here, I'll show you how to fly!' her husband would growl, kicking her with his heavy work boots. But even with ugly bruises all over her body, she never complained. A good five feet seven inches tall, she had the nicest figure I'd ever seen, with long legs and a long, graceful neck, which left such a strong impression with me that now I can hardly recall her face.

If not for the bruises on her face, she'd have been worth any amount of money, except for the fact that she was barren – people said that was what being a prostitute had cost her. I seldom heard her say anything, and few people cared to have a conversation with a woman whose past as a prostitute was known to everyone. From time to time she'd be seen bending over on the balcony to pick up the potted plants smashed by her husband; then when she had finished, she'd go out and buy new ones.

Auntie Zhang had an adopted son who owned lots of thick books whose pages had yellowed with age. He'd stolen them during the chaotic years of the Cultural Revolution. At the time, any book of even moderate interest was proscribed, so there was never anything good to read. And even when a half-decent book turned up in the bookstores, who on our street would have spent money on it? A piece of candy to suck on or a pair of polyester socks was a hundred times better than any book. The only books you'd ever find in my house were my textbooks.

But Auntie Zhang lent me books behind her son's back. One day I discovered a hand-written book with the first page missing. The handwriting was sloppy, but clear enough to read with difficulty. It was all about Kuomintang spies who planned to blow up Chongqing in the early years after Liberation. The prelude went like this: One night a watch-man heard strange noises in a deserted, cobweb-covered building on a dark gloomy street. He went in to see what was going on, and got the shock of his life. At this point in the story I was pretty scared myself, and thought I heard ominous muffled footsteps in the deserted courtyard. I forced myself to keep reading, and by the time I was finished, everyone in the compound looked stealthy.

I heard about a novel called *The Heart of a Girl*, which had found its way into the city. A thin book with a simple plot all about what men and women do together, it was the most poisonous weed of all. To stop the evil spread of bourgeois decadence, the police launched a series of raids on every school in the city, searching schoolbags and ferreting out anybody caught with a copy of the book, then extending their search to the bad elements who hand-copied it and eventually to the one who actually wrote it. I just hope there is a record kept somewhere of how many people went to prison or were executed because of this book. Bursting with curiosity, I waited for Auntie Zhang to lend me a copy. Since she was illiterate, she'd give me any book I asked for. But her son must have hidden this one skilfully, and it was probably my good fortune that I never saw it.

Two policemen came and dragged Auntie Zhang's son out of the compound one day, and he spent the next several years in a labour-reform camp, quite likely because of this book. She cried and fumed, cursing his books, and turning them into ashes.

I remember seeing her one night, kerosene lantern in hand, walking all the way from the rear of the compound to open the gate for her son, who was embracing a peasant girl and wouldn't let go. Auntie Zhang stood there in her slippers, waiting for him to come in. I was standing outside my attic door watching them. Not daring to disturb them and reluctant to ask them inside, she shielded the lantern with her hand to keep the flame from going out, and I could see the tortured look on her face in the dim light.

Revolutionary novels about the Communist Party leading poor citizens on the road to revolution were always available at school. They too caught my fancy, even though they were all the same. I loved the spirit of rebirth among the liberated poor. I was going to be reborn, too, starting at home.

Mother had an old black flannel overcoat, which she let Big Sister, Second Sister, and Fourth Sister wear in turn. But she wouldn't even let me try it on. It was too long for me, she said. And Fourth Sister said she wouldn't let me wear it even if it was in tatters. 'I'm going to be reborn!' I said to her angrily one night.

'OK, go ahead,' she mumbled sleepily as she moved closer to the wall to give me a little more room.

I was eleven that year, and wanted to try on that coat more than anything. So one day, when I was alone in the house, I shortened it with a pair of scissors and hemmed it with black thread. Then I tried it on. It was so warm and toasty, I couldn't have been happier.

When Second Sister discovered what I'd done, she dragged me upstairs, took down the stool that hung from the ceiling by the door and set it between the beds, then bolted the door and laid me down across it.

Holding tightly on to the legs, I stared at the floor, while she took a piece of firewood out from under the bed, pulled down my pants, and started flogging me across the bottom. 'You won't own up to it, you're going to be stubborn, is that it? Why are you so hateful? What right do you have?' As I fought back the tears, I wondered where someone as small as Second Sister had found the strength to flog me so savagely. The firewood cut into my flesh and drew blood before she stopped.

I never told anyone about this vicious beating, not even my parents. Maybe that's why Second Sister started treating me differently. Once, when some schoolmates put lice in my hair, which they'd picked from a dirty little girl in our class, Second Sister saw me scratching my head and pulled me towards her to see why. Lice were crawling all over my scalp. So she doused my head with paraffin, then wrapped it tightly with a piece of cloth to keep the air out. After about a suffocating hour, she took off the wrapping. My skin crawled when I saw all the little black dots floating in a basin of water.

The paraffin killed the lice, but raised hell with my scalp and hair. Brittle and not particularly black to begin with, after this my hair colour was a ratty brown.

ELEVEN

1

Big Sister called me out. Don't go to school today, she said. She wanted me to keep her company. That was fine with me, I didn't feel like going anyway. Who wanted to see the history teacher after he stood me up like that? He'd seduced an innocent girl, then let her down.

After walking down several narrow, winding lanes, Big Sister stopped in front of a compound near the granary and told me to go in and call her schoolmate out. She seemed edgy on this trip home, as if she were looking for someone or something to help her forget her latest failed marriage. 'You never shy away from anything,' I said, 'why don't you do it?'

She begged me to help.

'It's a boy, isn't it?'

'You're quite a devil for such a little girl,' she said, trying to hurry me along. 'It's a girl. Now get in there!'

A flight of stone steps inside the gate led up to a compound that was much smaller than ours, and was home to several families. I went to the first building on the left, where an old woman was cutting up dried peppers. I had to repeat myself several times before she said, 'She's not at home.'

'When will she be home?' I asked her.

'Don't know.' The old woman ended the conversation.

I turned and walked down the steps to the gate, where I relayed the information to Big Sister. That old woman's her mother, she said. She wouldn't call her out even if she was home, the stinking old hag! Rat demon!

She said this schoolmate had been a fellow sent-down

urbanite in the village at Mount Wu. They'd been friendly until they got into a fight over some insignificant matter.

Big Sister said that, when she went down to the village in 1964, as soon as she saw the four city girls there, she knew there were hard times ahead. One's mother came from a landlord family; another was the daughter of a counter-revolutionary; the third girl's father had followed Chiang Kai-shek's troops to Taiwan before Liberation, making her a 'child of the enemy'; and the fourth girl was orphaned during the famine. Problem cases, every one, tricked into going to the countryside to be transformed into heroes who answered the Party's call. Apes and monkeys screamed at night, sounding like wandering ghosts, and the city kids were scared to go out alone. Once a richly forested area, political movements in the Commune, plus 'backyard furnaces' and hunger, had denuded the place of its trees. The village could still boast a single malus tree, which the city kids wanted to cut down for firewood.

But the villagers said it was a haunted tree, and there'd be trouble for anyone who cut it down.

Superstition be damned. They cut down the tree anyway, and released its demons. One of the girls got pregnant and died in childbirth on Mount Wu. Not long after that, one of the other girls was raped by a district cadre, but didn't tell anyone, and married a local peasant. She too died in childbirth. Local custom decreed that anyone who died in childbirth must be buried after midnight. It rained heavily that dark night, turning the roads to mud, and the pall bearers and the coffin they were carrying fell over a cliff.

Two of the city boys, unable to tolerate the unjust treatment by local-government officials, recruited twenty or so like-minded youths to go up into the mountains as a guerrilla force, armed only with swords and spears. Figuring that life would be even worse where they were going, Big Sister decided not to join them. The rebel band didn't even make it to the mountains before they were caught, and the two leaders were sentenced to fifteen years in prison.

'Were they rehabilitated?' I asked. 'There are newspaper stories every day about righting political wrongs.'

'Rehabilitated? It doesn't take long for the labour camp to turn you into a wreck.' Big Sister quickly returned to her schoolmate. Only by finding her could she locate a boy who had once been interested in her. She hadn't thought much of him at the time, but now things were different.

Big Sister's first husband was a low-ranking cadre at one of the county's coal mines. They argued constantly, until one day he stormed over to the Party Committee to report that they stood on different class lines and revealed the story behind her natural father. Large posters went up the very next day, attacking her for 'Subversion by Offspring of Class Enemies from the Five Black Categories'. During the struggle session that followed, he stood below the stage to witness her torment.

'Enough about him,' she said. 'I should never have married a man like that.'

'He wasn't that bad. At least he was better than your present husband.'

'One's as bad as the other. And my next one won't be any better. The goal of marriage isn't to find a good man.' She tossed her head and started walking away. 'Besides, divorce has to be approved by so many levels of Party committees, and takes several years of desperate fight.'

A cable car piled high with sacks of grain was heading up the mountain; an empty one came down the other way. A team of stevedores was unloading grain from a boat, while another team atop the mountain was unloading the sacks from the cable cars, carrying them past a black iron gate, and stacking them in the granary. Houses near the granary were sturdier than most others in South Bank. Everywhere you looked you saw warning signs in red: 'No Trespassing', 'Guard Against Fires', and Chairman Mao's famous quotation, 'Dig Deep, Hoard Grain, Claim No Hegemony'.

Big Sister and I were under the bridge beneath the cable track. 'You haven't told me everything,' I said. 'Last time you complained that it was getting late, and you'd tell me some other time.'

'I've already told you more than I should have,' she said. 'Your future looks much brighter than mine. You weren't even six that time when Fifth Brother was run over by the cable car, and hadn't started school, but you knew enough to take a boat to the shipyard at White Sands Bank, a place you'd never been, to tell Mother. None of us thought you were capable of that.'

'You're wrong. I walked the whole way. Where would I have got money to take a boat?'

'OK, I'm wrong. But what's important is that a five-year-old girl could walk that far without getting lost. It looks like you're a member of this family, after all.'

'What do you mean by that?' Suddenly I was on my guard. 'Why did you say "after all"?'

'Because that's what I mean.' Her tone of voice didn't waver. 'What you did for Fifth Brother proves it. I was twenty-two that year, just back from the village at Mount Wu to have my first child, and I knew you belonged to this family, not like me.'

'How come I'm not "like" you in this family?' I nearly grabbed her sleeve. I didn't know if she had let something slip or was just leading me on.

Fifth Brother was holding a small winnowing basket filled with dried peas and mung beans, all of which he and I had gleaned from the ground and among the cracks between rocks under the cable tracks. Kids still lay on the ground as cable cars went up and down the mountain and picked grains from leaking sacks, but not with the desperation of the famine years. Even though the famine was over, there was still a shortage of grain, so children were sent out to scavenge. Every little bit helped; several days of scavenging could produce half a bowlful or more, which was enough for a meal. In the early summer of 1968, I spotted a clump of wild onions on the sandbank near the cable track. In the midst of my excitement, I heard the warning bell of an approaching car, and stood up to let it pass, my hands caked with mud.

That morning the cable cars going up the mountain were empty, those coming down were piled high with grain to be loaded on to ships tied up at the pier. Four or five kids were sitting in the empty car, including Fifth Brother, who was at the front. The operator and stevedores ignored them, since they saw them nearly every day. One of the kids grabbed a handful of beans out of Fifth Brother's basket; Fifth Brother, who never fought, returned the favour. The other boy shoved him out of the car, and the rear wheel ran over his left leg. The operator quickly threw on the brake.

I saw it all from where I was standing, and the screams started me crying. He was the only brother or sister who was nice to me; he never took advantage of me, he taught me how to read, and he often shared his food with me. Because of his hare lip, he avoided other people, and never argued with anybody in the family, even if they egged him on.

Second Sister, who heard the commotion, ran over to carry Fifth Brother, who was bleeding badly, on her back, after first tearing off his belt and wrapping it tightly around his bloody thigh. Having snapped out of my terrified trance, I fell in behind her.

The worst part of the factional fighting was over by then, and people were turning in their weapons; but artillery pieces, machine guns and tanks were still being used by some. Transport often came to a standstill, land and water, and power and water were intermittent at best. Both the clinic at Stonebridge and the District One Hospital were closed that day, out of fear that if they treated the wounded of one side the other side would retaliate.

Second Sister pounded on the hospital door, insisting that her brother's accident had nothing to do with the factional fighting. Overwhelmed by her persistence, the doctors were considering admitting him when I ran out of the hospital, not to go home, but down to the river. A cloudburst struck without warning, and the dark rain clouds skittering through the sky pulled distant mountains closer and pushed nearby hills away.

I don't know how long I walked, but by the time I got to the shipyard where Mother worked, the rain had nearly stopped. The light drizzle kept the sky dark. Mother and her partner were lugging a barrel of paint ashore from a ship, and when she saw me, looking as if I was made of mud, she threw down her carrying pole and ran towards me.

Big Sister was outdistancing me, so I ran to catch up. I couldn't make sense of what she had just told me, and this time I wasn't going to let her off.

'Why are you so impatient?' She didn't seem as hesitant as she'd been the last time. 'I haven't told you what life was like for me in the new society after Liberation,' she said tantalizingly.

2

The Triadman was arrested. In 1950, the Communist Party had decided to throw everything at the Sichuan anti-Communist forces, and at the same time launch a reign of red terror in the cities. The ensuing Counter-revolutionary Suppression and Counter-revolutionary Liquidation campaigns went on for several years. All the Triad leaders and the heads of religious sects in Chongqing were rounded up; hundreds of people were shot at the city's execution grounds every day, and the unclaimed bodies were buried in common graves. The South Bank execution ground was located at Persimmon Ravine. People shot there included the abbot of the local Buddhist temple, who had never involved himself in worldly affairs. Pious old men and women wept silent tears for him amid the excitement of the common folk, who filled the area's teahouses. People from Chongqing love excitement as much as they love the hot peppers they put in their food.

'Where killing is concerned, the Communists have it all over the Kuomintang,' Father said with a sigh.

Mother told him to shut up. Pregnant again, she hugged her daughter.

Someone brought word to Mother that the Triadman was in prison and wanted to see his daughter. Not sure what to do, she tossed and turned that night, unable to sleep. In the morning, her eyes red and puffy, she went, but alone.

Clumsy with pregnancy, she registered in a small room near the prison gate; not only was she denied visiting privileges, but her relationship with a reactionary was noted. On the trip home, she could hardly contain her anger, but didn't regret going.

The message regarding his fate took several months to reach her, long after the Triadman had been sent to his death. It was one of those Great Suppression Days, when condemned prisoners in a truck taking them to the execution ground had rebelled, only to be mowed down by machine-gun fire as they tried to make their escape.

In the stuffy, crowded below-decks cabin, Mother dried her eyes and tried to calm herself. Why shed tears over a man like that? But the tears kept coming. She was rocked back and forth by waves slapping at the hull.

One day, many years earlier, Mother and the Triadman were riding in a rickshaw when a passing funeral procession stopped traffic. Wailing sons and grandsons in funeral clothes walked in front of the coffin, followed by white-clad hired mourners carrying papier-mâché sedan chairs and horses, brocade ritual gowns, official robes, and silk funeral banners. The band played, firecrackers exploded, red lanterns swayed in the air.

He turned to Mother, who watched the procession with staring eyes, and said, 'Don't envy those people. When your

160

mother passes away many years from now, I'll arrange a grand funeral, with Buddhist monks and Taoist priests sending her spirit safely into the afterworld. Then I'll select a propitious day and the proper site for burial, which will bring fame and glory to her descendants.' He had guessed what she was thinking, that she wanted to carry out the filial obligations to her mother.

Grandmother died not in her village home, but in Chongqing, in Mother's house. Her two sons had cut down bamboo to make a litter for their dying mother, and carried her to Chongqing, begging their way to the city. After four arduous days and three wearying nights, they arrived in the city. Mother burst into tears when she saw them. 'Why didn't you write to tell me you were coming?' she asked them. 'I'd have paid for you to come by boat, even if I'd had to borrow the money.' The white headbands they wore, as village custom dictated when visiting relatives, had turned a dirty grey on the road, and neighbours in the compound complained that the mourning garb was a bad omen. Mother scraped together twenty yuan for boat fare for her brothers, who were anxious to return home.

But they told her they'd prefer to walk and save the money for more important things back home.

At the hospital, the doctors told Mother there was nothing they could do for the old woman. So she bought some Chinese herbal medicine and prepared it at home; for days our house reeked of strange smells. By then Grandmother was skin and bone, for her digestive tract was ravaged by worms, long, flat, colourful things that emerged with her stool. Poor Grandmother spent her days curled up in bed, her arms wrapped around her middle, neither sleeping nor able to sit up properly. She tried to hang on through the winter, but one cold night just before lunar New Year's Day, she groaned in agony on the chamber pot and collapsed. Mother helped her over to the bed, where her last words were for Mother to bring her starving youngest brother to Chongqing from the countryside, to feed him and teach him to read. After seeing Mother nod her assent, she stopped breathing.

On that day in 1953, when Grandmother died, Mother washed the corpse with warm water, then pressed one of the cold hands against her own chest. Grandmother, dressed in funeral clothes that Mother had sewn for her, lay on top of a bed of old boards in the hall next to the door. No one wailed over her passing, no Taoist priests were invited to chant over her body, no funeral wreaths or scrolls were hung, and no bier was set up. A lone oil lantern cast flickering light on Grandmother's corpse. She was buried among untended graves at Three Stones Gulch.

Even on her deathbed, Grandmother could not forgive Mother for fleeing from the arranged marriage. It was something that still troubled Mother, who often dreamed that Grandmother came to her bed, but never mentioned the marriage, and even as she lay dying, the topic went unmentioned. She would only complain that Mother had abandoned her, leaving her to face hunger and loneliness, and be at the mercy of others. She also wanted Mother to search for Third Aunt – her niece – but try as she might, Mother never found the grave. After Third Aunt died of starvation, in 1961, she was said to have been buried on a mound at the southern head of the Yangtze River Bridge. The bridge had not yet been built, and the rocky mound was overgrown with trash trees and weeds. With no stone to mark the spot, it was simply lost. Then when the bridge went up, the mound was levelled by bulldozers, which swept away every last bone.

Seventeen years after Grandmother's death, Mother opened her grave, wrapped her remains in white cloth and placed them in a small wooden box, then had her brothers return them to the village where she was born, to be reburied beside her husband on the hill behind their ancestral house. The dreams stopped. A villager who came to Chongqing later told her that black fungus grew in front of the grave every

162

time it rained, and on moonlit nights, they would pick them and bring them home to be eaten without washing, since no mud stained them.

3

Even before she'd become old, Mother could not keep her eyes clean without wiping them frequently with a handkerchief; if she didn't, a greenish fluid would gather and dry in the corners, making them itch painfully. 'That's what pregnancy did to me,' she told us. 'Try not to cry when you're pregnant. Don't be like me. Nothing in the world can make this better.'

Big Sister's recollections now reminded me that Mother was referring to the time she went to the prison, and nearly cried herself sick on the way back.

Big Sister, however, doubted that Mother actually got up the nerve to go to the prison, and I think she had reason to be suspicious; as her own daughter, she was especially sensitive to such things.

'So that's how your father died, is it?' The man had little to do with me, but I was sad nonetheless, and was holding her hand more tightly than I ever had before.

There was silence for a moment, then she blurted out something in a tone that really surprised me: 'If only that were how he died.'

She sat down on a rock, her back to the river, and, without my even asking, went on with her story.

It was a Sunday. Father had been out on his boat for many days, with no word, so Mother picked up Third Brother, who was three at the time, and, with Big Sister at her side, crossed the river to seek news at the shipping company. At Heaven's Gate, pedestrian and vehicular traffic was heavy on the slope near the harbour, making it treacherous even on sunny days. Caught up in her thoughts, Mother didn't see the handcart careering down the road until it was practically upon her.

Holding Third Brother tightly, she jumped to the side of the road, and screamed at Big Sister, who stood there frozen with fear. 'Get out of the way! Run!' She squeezed her eyes shut, unable to watch the collision that would surely kill or maim her daughter, and probably do the same to the driver when his cart flipped over. But, miraculously, the cart braked to a stop at the last second. Everyone was scared half to death.

But the terror quickly turned to stunned disbelief, for the driver was the Triadman's uncle. He called out Mother's name. 'It's you,' he said. 'You don't know how hard I've tried to find you two.' His temples had turned grey, his sleeves and trouser legs were rolled up, and he was wearing a pair of muddy rubber shoes.

It was a dramatic moment, but one more remarkable coincidence, or one less, would have made little difference in Big Sister's life. The upshot of it all was that the Triadman had not been shot, after all. Taken to the execution ground, he shat his pants when they fired a blank at him, and immediately agreed to co-operate. He gave them everything they wanted, names and all, and in the process came to hate the Kuomintang for treating him like a pawn after he had put his life on the line for them. Since he had a clear picture of his fate – a sacrificial pawn – why cover for the others?

He felt no pangs of conscience in his prison cell, even though everyone he named had been rounded up. It was just a matter of time, he thought, before he'd be a free man. It didn't take long for him to realize he'd been duped, for not only did his captors not set him free, they soon came with demands for more names.

'I've already told you everything I know,' he said candidly.

'No, you haven't. You must come clean and hold nothing back.'

He heard but didn't understand; he still understood nothing of Communist tactics.

At first he was locked up in a building near White Mansion,

which, along with Residue Cave, had been used by the Kuomintang to lock up members of the 'democratic parties' and the Communist underground. The Sino-American Co-operative Training School for secret agents, created in 1943, had been headquartered there. After Liberation, the Communists turned the place into a museum: Here we see the monstrous crimes committed against the Chinese people by the American Imperialists! Here is ironclad evidence that the butcher Chiang Kai-shek and his minions made martyrs of our comrades! Every year, on 27 November, Martyrs' Day, Young Pioneers lined up at the martyrs' graves, raising their fists and taking solemn vows in the name of the red scarves around their necks and the five-star flag fluttering above their heads.

But the list of martyrs needs to be revised too frequently. The Democrats were the first to go. Then, during the Cultural Revolution, many of the erstwhile martyrs were discovered to have been traitors. Then that judgement was reversed, and they were all martyrs once again. Investigations of the dead were more difficult than those of the living. The authors of *Red Crag*, a revolutionary novel about the jails here, were labelled traitors during the Cultural Revolution; one of them jumped to his death, splitting open his skull when he landed on the pavement. One of his eyes was shut tightly; the other was swollen to twice its normal size and about to pop out of its socket. That remains the most frightening photograph of the dead that I have ever seen.

The Triadman must have realized when they brought him there that history loves to play jokes, and that prisons need their revolving doors. During the day he was taken out at gunpoint to dig coal. Only at night did he have time to ponder the twists and turns of his fate. He began to crumble under the unbearable weight of his confessions, which went against all underworld protocols, not to mention his own standards. When remorse took hold of him, he knew it was too late.

4

There would be no second try to see the Triadman in prison, for he was moved to the Sun-Family Gardens in South Bank, one of two provincial prisons for hardened criminals.

Big Sister's natural father lived on as a spineless ex-Triadman, but not for long. In 1960, once he had outlived his usefulness as a collaborator, he was transferred to a labour-reform camp near his ancestral home in Anyue County. Any hopes that he might finally live out his days in freedom were quickly dashed by the famine that hit that year. There was no food in the camp for prisoners, unless they were made of stone, and in late October, he contracted dropsy and could no longer work. He was left to die.

That was a particularly cold winter, the ground frozen. If you didn't work, you didn't eat. When he breathed his last, his fingers were caked with blood from clawing at the rammed-earth wall, residue of which was still in his mouth. His dead eyes stared blindly. Not even thirty-six at the time, he was buried unclaimed in a common grave. Long after his death, someone who had survived the catastrophe revealed all this to Mother when passing through Chongqing.

That year everything edible disappeared in and around Mother's home town in Zhong County, and people began eating a chalky white clay called bodhisattva earth to relieve their hunger, at least for a while. But in the stomach it swelled and hardened, producing fatal constipation. My great aunt was the first to starve in the village; my cousin rushed home from the mining school where he was a student to carry out his duties as eldest son. On his way there, he passed through Fengdu County, and saw the famine's great toll on the populace. Children were being sold openly, whole families were fleeing for their lives, and corpses lined the roads without even a tattered straw mat to cover them; it got so bad that some families were reduced to eating the bodies of

166

dead relatives. A passer-by said to him, 'Don't go any further, comrade. You can't find food here at any price.'

After this filial young man returned to his school, he told no one that his mother had starved to death, or that famine raged in the countryside; instead, he wrote a new application to join the Party, in which he praised Party leaders for their wise agricultural policies. Personal advancement was what he sought, not a return to the starving countryside. His mother was dead, and all the complaints in the world wouldn't bring her back. His only hope was to climb the political ladder the regime had erected. Lies by cadres at all levels had caused the famine, and it was only by keeping to the lies that one could hope to join the cadres.

5

The more deeply I probed, the greater the mystery of my ties to the famine. In the years just before my birth, Grandmother, Third Aunt and her husband, First Aunt, and my mother's first husband, all those relatives, were swept away by the famine. But not me. How had I survived?

My silent musings always ended with question marks.

In the 1950s, people on this street, like people all over China, heeded Chairman Mao's call to have as many children as possible and earn the red garland of 'glorious mother'. Some women bore a child every year; some delivered twins. Mother's reproductive talents did not count for much by comparison. Yet by 1958, the family had been expanded by the addition of three children. Another brother preceded Fourth Sister, but he was stillborn. Induced labour had caused profuse bleeding in Mother, who slipped into unconsciousness and couldn't be awakened for a long time. This was in the spring of 1954.

'What a cruel mother you are. Why did you do laundry in the river only three days before the baby was due? You suffocated your own child, you killed him,' a nurse complained to Mother on her sickbed.

167

Mother smiled weakly and said in a thin voice, 'That's one less to take care of, and one less to suffer.'

The puzzled nurse walked off. It was probably the first time she'd run up against such a cold-blooded mother.

Mother had to laugh at herself, maybe to make herself feel better. Her fate and that of her offspring had already been determined. If her children entered the world dead, at least they were spared a lifetime of misery.

The reproductive craze swelled China's population dramatically. I wasn't the only superfluous one in the family; my brothers and sisters became just as superfluous as I, along with most people in China, and superfluous people are ill-disposed to treat others just like them with human warmth and compassion.

All this talk brought us right back to the famine years. Big Sister, who had a volatile personality, was sixteen when it began. When she learned the story of her birth, her loathing for Mother knew no bounds. But soon after that, it would be my turn to be born; my heart began to race in anxious anticipation of what Big Sister would say next.

TWELVE

1

Big Sister stood in the late spring drizzle of 1962, wearing a straw conical hat, as she waited for Father at the Alley Cat Stream cargo quay.

There were far more cargo ships than passenger ships on the river, making their way slowly through the mist and sounding their horns. She didn't know which ship he was on, and as the drizzle turned into a downpour, her impatience grew; she began to pace up and down. And the longer she waited, the greater her rage against Mother.

Father hadn't been home for three months, and when she finally saw him walking down a gangplank with a duffel bag over his back, she ran up to meet him.

Father started beating Mother as soon as he walked in the door. He had never raised a hand to her before, not in fifteen years of marriage.

Mother's eighth pregnancy – the sixth if we counted only those that survived – had begun to show in only the fourth month. She didn't try to avoid Father's blows, except to protect her unborn child. 'Don't, please, you'll hurt the baby.'

He stopped and sat down on his haunches in agony. Mother wanted to help him up, but didn't dare. Grasping the bedstead, she said tearfully, 'We'll do whatever you say, isn't that enough?' Father stood up and shook the thin door until it creaked. Second Sister and Third Brother quaked fearfully; Fourth Sister and Fifth Brother were crying. Father shoved and shouted them out the door.

But the bolted door couldn't keep in my parents' shouts or

their sobs. Second Sister took four-year-old Fifth Brother out of the compound; Third Brother and Fourth Sister ran away, and Big Sister didn't show her face. When none of the kids had returned home by nightfall, Father went out looking for them. The rain, which had fallen all day, had finally stopped. Big Sister, hat in hand, sauntered into the house, hoping to slip unnoticed into the attic. But Mother saw her and led her into the family room.

The minute they crossed the threshold, Mother told her to kneel down, but Big Sister flicked the water off her hat and pretended she hadn't heard. Mother snatched the hat out of her hand and aimed a slap at her, which missed when she lurched backwards with an angry curse. With ashen-faced rage, Mother grabbed her. Big Sister grabbed her back. Even though Mother's movements were awkward because of the pregnancy, she was still bigger than Big Sister. The two of them wrangled noisily, drawing a crowd of curious neighbours, none of whom tried to intervene. Eventually, Father walked in, drenched to the skin, all four children in tow, and jerked Big Sister away.

'How dare you hit your mother!' he scolded her angrily. 'It's one thing if I do it, but not one of her own daughters.'

'I was helping you, Papa,' Big Sister said through her tears. 'Why are you taking her side?' She spun around and ran into the darkened hall, where she elbowed her way through the crowd and ran away.

At that point Big Sister stopped; this was as much as she would tell me: Mother was pregnant with me, and she had fought with Mother.

I tried to cajole her into telling me more, but she just turned and walked off, leaving me with a major problem: like her, it seemed, I had to find out just who I was. For such an ordinary family, we certainly had more than our share of secrets. But maybe every rundown rooftop in South Bank covered up a houseful of secrets. Big Sister had dried up as a source, Fourth Sister was too busy with her own problems, and Second Sister wouldn't tell me even if she knew. The people around me kept skirting the issue, and I had a feeling that the answer to the riddle might be very embarrassing to me. But I couldn't let that stop me.

I remember once several years earlier, when Big Sister came home after a long bus ride, and there were bloodstains on her sleeve. She said she'd fallen in love again and wanted to divorce her husband, who tried, but failed, to catch her in an adulterous act. So he threatened to report her to the Party Committee and have her criticized for an immoral lifestyle. A fight broke out between them, and she threw a bowl at him, drawing blood.

Mother asked why she couldn't stay married to one man, and why each divorce was messier than the last one. When would she ever learn? Big Sister pulled me away and said to Mother, 'It's all your fault, you're a bad mother, and you have no right to demand anything of me! Your blood runs in my veins.' Their quarrel had something to do with me, it appeared, but once they started screaming at each other, they joined forces to drive me out, then resumed their argument.

Bewildered, I just stood outside the door until Father walked up and took me with him to the top of the crag below Compound Eight Beak. He sat down beside me. Back then he could still see ships on the river on overcast days, not clearly, but as moving black dots. But he knew they were the ships he loved and that they were sailing downriver to the home town he'd never see again.

2

After the dismissal bell for the afternoon's last class sounded, I was putting things in my schoolbag when the history teacher came into the classroom and we walked downstairs together. Out on the schoolground he didn't mention standing me up two days earlier, as if it had never happened. No apologies, obviously. He asked how my studies were going, as feelings of hurt rose up in my heart again. I turned and walked off quickly.

'I need to talk to you,' he called out.

I stopped, and regretted it immediately. I shouldn't have given in so easily. But since I'd stopped, I couldn't just start walking again.

He apologized for standing me up. The police and school authorities had come to see him at noon that day, he said, investigating the gatherings at his house. The police said they didn't believe that all they did was read, and suspected him of organizing some sort of reactionary clique to spread bour-geois-liberalist thoughts. School authorities, intimidated by the charges, were considering firing him. As soon as the questioning had ended, he rushed over to where I was to meet him, but I'd already left. The police then interrogated his friends, who no longer dared meet at his house.

Cars sped past, raising clouds of dust around us, but we were too caught up in our own thoughts to move out of the way. We walked and walked before I realized that we were heading west.

'Let's get something to eat,' he said. Without waiting for my reply, he took me to a little restaurant down a lane far off the street. There were three empty tables, so we sat down at one under the window. While we waited for our food, he asked, 'Still angry with me?'

'What will you do if they fire you?' I asked.

'Be a labourer again,' he said with a smile. 'Go back to my roots.'

When two bowls of soupy rice with green beans, a small dish of pickled vegetables and a plate of water spinach arrived, he ordered some bark-flavoured alcohol. He told me that when he was a temporary construction worker, he'd fallen off a roof and injured his lower back; it still bothered him years later, and alcohol was the only thing that eased the pain. I hesitated when he offered me a drink, since I'd never tried it

172

before, except for a sip of Father's wine at New Year, and I didn't like the taste. But to take the history teacher's mind off his troubles, I had a drink. It wasn't as bad as I thought – sweet and not much of a bite.

'Like it?' he asked.

I smiled.

I started talking about how my Mother and Father had met in 1947 and what things were like when the Communists took the city two years later. I did my best to reconstruct what people were wearing then, what the weather was like, and all about the stone steps and the river. He listened attentively without interrupting, except to order another bowl of rice for me.

I felt so self-absorbed when I saw the look in his eyes. I'd been pouring out all the misery that crowded my heart, without a thought for him. I stopped eating.

'How did you make it through the years of famine?' I asked.

'Every family's story was more or less the same, I think,' he said with a smile. 'But in the telling they were all different, too. Everyone's experience was unique.'

He said he'd like to write a book on the subject, all his thoughts on life and fate. Big Sister had said the same thing, but what she yearned to do was to pour out her grievances against the unfairness of her fate. He, on the other hand, wanted to find some new way of expressing his ideas. A group of young writers in Beijing were doing just that at the time, posting their works on a wall in the Xidan Crossroad as part of a mimeographed magazine called *Today*. It was now banned by the authorities. In fact, the Chongqing police were following Beijing's lead by putting pressure on his reading group. So even if he wrote something, he couldn't get it published.

I slid his glass across the table, but he slid it back to me. I held it in my hand. When he started talking about writing a book, my thoughts began to drift.

'Don't worry, you won't get drunk,' he said. He was watching me closely.

I set the glass down in front of him. 'You drink it,' I said. 'One more sip for you, then I'll finish it off.'

So I took a drink, then another. I could feel my face turning hot. My mind seemed especially sharp, and my speech was unblemished by a single stammer. I told him about my relatives who had starved during the famine, before I was born, and how my eldest sister had stormed through one marriage after another.

His view was that she was trying to change her life. But even by exhausting all her strength to fight society's power, she could not alter her fate.

The haves in our society had formed a ruling clique, he said, a new privileged class. While we common folk dreamt of adding another hole to a public privy, the cadres had their own flush toilets, bathrooms, telephones, servants, and nannies. 'Did you ever hear of a cadre starving during the famine? These people's first priority is to consolidate the common interests of their class and pass these on to their sons and daughters. Their second priority is to climb over others on their way up the ladder. The inevitable clash between these two priorities is what leads to the endless political upheavals that bring disaster down on the heads of common people.'

There were two Cultural Revolutions, he went on. The first involved cadres who attacked each other. People in the political arena carry their heads in their hands, he said. In order to enjoy special privileges, they must risk having their throats cut. Therefore, they have no right to complain, since that was the choice they made. Those people and their descendants, who now write angry denunciations against the Rebels who persecuted them, are laughable. The other Cultural Revolution belonged to the common folk who took advantage of the power struggle between Chairman Mao and State Chairman Liu Shaoqi to attack Party committees in an act of revenge. But as early as 1969 Mao turned on the Rebels, and for the last eleven years they have been under attack. The cadres aren't yet through with the people who dared challenge them.

I stared at the history teacher without blinking. He was talking so excitedly his hands were moving all over the place. I'd never heard him say so much at one time, and he didn't seem to care if I understood what he was saying or not, nor did he care whether or not I agreed with him. Seeing the look on his face, I felt a degree of pity for him. He knew so much more than I, but suffered from the same deadening lack of understanding. Where emotional needs were concerned, we were equals.

The small bottle of drink was empty, but there were still a few drops in the glass. He kept picking it up and putting it down, apparently unable to make up his mind to drink it. He laughed self-consciously, telling me I was the first female other than his wife he'd ever eaten in a restaurant with. Most of the time he ate a simple meal at home, alone. I couldn't tell if the drink had turned his face red or if he was blushing over this admission. I turned away and watched the proprietor go in and come out of the kitchen. The other two empty tables were now occupied.

The restaurant was still quiet. The sun was sinking behind the mountains, so it must have been five or six o'clock. The proprietor was fanning a fresh pot of soupy rice. Most customers would arrive at seven or eight.

This was the first time he'd mentioned his wife, and then only in passing. I'd overheard other teachers say that she worked in an elementary school, as an administrator, not a teacher. His seven-year-old daughter was a student at the school, which apparently wasn't in South Bank, but in some distant suburb. He wanted me to know that he was usually alone at home, and I knew what he was driving at, although I didn't let on.

'Your eyes give you away,' he said a little too quickly. 'You can't hide what you're thinking, not even the tiniest thought. They tell me everything.'

I shook my head spiritedly.

Don't you know, I said to him, but only in my mind, that the only thing I'm hiding is my loneliness, because I have to keep everyone at a distance? I yearn to give myself to someone. But I can't let my eyes reveal this yearning, since that will expose too much of my heart.

3

The younger boy is a little taller than his elder brother, and both have faces with a touch of sadness. After the death of their father, they are raised by their mother, and it isn't easy. They are four years apart in age, but as much alike as two peas in a pod. When the Cultural Revolution begins and Rebel factions are formed, they stay home to practise Chairman Mao's quotations and to use them as oratorical weapons. Then they leave home and become Rebel activists, and when the Rebel organizations split, they wind up in opposing camps.

This sort of thing was commonplace in this city of several million. In the early years of the Cultural Revolution, even old women who eked out a living mending rags and cutting shoe soles could recite quotations from the Great Leader, Chairman Mao, or his Great Second in Command, Lin Biao, and silence their critics with revolutionary slogans. Families that had split into opposing factions fought like cats and dogs.

It didn't take long for the army generals to take advantage of the situation to settle old scores. The 'August 15th' faction was supported by the Fifty-Fourth Army, which had been stationed in Chongqing. But then the Fifty-Third Army was sent to Chongqing, and it backed the 'Rebel to the End' faction. That was when the populace realized just how many armament factories there were in the city, since they fell under the control of opposing factions, who were encouraged to make best use of them. Chongqing would become the most notorious battlefield of the Cultural Revolution, with nightly curfews, fortifications on the commanding heights and major roads, and loudspeakers blaring night and day. During the first six months of 1967, battles were fought with knives and clubs, but in July, live ammunition began to be used.

During those days, most people on the three banks of the two rivers dragged the junk out from under their beds and replaced it with straw mats. They slept under and not on their beds, which were piled high with quilts and pillows. That was their protection against stray bullets or artillery shells that could come flying across the river at any time. Air-raid shelters built into the sides of hills during the war with Japan had held up well over the years, and were probably the finest in the world; they served as a refuge from the street fighting. Later, in the 1970s, under the threat of nuclear war, they would be reinforced and extended, until the city was honeycombed with shelters. But in the summer of 1967, every day, after darkness closed in, no matter how hot and steamy it was, people closed and bolted their doors, turned off the lights, and armed themselves with steel rods, scissors, and cleavers.

Then there came a fierce battle which raged all night long at the Medical College, with machine-gun fire and tanks. Few had expected to see a battle like it, especially the high-school and college students, who fled in panic, with so many scrambling over a wall that it collapsed on top of them; as many people were crushed to death as died in the fighting.

In August, the fighting entered the white-hot stage.

Both the 'August 15th' and 'Rebel to the End' factions prepared for a decisive battle on the Yangtze. Fortresses were set up in South Bank, in the heart of the city, and on the north bank. Cargo ships and ferries stopped plying the river, turning it into a deserted waterway. Even the loudspeakers of the 'So What if We're Finished' propaganda station of the 'Rebel to the End' faction, which were atop the Liberation Monument Tower in the centre of town, were mute. A white silence filled the sky, and no one noticed the rising temperature.

Sensing the approaching danger, people who lived on the banks of the river took refuge under their beds or in air-raid shelters.

A bunch of kids were outdoors reciting some silly proverbs on 8 August 1967. When shells began landing, my fearless third brother, who was sixteen at the time, ran over to Compound Eight Beak, which had a clear view of Heaven's Gate, and lay prone beneath a crag to enjoy the spectacle.

Father went after him, clinging to walls and crouching the whole way to avoid getting hit. 'Son! Son!' he shouted, sweating from anxiety. Not quite five years old and driven by curiosity, I sneaked along behind him.

At the convergence of the Jialing and Yangtze Rivers, smoke rose from the burning skeletons of abandoned ships. A landing craft had run aground on Turtle Rock, its stern deep in the water, the bow still afloat, but sinking slowly. Another escaped the same fate only by steaming downriver at full speed.

At Compound Eight Beak, Third Brother was nowhere to be found. As Father started down the steps to the riverbank, he spotted me behind him. 'Beat it, you!' he yelled, pointing towards home. 'Scram home!'

Stopped in my tracks by the anger in his voice, I turned and ran home as if my life depended on it.

Third Brother said that when he saw the landing craft sink, he ran down the steps all the way to the river and dived in, then swam back to the bank with something he thought would be interesting; it was a plastic tube containing a dozen shuttlecocks. It turned out that the sunken craft had been manned by student badminton players. Amid flying bullets, Father dragged Third Brother home and shoved him under the bed, where he continued smoothing the feathers of his precious shuttlecocks.

A fierce battle raged between the 'Rebel to the End' faction, which had sailed its landing craft upstream from the armaments factory, and a gunboat and small steamboat of 'August 15th', which had come up from the Jialing. The warships had been outfitted with armour plating, with portholes for rifles and cannons. Most members of 'August 15th' were students, with a few workers mixed in, and were fairly well equipped. But they were no match for the 'Rebel to the End' landing craft, manned mainly by former navy sailors. The 'August 15th' gunboat took twelve hits, including one on the main engine. Before they had time to turn and run, their boat sank and took them with it.

The history teacher saw the little steamboat meet its fiery end.

At the time he didn't realize that his younger brother was aboard. According to surviving members of 'August 15th', an effete scholar like him should have stayed ashore, but he had come aboard on his own. After they brought the bodies up out of the water, he found his brother's thick glasses with transparent rims, which were buried in the Red Guard Martyrs' Cemetery at Sandbar Park along with a host of unidentifiable corpses. In Chongqing, where the fiercest battles of the Cultural Revolution were fought, no fewer than twenty cemeteries were reserved for those who had died all in defence of the Great Leader. But only Sandbar Park remains, and the vast majority of graves bear no names. Once a stately memorial, it had boasted etched lines of Chairman Mao's poetry and quotations in his own unrestrained calligraphy. But halfway through the Cultural Revolution, the factions were disbanded by the military, and the cemetery fell into disrepair, with toppled tombstones amid clumps of weeds, to become just another deserted graveyard.

The history teacher's mother was home knitting a sweater when she heard the awful news; her knitting needle jabbed into the palm of her hand, and she died of a stroke on the spot, without so much as a yelp of pain.

The history teacher withdrew from the factional fighting and returned home, which had been ransacked out of revenge by his brother's comrades.

'Eighth month, the eighth day, citizens had the devil to pay' became a new proverb in the city, one filled with ominous implications. Thirteen years later, when relatives of one of the dead Red Guards came to Sandbar Park to dig up the remains and bury them elsewhere, they received the shock of their lives: 'Wronged ghost!' they screamed. 'Wronged ghost!' The skull had turned completely green. They were later told that the bullet that had killed the young man must have been made of copper, which had oxidized in the liquefied brains and dyed the skull.

I'd have had to be blind not to see that the calmness with which the history teacher related these events as we sat in the restaurant was an act, and that he was struggling to suppress his pangs of conscience. For the first time I sensed something contradictory in his eloquence. He was clear and persuasive when he spoke of the 'two Cultural Revolutions', but his argument had a flaw. For if the Rebel organizations had been engaged in the 'common people's Cultural Revolution', why were they so intent on killing each other?

'All we ever heard was the Rebels were savages,' he said, 'yet when they were in control of the situation, few intellectuals or ordinary citizens were persecuted or driven to suicide. But when Mao let the military take control and usher in the "Class Purification Movement" in the 1970s, that's when the common people really suffered.'

He was right, of course. During my second year at school, people accused of joining the 'May 16th Conspiracy' were committing suicide all over the place, and 'Kuomintang dregs' and 'reactionary literati' were ferreted out daily. So many bodies floated in the river during those years that people lost interest in going down to see them.

I sat across from the history teacher, cupping my head in my hands, the food completely forgotten as the time slipped away. Night had fallen.

I didn't even think about the book *Human Anatomy*, which

was in my schoolbag, until we had said goodbye. All the profound things he'd said and his far-sighted point of view were so far removed from the book that I'd forgotten to return it and shame him for being so base. I called him back, and we walked towards each other under the streetlight. The shadows of branches on nearby trees obliterated his features, transforming him into a faceless spectre.

'What is it?' he asked. He could see I was breathing heavily.

'Your book,' I said calmly and in measured tones. 'I read it, and I understand it.' I produced it from behind my back and handed it to him. He took it from me, turned, and walked off, clearly alarmed and a bit panic-stricken.

My very first moral victory. As I watched him hurry off, for some reason I suddenly felt an onrush of desire. My heart was beating wildly, my pelvic muscles were twitching, and my nipples grew painfully taut. I had to hug myself tightly.

4

On the way home, not even the chilled winds calmed me down. The sound of an organ drifted over a wall from a nursery school.

> Looking, always looking,
> Looking for a friend,
> Nodding our heads and holding hands.

The children were playing drop-the-hanky on the play-ground. What were they doing out at this time of the evening? The stench of shit drifted up and down the streets from the droppings of the peasant nightsoil collectors or from a nearby public toilet. It was hot; the trees were rustling and water dribbled silently in the ditch.

There were more people than usual in Compound Six when I walked in, including some from other compounds and other streets. It was a crowded place to begin with; now people were nearly knocking each other over. 'It's a boy!' 'Lucky Mama Shi, she has a grandson!' Fourth Sister and Dehua were on stools in the hall eating dinner, Fifth Brother was there, too, and Father was fiddling with his transistor radio.

I tossed down my schoolbag, picked up a basin, and went into the kitchen to get some water. A pot of soup was cooking on Mama Shi's stove, releasing steam with a meaty fragrance; kettles were heating on the other stoves. The visitors who had come for celebratory red eggs had said their noisy goodbyes and gone home. Mama Shi's house, the first in the rear, was nearest the kitchen, so I could see her daughter-in-law lying in bed through the open door. 'Why isn't the soup ready yet?' I heard her complain. 'Do I have to wait till I become an idiot before I get something to eat?'

'It only works if you eat it in the middle of the night,' Mama Shi answered her.

They were talking about eating the placenta, which was a custom around here. You brought it home from the mid-wifery, washed it in the river with salt and soda, then chopped it fine and cooked it in pork broth. People believed that the placenta was the site of all the new mother's nutrition, and the logical means for her to regain her strength. Greedy women gathered round any stove where placenta soup was being prepared. Most would stand at their own stoves and dip into their neighbour's pot with long-handled spoons, but the bolder ones would walk right up, dish up a bowlful, and quickly blow on it to cool it enough to slurp up. 'I'm just tasting it to see if it's salty enough,' they'd say if they were caught.

I felt like throwing up every time I heard someone talk excitedly about eating placenta soup, and I recall one time when Big Sister, who had just delivered, got into an argument with Mother over it.

She refused to eat what she was given, banging the side of the bowl with her chopsticks and complaining to Mother, 'This is pig's stomach. Ma, you threw my placenta away, didn't you?'

182

Mother didn't say a word.

'The soup's the same milky colour and tastes about the same,' Big Sister complained angrily. 'But you can't fool me, there's no placenta in this!' She knew that Mother didn't believe what they said about the placenta, and considered eating it barbarian. She'd never cook it for one of her own daughters. Mother may have been uneducated, but she had her principles, and not eating parts of the human body was one of them.

<h1 style="text-align:center">5</h1>

But Mother did believe in witchcraft, and considered witch healing more effective than Western medicine. Once, when I was thirteen, I missed a step when I was carrying a load of sand and tumbled down the steps, badly wrenching my left wrist, which swelled up horribly. In the middle of the night, when the pain grew unbearable, Mother sneaked me out of the house and over to a street behind the water ditch, where she knocked anxiously on a door. Both the door and the windows of the place were incredibly small. A woman was sitting in the pitch-dark room smoking a cigarette. She lit a lantern after we came in, but it gave off only a faint light. When she put it on a dresser in the corner of the room, I couldn't make out her features, and all I could see clearly was the cigarette dangling in her hand; she never took a puff. Unhappy about our coming to see her without asking her first, she said we couldn't afford her services.

Mother asked how much she charged.

She flipped her cigarette away and raised fingers to show a figure.

Mother nodded without saying a word.

The woman stood up and told me to sit on the bed, where she applied a strange-smelling ointment to my wrist, mumbling an incantation while she rubbed it in. Then she lit a stick of incense and held it close to the injured spot, sending what felt like electric currents racing through my body.

'All right, you can take her home now,' the woman said breathlessly as she sat down again.

I hopped down off the bed, my wrist already feeling as good as new. Mother handed her the money, which she refused to accept, to Mother's puzzlement.

The woman said she liked the way Mother had agreed to the price without hesitation. She knew we were poor. But she told us not to tell anyone. 'You never came here, understand?' she growled.

That was the winter when blood seeped from my body for the first time. I hid behind the curtain around the chamber pot, not knowing what to do, while Big Sister stood outside with a full bladder. Wondering what I was doing, she parted the curtain and saw me sitting on the pot, trembling. After handing me some toilet paper, she told me to stuff it into my underpants. From then on, when my periods came, especially in the winter, the increased flow of blood made me extremely tense, but all the curses in the world had no effect. Some days I had to run home while school was still in session because my underpants, my flannel lining, even my trousers would be wet to the touch. Ashamed and uncomfortable, I'd walk in the house and change into something else while I dried my flannel lining over the stove – I didn't have any spares – and as I waited for them to get dry enough to put back on, all I could think of was how my teachers might punish me again for leaving class.

I have a mole on the palm of my right hand, which a fortune-teller found troubling. 'It blocks the vein where several energy passages intersect.' I also have a scar above my navel from an operation to remove a boil when I was little. It's like an eye that keeps staring back at me, and whenever I take a bath, I trace a question mark around it with my finger.

THIRTEEN

1

I opened the attic door and stood barefoot in the entryway. The compound was just beginning to come awake. Someone was urinating into the drain hole in the courtyard. The overnight build-up made a loud splashing sound.

Rays of sunlight passed through laundry drying in the courtyard and fell on the low bamboo stool in the corner of the hall. I put my schoolbag over my shoulders and had got as far as the door when Mother came out of the room, combing her hair. 'It's Sunday,' she said impatiently. 'Where do you think you're going?'

No wonder I didn't see anyone on their way to school. Mother looked exhausted, as if she hadn't slept all night; her eyes were puffy, but her gaze was sharp as ever, and, stung by the feeling that she could see right through me, I panicked. Her face softened, as if she wanted to say something to me, but she just coughed once, then turned and went back into the room. Our neighbour was eating some rancid-smelling porridge and pickled beans. I took a book down to the river to review my schoolwork, but couldn't concentrate. So I went home, where Father was alone, washing dishes.

'Where's Mama?'

'She said she was going to see your second sister,' Father said. After a moment's thought, he added, 'She also said she was going to burn incense at the Arhat Temple in town.'

That was strange. Had something bad happened? Whenever she was up against a problem she couldn't deal with, she would burn incense at the Arhat Temple, sometimes taking me along. She said I went there when I was three years old, but the first visit I actually remember occurred when I was four or five, I think. The smell of lotus root filled the quiet, deserted temple.

Cobblestones crunched as we walked down the path. Stone statues every four or five steps had been turned faceless by the relentless wind, pitted and scarred like leprous beggars.

We turned a corner and walked up to the main gate, where Mother told me to stop, straighten my clothes, and pull up the straps on my shoes. Each Buddhist statue, she said, controlled one fate. If you kowtowed to the arhat that governed your life, luck would be with you throughout your days. She patted me on the head as a sign that the choice was now mine. When I entered the temple, she said, if my right foot crossed the threshold first, I was to count statues from the right. The five hundred arhats were aligned in a double square, and I was to count in accordance with my eight natal numbers – year, month, day and time of birth – with no skipping and no choosing. The one I landed in front of was my personal arhat. If, on the other hand, I entered with my left foot, I was to begin counting from that side.

The threshold was so high I had to steady myself with my hand to climb over it, and in my nervousness I forgot to notice which foot went over first. Suddenly, arrayed before me in the double-squared temple, were stone arhats of about the same height, but different in every other respect: glaring, laughing, solemnly seated, cradling a phoenix, holding a good-luck symbol, or with a lotus flower growing out of the head.

'Kneel, Little Six!' Mother said firmly, leaving no room for argument.

I did as I was told, kneeling fearfully on a straw mat, without so much as looking up, afraid that the arhat that controlled my fate might be pot-bellied or red-faced. Finally screwing up my courage, I looked up and saw a statue that seemed to touch the ceiling: benevolent features, merciful expression, generosity suffusing its pale face, silver sword in hand, standing on a golden-maned lion, different from all the others. It was gazing down at me, its eyes clear. I had no idea how to figure my eight numbers, and didn't want to ask Mother how she'd done it, yet I had the feeling I already knew this arhat, that I'd seen it somewhere before.

Mother knelt beside me and lit three joss sticks, then told me to kowtow with her. Her blue cotton shirt rubbing roughly against my face felt wonderful. 'This is Manjusri,' she said. 'Say whatever's on your mind. He's your protector. Tell him what sort of fortune you want, but don't say it aloud. Just repeat it three times to yourself.'

With my head touching the floor, I told him what I wanted, ten times at least. And when I turned my head, Mother was looking at me with tenderness in her eyes.

My fate had never been good, not since the day I was born, and it would likely never change all my life. Whatever it was I said to myself that day has, in the intervening years, completely slipped my mind. During the Cultural Revolution, not long after we visited the temple, the statues were all smashed and the temple was sealed. Later on it was restored, and I made a special trip back to see the reconstructed arhats. Gold had been donated to paint the face of the Buddha, and there was a new Manjusri, an exact replica of the original one. But it seemed alien to me, and I doubt it remembered the wish that by now even I had forgotten.

It's a question I've never been able to answer: Why had Mother chosen the Manjusri arhat to protect her eighth child – the sixth to survive – and not Samantabhadra, god of rationality, or the merciful Guanyin, goddess of benevolence, or even the almighty and omniscient Sakyamuni, the Buddha himself? She was barely literate enough to read simple letters or write a greetings card – with plenty of miswritten characters – so maybe it was pure luck. Manjusri's sword is the sword of knowledge, the lion the source of intelligence. Maybe she knew all along that I would spend my life suffering over my yearnings to know, that I needed an answer for everything, and that a yearning to understand could only add to my troubles and take a heavy toll. How fortunate to go through life ignorant, letting nature take its course, bearing children and avoiding complications, then dying in peace and letting your ashes flow to the sea.

But in the years to come, Mother removed herself from her children's concerns, including my need for knowledge. None of that mattered to her, and I never again felt the warmth and tenderness she had shown me that day in the temple. She saw no need for me to learn the family's secrets, especially those surrounding the circumstances of my birth.

2

I yearned to see the history teacher! I hunted all over for the little mirror, digging through all five drawers out of the bureau. In the clothing drawer I found a blue baby's cap that I'd never seen before. It would have remained hidden if I hadn't taken the drawer out. Something hard was wrapped inside it – a tiny harmonica. The cap was old and moth-eaten, but I liked the colour and the little dark embroidered flowers; the satin cover and flannel liner were soft and warm to the touch. Then I recalled seeing the harmonica once before, but Mother had snatched it away from me.

I went up to the attic for Fourth Sister's little mirror, which she'd taken from the drawer and hidden under her pillow. I hated my jaundiced face, but tried to improve my looks with some of Big Sister's daughter's prickly-heat powder. I dabbed it here and there, then spread it around evenly. Another look in the mirror: one powdering can cover ten ugly faces, and I was pleased with what I saw. I quickly laid the mirror on the bed, upside-down; my fear of the damned thing certainly equalled Mother's.

The history teacher was sure to ask me: Why is your face so

pale? Afraid of something? I began to wish I hadn't used the powder, because once I started blushing I couldn't stop. I'd always sensed that my youth, my golden years, would pass quickly, like a ray of light locked away in a box. And on that day in my eighteenth year, I felt like opening up the box to look at that ray of light, hoping to see it shine brightly.

The miracle of love is not easily come by in life, and I'd been waiting an awfully long time; now it had appeared, and I couldn't bear to shrink from it. I was in love with him, untroubled by the knowledge that he was married. Unconsciously, that may actually have been the deciding factor. I had always loved what I could not have, and the more remote the possibility, the stronger my emotional attachment. Thoughts of him came when I opened my eyes in the morning. What's he doing now? How did our last meeting go? What will I do when I see him again? I'm a lost cause, I thought to myself, absolutely hopeless. Before even letting love gain a foothold I had nearly exhausted most of the fondness two people in love are entitled to.

Over and over I took stock of my tangled thoughts. You're too lonely, I chided myself. It's common for students to have a crush on their teacher. But how do you know you won't turn and run away as soon as you're face-to-face with him? If you do, your heated passion of a moment ago will simply go up in smoke.

Instinct told me he wasn't at school, though he sometimes spent Sundays alone in his office. But today he's home, I just know it. I boarded a bus at Stonebridge Square, but it was moving so slowly that I got off and walked down the slope, along the bank, and across the creek. Mud formed little mounds on the bank, which was covered with downy soft reeds. I saw the cluttered rows of houses on stilts he had described to me. He lived in a hillside bungalow with plastered walls; the wood had turned almost black under the constant assault of rain and the blazing sun.

My heart beat wildly as I stood at the bottom of the hill; I couldn't believe how brave I was. What if he asked why I came? I could say I wanted him to write a wedding scroll for Fourth Sister.

But no, why should I lie? I'd simply say I wanted to see him, so I came over. The stone steps at Crabapple Creek went all the way up the hill, and I had to stop several times to catch my breath. But the thought of turning back never entered my mind. He had ignited something deep inside me. Colour had appeared on my haggard face and bloodless lips, and my hair, blowing in the wind, had turned from a mousy brown to a rich black. My scaly skin had become smooth, my nails had turned glossy. If I could have seen myself, I'd have known that on that day when I had just passed my eighteenth birthday I used up all my youthful beauty, something that ought to be enjoyed in a measured pace over the years.

When I reached his street, where all the houses faced away from the river, I didn't even have to look at addresses; I found his house by instinct.

I didn't run away. My heartbeat was normal, my calmness downright scary. I raised my hand and knocked on his door.

3

He was shocked to see me standing there when he opened the door, but he quickly regained his composure. 'Come in,' he said with a tilt of the head.

As I'd figured, his wife and daughter weren't home – he was alone. In my dreams I'd seen a house filled with books, and there they were, on a bookcase that divided his thirty-square-metre room into two rooms, one large, one small. Wet laundry hung from a bamboo pole on the veranda. A small door off to the side led to an add-on kitchen. With only a bed, a wardrobe, and some stools, the place didn't appear cramped. An ancient gramophone sat on a table by the bookcase, an old porcelain vase stood in the corner.

Instead of asking why I'd come, he just smiled, as if he'd read my mind. That smug grin of his was so humiliating; I hated it. I sat down on a stool next to the wall, and he poured me a glass of cold tea. Then he bent down, took a gramophone record from a pile of records, newspapers and books and put it on the gramophone.

There was indeed a picture of his mother on top of the bookcase. She looked blankly down at me. What was this deceased woman trying to tell me? 'She looks a lot like you,' I said.

He nodded and came up to me. In my panic I drank half the glass of tea. He took the glass from me and set it on the bookcase, looked me in the eye, and bent over to kiss me lightly on the forehead. I leaned towards him and opened my mouth breathlessly.

As he took me in his arms, my body pressed up against his; I was so dizzy I closed my eyes and suddenly lost sight of where I was. I didn't struggle, I was ready to give myself to him, whether or not he wanted the gift I was offering him. Take me, I said inwardly, I'm yours completely. A kiss gave me the answer I sought, as his quivering lips brushed against my burning skin.

I suddenly realized that this wasn't a new me, that I had always been like this; these inexplicable urges were in my nature, and I was willing to abandon everything or be totally abandoned, all for love. With no thoughts for tomorrow and no regrets over yesterday, I would have gladly given up my life at that moment. I felt myself being carried naked over to the bed, where he began touching forbidden places, places even I dared not touch. But his hands and lips stopped abruptly and nothing happened for what seemed like an eternity. I opened my eyes and looked at him. He seemed strangely hesitant.

My face was burning; I was ashamed by my uncontrollable desire.

'You're still a virgin,' he said.

'Not because I want to be,' I said.

'No man will want to marry you, and even if one does, he'll make life miserable for you. In our society, few men can break free of traditional concepts, even now.'

'I'm going to live alone, that's the way I want it.'

'Because you know I won't be with you?'

'That never crossed my mind,' I said almost defiantly. 'I just want to be yours today, to be with you now.'

I must have shocked him, but my words put him at ease. He called me by name. 'You'll get married some day.'

I wanted to tell him that, ever since my childhood, not a single married person I ever saw, including my neighbours and my brothers and sisters, was truly happy. If marriage was that bad an institution, why would I want any part of it? But love, that was everything to me. It was all I wanted, just that little bit.

But I didn't tell him. I just shook my head, over and over.

I was a girl blinded by desire; I knew I loved him, but couldn't find the words. Maybe one day I'd fall in love again, but that was 'one day'. My present love for him was unique, and would cast a shadow over the rest of my life.

He put my fingers first into his mouth, then between his legs. His penis was hard and hot. I never knew that a man's sex swelled up and turned purple like that. It was much larger than I'd imagined; its veins were pulsating, like a caged animal that has been set free. My hand was trembling, but I didn't pull it back. I never dreamed I was capable of the brazen act of holding a man's penis. He hugged me tightly, as if he wanted me to pull me into him. Spots of sunlight filtering through the bamboo leaves fell on to my naked body, which seemed to know the joy of a leopard on the run; the spots of sunlight bound our bodies together like a ring of fire, as the mighty Yangtze flowed past the window, turning the city on the opposite bank into a mirage; the cliff outside his window was a vast shade-covered flatland. Some little girls were singing as they skipped:

One two three four five six seven,
All horse orchids grow up to heaven.

Accompanying the girls' crisp giggles up the cliff were the
happy horns of steamboats edging up to the pier below. For
the first time I understood why they sounded their horns to
each other. All those sounds beyond the window were an
accompaniment to the music swirling from the gramophone.

With great joy I grabbed his hand and lay down, pressing
my breasts against his chest. I could feel his rhythmic heartbeat. He kissed my ear. 'Your heart is more fragile than other
girls',' he whispered, 'so delicate that a mere touch opens a
hole.'

He spread my legs open, and I felt something hard enter the
space, like a thief moving in when no one was looking.

He asked me if it hurt. I told him no.

He sighed and said it hurt him a great deal. Down below it
was so painful he thought it might explode, and in his chest his
heart ached. But pain is good, he said. Love isn't sweet, and
loving me was more painful than he had imagined.

His tongue pressed into my mouth and merged with mine;
our fingers were intertwined. When his body pressed down
on my breasts, he filled me up down between my legs. Now it
hurt; a pain I'd never felt before had me in its grip, and I nearly
cried out with every move he made. I was breathless, but I
didn't scream – I'd have been ashamed to. I wanted to look at
his organ and see how anything could do this to me, but my
eyes seemed frozen shut. It was as if we had fused together,
and I could hear gnawing sounds coming from my womb,
which suddenly caught fire and began to seethe.

The river turned upside-down, with ships sailing in the sky
and mountains hanging from the heavens, crashing down on
his tongue, his fingers, his gaze, his angry face, his ecstatic face.
I was in the sky's embrace, waves were rising and falling
around my head and ruthlessly swallowing me up.

Without warning my tears began to flow, and I couldn't

stop them. I was quaking. A rich sheen covered my skin, the fragrance of my own body filled my own nostrils. It smelled like orchids or gardenias. But most miraculously of all, my breasts swelled tenaciously. There's no doubt that my breasts ripened that day, grew full and resilient.

4

Slowly our breathing returned to normal; locked in a sweaty embrace, we didn't say a word. He kissed me and asked why there was no blood. I detected a note of surprise in his voice. I checked the straw mat, and indeed there was no bloodstain. Instead of asking if another man had touched me, he merely said I must have broken my hymen while engaged in heavy labour.

As he stroked the scar around my navel, I closed my eyes and listened to our hearts beat in harmony. With my arm around his neck, I rested one leg against him and wrapped my other leg around his. I knew that all virgins carried a certificate of authenticity – their maidenheads. Had I come into the world without one? Maybe I never needed one, maybe I was born a non-virgin!

'Is this what you wanted?' he asked as he held me tight. 'To lie naked with me?'

I said it was.

He said it was definitely what he wanted. In his dreams he always woke up after we had taken off our clothes, to his great regret.

I asked him why.

He said because when he saw me naked sitting on the bed in front of him, there was blood on my thighs. He couldn't finish the dream because he was afraid he'd hurt me. Deeply moved, I pressed my face against his, happy with the thought that I'd fallen in love with a man deserving of that love.

He told me to sit up.

Always obedient to him, I did as he said, sitting on my heels and resting my hands on my knees, just the way he'd seen me in my dreams. Naked, he seemed taller and huskier than usual, except that his penis hung slack. He picked up a drawing board and sat on the stool closest to the bed. Telling me not to move, he began sketching with a pencil. After a few minutes he walked up to the bed and showed me what he had drawn.

My naked body! My nipples and navel were drawn with great care, so was my pubic hair. The face was the one he had drawn in his office, with the body added. So that was me, the woman, more natural than when I had clothes on, a wild erotic animal. To me, being that brazen was right on the mark. And that's why he'd drawn the head at the top of the page, waiting to fill in the rest later. He had been manipulating me all along! How wonderful, I had aroused him from the very beginning!

I wanted the sketch.

'Aren't you afraid someone will see it?'

'This is me. What should I be afraid of?' I said. 'Will you sign it for me?'

He signed the sketch with a flair, removed it from the drawing board, and laid it on the pillow. I couldn't help noticing that, while he was looking at the sketch, his penis grew hard again. He turned around in embarrassment and started to get dressed.

I jumped down off the bed and put on my underwear, then my blouse and skirt. By the time I was slipping on my sandals, he was cinching up his belt.

He walked over to the gramophone and turned off the music, and when he came back, he had a strange look on his face. He pulled me over to the bed, sat me down, and put his arm around me. He said his wife and daughter wouldn't be home till after dark and asked me to stay a little longer. I was neither jealous nor despondent. On the contrary, I was delighted that I'd done something I'd wanted to do for so long, and it was so much more beautiful than I'd thought.

We were lying side by side on our backs when he propped himself up on his elbow and began to talk. But his voice was different now, tired and flat: 'Forget me,' he said. 'I'm not worth it. I'm just like all other men, worse even, a real bastard.' I tried to say something, but he put his hand over my mouth. 'Don't say anything, just listen. And remember what I say.'

He stood up, to get some tea, I thought, but it was a cigarette he wanted. He lit it and took a deep puff. I'd never seen him smoke before. He said that Cultural Revolution activists had been receiving notices from the District Party Committee to report to a 'study class', and he was waiting for his. The school had already informed him that he was to come in for a talk the next week, and although he couldn't say for sure what they wanted to talk about, instinct told him that he would soon be incarcerated in one of those makeshift prisons.

I sat up and shook my head.

'You don't believe me?'

'You can't mean it.'

He flicked his ashes on to the floor. 'You'll understand one day,' he said. 'Certainly by the time you're my age.' If I'd been a little more attentive, I'd have noticed that something was wrong in the room, something about the atmosphere. But I was too busy looking at him.

'The time has come to settle scores,' he said. 'The vested interests aren't about to forgo the pleasure of getting their revenge against those of us who went after them.'

I stood up. 'No,' I said. 'You didn't do anything wrong, you were a victim of the Cultural Revolution.' I must have sounded surprisingly serious, because he stopped to listen to me. But I just kept saying the same thing over and over. He sat on the stool near the bed.

'I'm considered a "murderer".'

'Nonsense!'

'They say I killed my brother, that I ordered the shelling.'

'That can't be.' I was nearly crying.

'It's true, I murdered my own kid brother.' He looked at me calmly. 'You should leave.' That was what he said, but he was holding my hand tightly in his.

Finally he let go of my hand and walked over to the bookcase, where he picked up one foreign novel after another until he had a stack of them. Some of them I'd read, some I hadn't. They were for me.

I reached out to pick the sketch up off the pillow, but he stopped me, grabbed the piece of paper and looked at it one more time before wadding it up and taking it into the kitchen.

'That's mine!' I shouted. 'It's me!' I ran after him.

Taking my head in his hands, he said, 'You have your whole life ahead of you, and you need to live it as cleanly as you can.' He walked to the stove and lit the paper.

I left his house alone, carrying a bundle of books, and still somewhat dizzy, unable to be free of the feelings of a girl who has just become a woman. It was as if he were still inside me, and the scorching semen that had spurted from his wonderful sex leaked out with each step I took, sweetly lubricating my labia and wetting the insides of my thighs. I hugged the books tightly as if they were his body.

But then I thought back to what he had said to get me to leave, things I really didn't understand, and my heart trembled. For some reason, I sensed how resolutely he had made love to me, with a reckless, frenzied passion that had seemed about to crush the life out of me. It was a bad omen that signalled the long night ahead.

He did not speak to me of the future, nor did he say that he wanted to see me again.

FOURTEEN

1

I laid down the bundle of books, looked into the bedroom, and listened for sounds in the attic. 'Has Big Sister left?' I asked.

'Yes,' Fourth Sister replied without even turning to look at me.

That was just like Big Sister, coming and going without a word to anyone. 'Have you been out chasing ghosts, or what, Little Six?' Mother yelled from the room. 'I've been looking for you all day. Do you know how much work there is to do around here?'

I walked into the room and greeted her warmly. She was straightening up the bottles and cans under the bed, and acted as if she hadn't even heard me. Then she stood up and gave me a strange, cold look, one that said: I knew that as soon as that one came home, there'd be trouble. You think I can't guess what you two have been talking about?

Ignoring her silent response, I asked how Second Sister was getting along.

She said that Second Sister's child had diarrhoea, so she hadn't been able to burn incense, as she'd planned: I knew she was lying. She'd gone across the river to take care of things she didn't want anyone else to know about.

After getting a drink of water, I carried my books up to the attic, where Big Sister was lying on the bed, having apparently just come in. Strands of hair were still stuck to her recently washed face. She laughed when she saw the look of surprise on my face. 'You're the easiest person to trick I know.'

'Go ahead, trick me,' I said as I sat on the bed, without anger.

Her mood changed abruptly. 'This family,' she grumbled. 'You can't wait till I'm gone. I know you all think I'm in the way.' She said she'd be leaving in a day or two, but would be back before long, and then for good. She wasn't going to spend the rest of her cursed life in that stupid remote mountainous corner.

It was afternoon, at least I think it was. Time had ceased to exist for me that day; I wasn't even sure I still existed. My head and my heart were submerged in breathless ecstasy, a feeling I'd never experienced before.

Someone downstairs was calling for Big Sister. She got up to see who it was, then came back and said she had to go out.

'Are you leaving?' I asked inattentively.

'Just for a while. Don't worry, I'm not going to leave today.' She patted me on the head, as if the thought of her leaving were too much for me.

I walked over to the landing. Big Sister was laughing and talking with some man as they walked out of the compound. She was putting on a show for us and for the neighbours. Her companion was tall, like a basketball player. Big Sister's in love again, I was thinking. She'd carry out her promise to leave the coal district where she lived and return to the city, even as a beggar, if she had to.

Fourth Sister came up to the attic, clearly unhappy. 'What do you think you're doing up here? Get downstairs and dump the stove ashes.' She and Dehua were at it again, and she was taking her anger out on me.

'Who's that guy?' I asked her.

'What guy? Oh, him, he and Big Sister were in the countryside together.'

'Is that why she came home, to look him up?'

'How did you know?'

'Just a guess,' I said as I walked downstairs. I had to admire Big Sister. She'd found what she was looking for.

199

She'd talked about him before. They were old acquaintances, maybe a little more than that. That time she'd taken me along to look up a schoolmate was to help her find him. His former wife was half Japanese. In 1953, all Japanese married to Chinese were forced to leave the country, and not permitted to take their children with them. When two policemen showed up at their door to take the Japanese woman away, she refused to go with them, and her husband blocked their way. They had three daughters, one of whom held on to her arm, while the other two wrapped their arms around her legs. Her tears flowed in an endless stream. High School Avenue had never witnessed a more heart-breaking scene.

After the Japanese woman had been taken away, the family was victimized in every political movement that came along. The husband was invariably grilled over why he had become a 'traitor', and his children were cursed on the street as 'Jap brats'. Well, the tall fellow married one of the mixed-blood daughters, and often had to defend his choice with his fists. When that turned to knives, he was sent to a labour-reform camp. Misery dogged the couple for years, until the 1970s, when Sino-Japanese relations turned from hostility to friendship, and life improved dramatically for anyone with overseas connections. Now that his half-Japanese wife's worth had skyrocketed, she left him, and all that remained was for them to sign the divorce papers.

Big Sister came home late that night. 'You're quite a couple,' I said. 'First prize in the divorce contest.'

'Who'd want me, with all those kids of mine?'

Not wanting to say any more on the subject, she began humming a Sichuan folk song in her sweet, deep voice. She didn't give a damn about men, she said. There isn't a good one in the lot. She was probably seeing several men at the time. She wasn't happy unless she was in some sort of jam.

2

I don't think I'd ever slept as soundly as I did that night. When I finally got up late the next morning, reluctantly, I was alone in the attic. Uncharacteristically, I looked at myself in the mirror before getting out of bed. It wasn't the same old me; I'd changed, especially my eyes: the perennial look of fright had been replaced by a serene lustre. I was pleased with what I saw. Mother and Big Sister had noticed something different about me the day before and must have wondered why I seemed so happy. My infatuation with mirrors began that morning; their tiny images became my world, a place where unhappiness was forbidden entry. I walked around in it, passing through fog and rain, stopping from time to time to look at the images of familiar people and places.

Someone was beating his child in the street across the ditch, running after him with murderous intent: 'Go ahead, run, run all you want. Just see if I don't chop off those dog-turd legs of yours!' A man's harsh shouts poured in through the skylight. The boy, who was always running off to the city centre, had been caught again. He'd be chained to his bed and starved for three or four days, until, with nearly his last breath, he'd beg for mercy.

But sooner or later he'd run off again. I had no idea where that strange little boy thought he was going.

Only a few days after their decision to marry, Dehua had stopped coming home, and on those rare occasions when he did, he reeked of alcohol. After work, he and some of his buddies at the factory would start drinking and playing poker. He completely ignored Fourth Sister, who wept but got no sympathy from him. She bored him, he said, and she responded by taunting him: The last thing your pretty schoolmates want is a man with a marriage certificate in his pocket. That was the last straw: he turned on his heels and walked out, moving in with a co-worker. He not only stayed away from our house, but his parents' house as well.

Big Sister told Fourth Sister to follow her example and get another man, but she said she didn't have the guts to drop one man and take up with another. Unable to live without Dehua, she begged Big Sister to talk him into coming home.

The two of them left the house just as I came down from the attic. At lunchtime, Father said we didn't have to wait for Mother, since she'd left early that morning to go into the city centre and take care of Second Sister's sick child. 'She won't be back until after dinner,' he said. 'It's just the three of us today.'

Something was preying on Father's mind, and his back was more hunched than ever. When he told Fifth Brother to see if the fishing rod and net could be repaired, he was told that Third Brother had taken them away a long time ago. Father's brow creased in a frown as he packed tobacco into his pipe and, without lighting it, walked slowly out of the compound. He didn't say where he was going, and I didn't ask. Maybe the riverbank, maybe not. By now, everyone in the family had begun doing things without telling anyone else.

3

The sudden turn in my life appeared on my way to school. It was fated to appear, sooner or later it had to, but if I hadn't decided to rush headlong into it, it would have been delayed for quite a while.

When I crossed the street, the school gate was nearly deserted. It was quieter than normal, which is why I was able to spot the man who was always following me; he was standing next to the wall about twenty paces from the gate. It was him, all right. The minute he saw me, he scurried into a nearby lane like a scared rabbit.

I don't recall if it was a school day or not. A single thought occupied me: I had to see the history teacher again. Even the great mystery of my life – the events surrounding my birth –

had gone into hiding over the past two days. Now it suddenly resurfaced. After everything that had happened in recent days, from all that Big Sister had told me up to my first experience with love, I was no longer willing to await passively whatever fate had in store for me.

Once again I didn't get a good look at the man. His features flashed into my mind for a mere second, long enough for me to pick him out in a crowd, but not long enough to describe him. Then all of a sudden, remembering what Big Sister had told me, the pieces all fell together. I didn't have to pursue him, after all. I turned and headed home.

The sky was crimson, as it always was at dawn and dusk; houses and hills, near and far, looked fresh and bright. I walked in that light, my eyes unfocused, taking in this moment of extraordinary colour.

I strode into Compound Six. Mother was sitting in the hall in front of our door. Holding a fan, but not using it, she sat calmly, as if she'd been waiting for me.

4

I swaggered past Mother without looking at her. If she wanted to talk, it was up to her.

A clap of thunder rolled over the roof, promising lightning and rain. I sat at the table without turning on the light. The little bit of light seeping in through the window created a rainbow on the wall, where the clock patiently ticked away the seconds and minutes.

Mother couldn't sit out there for the rest of her life, that I knew. Sure enough, she pushed open the door, walked in, and sat on the edge of the bed. 'You wouldn't let them tell me anything, so now you have to,' I said.

She sat there looking at me, something she'd never done before; normally she was either yelling at me or was busy with something, or lay in bed exhausted, too tired even to open her eyes. Old as I was, this was the first real chance I'd ever had to talk with her, free of interruptions. My tongue seemed at war with itself, and the words came out garbled; my throat was parched. I longed for some water.

'The man followed me again,' I said through clenched teeth.

'There's nothing to fear,' Mother said matter-of-factly, not excitedly, like the time before.

'It's not fear I'm feeling,' I said. 'It's hatred. I hate everything and everyone, including you. I can't take it any more.'

The muscles in Mother's face twitched. She said she knew. 'Nobody's going to harm you while I'm looking after you. Especially not him.'

'It's a little late to be saying that,' I said. 'I've grown up without a mother, for all intents and purposes. Why should I believe you now?'

She stood up, but sat down again. 'Listen to me, Little Six.'

People who have gone hungry can never forget what it was like. Mother said I was the only one who had no such memory, because I went hungry in her belly. In the late 1950s and early 1960s, they nearly went mad from hunger. There were times when they went to bed at night without dinner, then got up in the morning and started thinking of ways to fool their stomachs. Then one day the government announced that Sichuan ration coupons were null and void, turning the coupons she'd worked so hard to save into worthless paper. She was so upset she saw stars.

Then a telegram arrived, informing her that Father had had an accident. The ship took him three hundred kilometres away and dumped him in a hospital in Luzhou. Taking Fourth Sister with her, Mother boarded a ship heading upriver, all the way to Luzhou. When she saw how gaunt Father was, she didn't have the heart to tell him that Third Aunt had died or that Great Aunt, who lived in the Zhong County countryside, had starved to death. She also withheld the news that Third Brother had been caught up in a whirlpool and would have died if a passing sailor hadn't jumped in and saved him, and the fact that the children were so hungry they'd have gone out to steal food if she hadn't stopped them.

When Mother turned around to dry her eyes, Father pulled Fourth Sister up close and asked her what she'd like to eat. Meat, some eggs, an apple, an oil fritter, and some hard candy, she said.

Father took out the little bit of money left over from his wages and told Mother to get Fourth Sister something to eat.

Out on the street, Fourth Sister was about to take a bite out of the flatcake Mother had bought when a white-haired old woman snatched it out of her hand, shoved it down the front of her jacket, and wrapped her arms around her shoulders, lowering her head as if prepared to protect the flatcake with her life. She shrank into herself, with the cold wind whistling around her, sneaking a look at Fourth Sister from time to time; wrinkles on her face and neck folded down over her collar like coiled rope. The food wasn't for her, that was clear. It was meant for children at home. The ferocity of the mugging didn't scare Fourth Sister as much as the old woman's suicidal determination to hold on to her booty, and she started crying.

Mother took her hand and walked off.

Forced to leave Father in the Luzhou hospital, they returned to Chongqing alone. With five hungry mouths to feed, Mother went back to work as a coolie labourer. One day, when she was carrying sand for a textile mill, she met one of our neighbours, Spectacled Wang, a fat woman who was in charge of the scales and was single-mindedly seeking admission into the Party. She hoped to get it by making life miserable for Mother. As she sat behind the scale, she insisted that each load weigh a hundred kilos. Mother was so weakened by hunger that Big Sister and Third Brother had to share her load until just before they reached the scale, where they dumped their sand into her baskets and tamped it down tight. Wobbling under the weight, she sprained her ankle, but hobbled up to the scale, where the load weighed in at only ninety-eight kilos.

Spectacled Wang told her she'd only get paid if the load weighed a full hundred kilos, and confiscated her work permit on the spot. Holding her anger in check, Mother said, 'We don't rob and we don't steal. We live by the sweat of our brow, so please let me keep hauling sand.' Spectacled Wang replied by dumping the sand on the ground and stamping all over Mother's baskets.

A young bookkeeper from a nearby plastics factory who heard the commotion came out just in time to see Mother being bullied, and walked over to help out. Spectacled Wang, who knew the man, shouted to him, 'Young Sun, don't you dare come to the aid of a reactionary's wife!' Rather than argue with her, he helped Mother, whose ankle was already badly swollen, make the trip home, where she collapsed as soon as she was in the door.

He was ten years younger than Mother, who was thirty-four at the time, and unmarried. His stepfather had owned a small business in town, with two workshops, where he made ox-horn combs. After Liberation it was nationalized into a joint state—private concern, and his capital was funnelled into a South Bank factory that manufactured plastic household articles. Even though his 'fixed profit' was barely more than his employees' wages, he was still labelled a Capitalist. After graduating from high school, Sun was assigned to the factory as an 'apprentice', but his class status was anything but clear: somewhere between a Capitalist Representative and a petty functionary. As the person responsible for preparing the daily work schedules for the coolie labour teams and reporting to the cadre in charge, he sweated much less than the labourers, of course, but he was a diligent worker. After finding some ointment to stop the pain in Mother's ankle, he did some housework and watched the kids for her.

Once her ankle had healed, Mother went to work as a

coolie labourer in Sun's plastic factory. Once, when carrying asbestos plates across the river, she missed the ferry and had to wait for the next; he met the ferry and helped her with her load.

He told her that he was the eldest child of a father who had died when he was two years old. His mother, who was working in the Sun home, married the recently widowed head of the household, who adopted him as his own son. He changed his name to Sun. His mother had five more children, but he always felt like an outsider in the family, and missed having a big sister.

'If you don't mind,' Mother said, 'you can treat me as your big sister.'

When she was carrying cement up the hill during her menstrual period one day, Mother spat up blood and passed out. During the two days she rested at home Sun looked after the kids all by himself; he even saved some of his ration coupons and, at considerable risk to himself, stole steamed buns from the factory canteen for the kids, who had known little but hunger for over two years. Now, finally, they were given the relief they needed to stave off the sort of maladies that would otherwise affect them for the rest of their lives.

When he bought provisions for the factory workers, he held back five kilos of rice for the family, something that, under other circumstances, he would never do. That much rice was like manna from heaven, and the kids ate well for at least a week. He was more like a brother to her than her real brothers; he did all the heavy work around the house, from hauling water and chopping wood to repairing the leaky roof. And when he played his harmonica for the kids, there was laughter in the house. He favoured Sichuan operas, and since Mother liked listening to them, she sang along with him. Still a young woman, she nonetheless had trouble believing that such pleasant sounds could come from her throat. No longer did she come home from work exhausted, nor did she so easily lose her temper with her children.

'You'd look different with a perm,' he said one day when he saw an old photo of her. He told her he had some unused permanent solution at home.

A permanent wave, that was ages ago, back when she was a newlywed, one of those rare periods of happiness in her life. In the desperate days of hunger and deprivation that followed, she had even forgotten what she looked like. Now he had returned all this to her, as if by magic. He was the first man ever to do her hair. His fingers were nimble, his work expert. The lamp cast a dim light, as a fine drizzle fell outside.

With Father away on his ship, and no letters, Mother had been alone for so long she all but forgot what it was like to have a man around the house. Now this 'younger brother' reminded her that she was a woman, and powerful desires and yearnings for love resurfaced in her heart. Just how it happened she wasn't sure. He was standing behind her, and she realized that their bodies were touching. The brief contact frightened and excited them. With the children away, the house was empty, and so was the bed. They were powerless to prevent the inevitable, and in the vast emptiness of the room their bodies were joined.

Soon after they finished their not at all unhurried love-making, there was a sound at the door, and the children returned. It all seemed predestined, prearranged somehow.

5

The very bed we were sitting on at this moment! As Mother recalled her past, she was not the thirty-four-year-old youthful woman of those days, but the one I was used to seeing: a worn-out retired labourer, old before her time.

What this all meant was that she was pregnant with the child of a man who wasn't her husband. Me, an illegitimate child! I should have guessed when I heard words like 'daughter of a slut' and 'bastard', which people hurled at each other but really directed at me. The signs were all there, I just hadn't recognized them. An unconscious fear, I suppose.

'That was at the height of the famine.' When she talked about this man, Mother was a different person, a stranger. No longer shrill and impatient, her tone was uncommonly gentle; she didn't even raise her voice as she passionately defended herself. 'You don't know what a shameful act that is in the eyes of the world. That's why I couldn't tell you. Back in 1961, I didn't know how the family would survive. He supported us, like a messenger from heaven. Whether you want to admit it or not, we owe our survival to that good and decent man.'

Mother said she didn't want to have the child. Not only would it be an awkward addition to the family, but with one more mouth to feed in the midst of a famine, life would be even harder. So to end her pregnancy she took on the hardest jobs, carrying heavy loads up and down the hills; but through it all, the child held on as if taking root in her belly. So she decided to have an abortion. Sun objected, but Mother was dead-set against having the child. Why subject a 'love-child' to lifelong disgrace and humiliation? After arguing back and forth, they finally agreed to draw divination lots at the Temple of the Arhats. The child's fate would rest on the results: up lot or down lot.

'What if it's a middle lot?' Mother asked him.

'It's the same as up,' he said.

'But we give it away,' Mother said.

It was a down lot, to their surprise and chagrin. They agreed to disregard the results. 'We can't just throw a life away,' he said. 'It's our child.' Yes, how could they let divination lots determine the fate of an unborn child? Drawn by two people, the lot could not represent the wish of the Buddha, who responded to the heart of one person only. But in this case, whose?

The divination lot had probably been drawn by me, for I had no desire to be born.

As Mother's belly swelled, they kept delaying a decision.

Then one night Big Sister got up to relieve herself, and when she was finished, she went downstairs to get a drink of water. She quietly slipped the bolt of the bedroom from the outside.

Still half asleep, she saw a pair of men's shoes at the head of Mother's bed, and assumed Father had come home. Papa, she said, startling Sun, who jumped out of bed, threw on his clothes, and ran into the courtyard. Lights snapped on in the rooms of our neighbours, who made a terrible fuss. Sixteen at the time, Big Sister had already been seen taking walks with a boy, for which she'd been criticized at school and at home, where she and Mother had had a terrible fight. To make matters worse, she was angry with Mother for not taking her to see her real father, who, as far as she knew, had recently starved to death in a labour-reform camp. She could never forgive her; in her eyes, Mother was the cause of everything miserable in her life. She called Mother a whore.

This so enraged Mother that she ordered her daughter out of the house.

Ignoring her, Big Sister picked up the meat cleaver, not to kill either of them, but to frighten Mother, who tried to grab it out of her hand. In the struggle, Big Sister was cut on the arm, which bled profusely. The other four kids were scared witless, especially Fifth Brother, who was only a baby. There was no sleep that night for the neighbours, who were ready to summon the neighbourhood policeman to 'educate' Mother. Seeing the seriousness of the situation, Big Sister clammed up. This is our business, Second Sister said, and I need my sleep. She slammed the door on the crowd.

From then on, if Big Sister was home when Sun came over, she turned her back and hurled curses at him over her shoulder. For a while he pretended he hadn't heard. Then he began leaving as soon as she walked in the door. Caught in the middle between Sun and her eldest daughter, Mother didn't know what to do.

Just the sight of her mother's protruding belly threw Big Sister into a rage, and when she heard that Father was on his way home, she ran down to the river to be the first to give him the news that led to the terrible row.

For the second time, Mother decided to terminate the pregnancy and bring the situation to an end.

But to her astonishment, Father objected, arguing that the sins of the parents shouldn't spell doom for the child, who was approaching full term. In Mother's view, he wanted to keep the child as a weapon to subjugate her, a thought that stiffened her spine: I'll have this child, and we'll see what you do about it later. For the second time, she changed her mind about going to the hospital.

Father's homecoming did not lessen the enmity between mother and daughter; their arguments actually got nastier. Big Sister even started talking to the neighbours about what was going on, transforming Mother into the neighbourhood's most infamous woman: not only had she had an adulterous affair, she was pregnant and actually planned to have the little bastard.

All this occurred just as the municipal government launched a 'Communist New Morality' campaign. Since the morals of South Bank residents were notoriously un-Communistic, our slum area became a primary target of the campaign. Under the urging and coercion of the Neighbour-hood Committee, Father took Sun to court, charging him with seducing his wife, trying to break up the family, and violating the one husband–one wife constitutional statute.

'You were born by then,' Mother said, 'and that bunch of meddlers wanted to give Sun custody, then throw him in jail and make his mother responsible for your upbringing. You and I had reached the end of the line.'

FIFTEEN

1

Before I was a month old, Mother had to go back to work, and the job of taking care of me fell to my nearly blind father. He had the right to cripple or smother or crush me, as so many people do with their own daughters, and all it would take was a claim that it was an accident. But he didn't. I weighed only two kilos at birth, a bag of bones under a mass of wrinkled skin, with two big round eyes. With six children to look after, Father often had to leave me untended and alone on the bed. Big Sister was always pinching me to make me cry. My cries were shrill but not particularly loud, my tears seemingly endless; my fists were buried in my eyes, most of the time. Fifth Brother, who was only four at the time, and ignorant of the adults' resentment, played with me when his brothers and sisters weren't around.

When I was still in swaddling clothes, Mother took me to the courthouse, where she handed me first to my father, then to my natural father. Our gossipy neighbours got a big kick out of that; always eager to blow things out of proportion, when there was a real scandal, they could be counted on to add plenty of fuel to the fire. And I was the prop in this particular farce, an ugly, beat-up ball anyone could kick around at will.

'In other words, after I was born, all any of you could think about was how to get rid of me, right?' This was all I asked, and it was more out of surprise than of anger.

'Don't say that,' Mother said. 'Your father's a good, kind-hearted man. Before the court case was settled, he decided to keep you, after all. Sun, who wanted you, too, was willing to accept the consequences.'

After helping Father write the complaint, Big Sister was his official witness in court, where he began to have second thoughts. Mother denied that Sun had seduced her, and took all the blame, saying she should be found guilty of any crime, not he.

Sun apologized to Father, a man he'd never met, and told the court that he'd pay for the child's upbringing, whether or not Mother asked for a divorce. And Father, who hadn't wanted to go to court in the first place, withdrew his complaint. Seeing that the case would not go forward, the court referred it to mediation.

Back home, Father said he shouldn't have listened to people who urged him to file charges, and it was up to Mother to choose. He'd let her go to Sun if she wanted, and she could take their daughter along with her; he'd stay at home with the other kids. Maybe he was just trying to impress her by making a show of his generosity, but Mother was moved anyway. She wanted to leave, but couldn't bring herself to do it; abandoning her five children was simply too much for her, and Father's failed eyesight would keep him off the ship from now on. The family needed her. This, however, would mean she'd have to give up Sun and not permit him to see their child, two unbearable consequences.

Knowing the agony Mother was experiencing, Sun was disconsolate. But what choice did they have?

The lights were off in the darkened room, and I couldn't see Mother's face. But I knew she was crying, and her sobs made talking all but impossible. But what could I do? Listening to her talk about the shameful circumstances of my birth gave rise to anger and loathing, and I was determined to hold on to those emotions.

Mother and I were sitting there speechless when the smokestack at the cigarette plant blew off a load of steam with a strange rumbling noise that nearly rocked nearby frame houses off their foundations. This happened several times a day, even at midnight. We were used to it and didn't let it bother us most of the time; but now it seemed to be an intentional impediment to Mother's recollections.

The way things were, all they could do was find a family that wanted me. First they sent me to a workmate of Mother's at a textile mill.

'They had two sons,' Mother said, 'but no daughters. And they were better off than we were. You'd have enough to eat, and since people wouldn't know you were illegitimate, no one would pick on you. At the very least, there wouldn't be a bunch of older siblings who resented you for taking food out of their mouths. And without you around, they'd treat me better, be more obedient, with fewer arguments.'

I seemed to recall a woman who changed my diapers at night – I was a bed-wetter – and who did indeed treat me better than Mother did.

'No, that didn't happen till later. The woman missed you after you'd left and took you home with her for a few days,' said Mother. 'But you were only six months old when you actually went to live with her. Not long after that, her husband was arrested, for embezzlement, they said. During the famine years people did whatever they could to put food on the table, and now the authorities did whatever they had to do to catch the culprits. If you got away with something, well and good, and if you could save yourself by framing someone else, that's what you did.' Whatever the case, someone snitched on him and he was sentenced to three years in a labour-reform camp. And since his wife couldn't keep me any longer, Mother had to bring me home.

I don't think she ever went so far as to leave me by the side of the road, but she must have given me to one family after another, maybe even an orphanage. But for one reason or another, I always wound up back in this family, where, eventually, I stayed, whether they liked it or not.

I vaguely remember an occasion when I was very young.

Missing Mother, I went to High School Avenue to wait for her on her day off, but got lost on the way. I sat on a stone step where anyone passing by could see me, not daring to cry, for fear that someone would think I was a lost child and kidnap me. I sat there as if nothing were wrong until, finally, Third Brother spotted me and took me home, and complained to Mother, who had taken another road home. I was rewarded by a couple of sound slaps and an earful that lasted all night. Shock replaced the fear of not finding my way home, but I couldn't say a word in my defence, and even if I'd tried, I'd probably have screwed it up. I was home, I had a home to come back to, such as it was, and that was all that counted.

As a child, I'd always shied away from strangers. Just being around someone I didn't know had made me nervous. Nothing changed after I grew up, most likely owing to a childhood fear of losing home.

And yet, the answer to the riddle had been there all along, plain as day, waiting for me to discover it. I guess I was too stupid to look in the right place.

I broke the silence: 'I want to see him.'

Knowing that's exactly what I'd say, Mother calmly stood up.

I huddled against the wall, not knowing what she was going to do. She walked over to the door to make sure no one was listening, then turned and said in a hushed voice, 'It's already arranged. I'll take you into town to see him tomorrow afternoon.'

So, over the past few days, when she'd gone into town, ostensibly to visit Second Sister, in fact she'd been making arrangements for the meeting. By my calculations, it had been at least seventeen or eighteen years since she'd seen my real father. Her hand was shaking so badly when she tried to open the door that it took three attempts to slide the bolt back, and she kept her hand on it, as if lacking the strength to push the door open.

Mother was going to see someone she must have missed terribly for a very long time, but couldn't bear to see, and all for my sake.

2

It must have been after my 'belonging' was decided that they agreed to meet one last time. He lived in an upstairs room in a two-storey frame house on New People's Street on the opposite bank. There they embraced tightly, finding it nearly impossible to let go. The street beyond their window was alive and noisy, as if half the town were on its way to market. A funeral passed, the mourners wailing to heaven amid the popping of firecrackers; a parade of celebrants, accompanied by gongs and drums, was carrying 'Congratulation Letters' to city residents who had 'volunteered' to return to the country-side in answer to the government's call following the famine-caused depletion of manpower in farming villages. But the sounds didn't exist for them, as they were drawn into each other's bodies, swallowed up by their breathing, their naked bodies covered with sweat.

I wonder which corner Mother had put me in.

Try though they might, the climax wouldn't come. It was the first time they hadn't had to worry that one of the children would burst into the room or wake up in the middle of the night; for the first time they didn't have to sneak around, and they never dreamed it would be so hard. When he rolled off her, she gazed at him, the look in her eyes saying: It's over for us.

This was not the first time for them to say: Let's not see each other any more; each time was always going to be the last. This meeting, however, had been a disaster, despite all his careful planning for them to be alone. Whatever romance was left in his soul had been worn away by his legal ordeals. This afternoon went by faster than any of the others.

When they left, they walked one in front of the other, as

usual, so people wouldn't think they were together, stepping on the litter from exploded firecrackers, threading their way through the still open market and continuing on to a Sichuan noodle stand tucked into a side alley and down a few steps.

When the steaming noodles were placed in front of them, they stared at their bowls and ate as if each of them were there alone. The bulb connected by wire to a house on the lane didn't even give off as much light as distant streetlamps, but was bright enough to cast their shadows on the table. Before her noodles were half gone, Mother's tears were flowing into the bowl. 'Don't cry, Sister,' he said. 'I fall apart when you do that.'

'It's nothing,' she said. 'I'll be fine in a minute.'

'You take the girl,' he said. 'Who knows, she may be the one you rely on when you get old. There's no hope for me, and the court won't let me see her before she reaches adulthood. See how much luckier you are than me? At least you come away with a child. Me? I have nothing and nobody. Only shattered dreams.'

He was hoping to cheer her up, but only succeeded in making her feel worse. 'I'm not crying over you,' she said. 'Don't think I can't live without you.' She forced back her tears. 'And you can live without me. As for the little one, she'll survive or she won't, whatever fate decrees. I'll be old soon, but you're still young. Find someone and settle down.'

Getting no response from him, she continued, 'Give me your word that you'll make a good life for yourself.'

He didn't want to cry, since men aren't supposed to do that in public. But he couldn't help himself.

Mother, who was barely literate, knew that the Chinese character for 'endure' was made up of a knife above a heart. To help them both end the relationship decisively, she left her job in the plastics factory and asked a member of the Neighbourhood Committee to help her get a job with a transport team that hired out to a factory on the other side of the mountain. It was so far away, she could only come home at weekends.

After they parted this time, Sun was transferred to a plastics factory near the crematorium at the other end of the city, taking a demotion from minor cadre to worker. His job was to cut asbestos.

Was it the last time they saw each other? I wanted to know.

One day, while she was carrying stones, Mother broke down and cried in front of everyone.

'This isn't the job for you if you can't carry those.'

'Take a break, and the fatigue will soon pass.'

They might as well have saved their breath, because she didn't hear a word of it. She was soaked with sweat – she often said she couldn't remember the last time her clothes were dry around her waist. She ate only two meals a day, and there were often rumblings in her stomach. Insect bites scarred her face. She simply wouldn't let herself listen to the faint sounds of his voice coming to her on the wind: he was saying he missed her, that he wanted to see her, that he needed her, and that he knew she needed him. She refused to listen. If she'd had a weaker constitution, been less resolute, if she hadn't forced herself to be deaf to the sound of his voice, she'd have thrown down her carrying pole and rushed down the hill and across the river with the single-minded determination of a woman in love.

Mother was capable of that, but she knew she didn't have the right to live for herself alone, that her first responsibility was to her sons and daughters. Her hair had begun to fall out, her waist was thickening, her back was getting more bent by the day, and the hump on her shoulder kept growing. She was shocked by how quickly she was ageing and how ugly she'd become. She was fast turning into the mother I had always known.

It wasn't until years later, after I'd taken plenty of knocks in my life, that I was able to patch together this picture that Mother had torn to shreds with cold reason. At the time I was too busy blaming her for just about everything to take time out and try to understand her. All the things she told me still failed to melt the wall of ice between us. Cracked it, maybe, but not enough to bring it down. In fact, it seemed to have even greater reason to remain standing, and there was nothing I could do about it.

3

Most streets in this city are too pitted and steep for bicycles or handcarts, and cars can't negotiate most of the little lanes and alleys. And so a group of labourers known as 'polers' waited patiently with their carrying poles and ropes at crossroads, stations and piers to be hired for odd jobs.

In addition to coolie labourers who sold their sweat as polers, the city was home to an army of idlers and the teahouses that served their needs. Every area had at least one, and on the main streets you could usually count a dozen or more old and reputable establishments. The customers weren't all old men; some youngsters mingled there as well. Once you were inside, the warmth from the steaming teapots was invigorating, and great pleasure awaited customers who cracked melon seeds, peanuts and, most importantly, dried peppers, chatted aimlessly with friends, and, once they had dawdled enough, stood up and stretched, took out their pipes, and walked off slowly.

No matter how poor people from Chongqing might be, they'll always find a way to get their hands on some hot peppers, which they'll eat until their mouth and face are red and puffy; this sort of masochistic pleasure was probably meant to show an unwillingness to knuckle under to fate, or perhaps an indulgence in defying that fate.

Mother and I sat down at a small table in a roadside teahouse in the upper city, and within two minutes, before the tea had even arrived, a lean middle-aged man walked in the door with the light in his face. Tall but somewhat stooped, he headed straight for our table and sat in the chair between Mother and me. I looked at him warily, my heart pounding so hard I saw stars. He had just shaved, and was wearing a clean shirt under a faded high-collar jacket, but none of that could hide his haggard appearance. There was no doubt about it, this was the man who had stalked me all my life.

There was a hopeful smile on his face – he probably wanted to hear me call him Father. But I couldn't say it, I didn't know what to say. I knew I was blushing. Mother didn't even look at me as she shifted to one side to stay clear of the arching water the waiter was pouring expertly from his long-necked pot into the cups. She covered all three cups with lids to let the tea-leaves steep.

No one said a word. He looked at Mother, who returned the look for a moment before getting up and saying she'd be right back. He watched her, an ugly old woman, with a look in his eyes the likes of which I'd never seen before: moist and warm. The father at home had never looked at her that way. The man seemed to relax after she left; he wasn't as stiff and unnatural in front of me as when he'd walked in. Mother's departure actually breathed life into his face.

Someone turned on a transistor radio, and the sounds of a Sichuan opera could be heard – I think it was *Autumn River*, in which a girl from olden times sits restlessly on a ferry boat, chasing after her lover. Just then a young dandy in bell-bottoms and permed hair strolled past the teahouse with his Sanyo boom box, from which emerged a Hong Kong pop song that clashed badly with the heart-breaking high-pitched aria from the local opera. Four customers sitting by the door were playing a game of Pai Gow.

When I looked towards the door the second time, he said, 'Your mother isn't coming back.'

I ignored him and kept my eyes on the entrance.

So we had to leave the teahouse, without so much as sipping our tea. After crossing the street and then the high-way, he took me into a department store and up to the fabric counter. He must have read my mind, knowing that if he asked me what I wanted I wouldn't tell him. So he picked out a blue polyester floral fabric – blue was Mother's favourite colour – thrust it into my hand, and told me to make a blouse out of it, since what I was wearing was so old and worn. It was a hand-me-down from Fourth Sister, something between a blouse and a jacket, shapeless and dull. What he had on wasn't much better. I didn't even thank him, but when I glanced over at him, the smile was gone, replaced, for some strange reason, by a nervous frown.

4

It was a little after four in the afternoon, not yet dinnertime, and most of the restaurants in the area hadn't opened for the evening meal. We passed several before finding a rather fancy place that was open for business. He hesitated for a moment in front of the flashy façade. Once inside, we followed the waiter upstairs.

I sat across from him and listened as he ordered the food: hot and spicy fish in bean sauce, tender bean curd, and shredded beef fried with celery.

When the food came, he hardly touched it, putting most of it into my bowl. I kept shovelling rice into my mouth, but it was hard and undercooked, so I washed it down with the bean-curd broth. Unfortunately, I drank it too fast, and started to choke. He reached out and patted me on the back, and as soon as I stopped coughing I put down my chopsticks.

No matter how closely I studied his face, I saw no resemblance; he was still a stranger. But he was completely focused on me, that much was obvious. So someone in this world actually valued me, wanted me to be happy, wanted to get to know me, wanted to talk to me, piled my plate high with meat and fish, and made sure no one tried to take it away or told me I was eating too much or gave me funny looks; and I had no appetite and couldn't get happy. My mood bounced between amazement and indignation, and my head was churning out strange thoughts that even I didn't understand. But one sentence said it all: There's no way I will recognize you as my father!

He ordered some grain spirit. To boost his courage, perhaps? We were both trembling inside; maybe his blood was in fact flowing through my veins. He took a drink and started talking.

'Today's your birthday.'

'My birthday?' I repeated. I felt like sneering. 'You're too late. My birthday was the 21st of September.'

'On the Twenty-Third Day of the Eighth Month that year, I watched you being born in the hospital,' he said. Obviously, I was counting by the Western solar calendar, while he and Mother went by the traditional lunar calendar. He said that eighteen years earlier the two dates had fallen on the same day, but that this year the lunar date came quite a few days later.

So that's it! The secret is revealed by something you planned, not by my relentless pursuit! You decided to tell me everything on my eighteenth birthday. That's what you had in mind all along! That was how things happened to me!

He'd waited eighteen years for this day, exactly as expected: told he couldn't see me until I was an adult, he'd patiently waited for this day. But maybe Mother had wanted to keep the secret, and only relented when she was convinced that it could no longer be kept from me. I had to admit that I was nervous, too, and apprehensive.

5

Since I seldom went into the city centre, I wondered why there were so many people on the street; it was as if the houses had given up all their occupants. Cars honked non-stop as they threaded their way through hilly streets. Colourful flags and banners fluttered in the wind, bright balloons floated gaily above tall buildings. The streets seemed almost too clean, and some of the houses had recently been whitewashed, with fresh red New Year couplets on their doors. Glittering ribbons made the whole scene unreal somehow. Everyone seemed to be dressed in his or her finest. It was like a festive holiday.

All that afternoon and evening my natural father tried his best to see to my needs and make me feel well-disposed towards him, and I wasn't the least bit grateful. His so-called father's love had come too late; I didn't need it any more. But I didn't stop him from trying, either. 'Want to see a movie?' he asked after we finished eating. 'Your mother says you love books, movies, and good food.'

I nodded without hesitation.

The theatre was showing a double bill, and we entered halfway through the first movie, a Chinese film about the war with the Kuomintang, with artillery shells exploding all over the screen and bugle charges sounding. Machine-gun fire left the ground strewn with enemy soldiers. But the death of any revolutionary soldier was accompanied by several minutes of soul-stirring music and the wails and cries of revenge by his comrades in arms. The second movie was a foreign film about a passenger liner that hit an iceberg and sank in the freezing water. He hardly took his eyes off me long enough to watch the movie. Finally I said I'd seen enough and wanted to go home. He looked at his watch. It's still early, he said, and told me not to worry, that he'd take me to the bus stop, then to the ferry landing, and from there to home. Getting no response from me, he said, 'I thought you wanted to see me.'

'Now I've seen you. Mama's probably waiting for me at home.'

'You're an adult now, so the court can't stop me from seeing you.' His overbearing tone sounded more like an older brother than a father. Now that we'd seen a movie, he insisted on taking me to Loquat Park, the highest spot in the city.

As we stood together in Red Star Pavilion, I could see that he'd done the right thing. There weren't as many people as there'd been in the shops below, and this hilly city looked so different from up here. Houses were lit up in both parts of town, and cars continued driving through the streets, but now only their headlights showed, like fireflies flitting around in the dark to illuminate the rolling hills and the city's skyline. Two parallel rows of lights on the Yangtze River Bridge stretched through the darkness to South Bank, and ships' lights were reflected on the calm waters of the two rivers, shimmering like stage lights when the wind raised ripples on the surface.

6

My natural father told me a great deal that night. I kept my distance from him as I listened, clutching the piece of blue fabric. He, on the other hand, wanted to shorten the distance to be more intimate, although he didn't go so far as to put his arm around me. When we were sitting on a stone bench in a quiet corner, I still kept my distance, repulsed by his attempts to come closer, and before long he gave up the idea. The smell of alcohol on his breath wasn't very strong, and what I detected was his sulphur soap. To be honest, I liked the smell; not pleasant, really, but clean. He'd trimmed his nails for our meeting; his fingers were long and thin, like mine, but the backs of his hands were scarred somewhat. What little hair he had left was a mixture of black and grey. How could he look so old at only forty-three? But his voice was strong and clear, and when I looked away and could only hear his voice, he seemed younger.

After he and Mother parted, he found a peasant girl from a nearby village with the idea of starting a family. Before the wedding, he went to Mother's workplace one last time. She refused to see him, so they talked through the closed door. He gave her a date and place and said he had to see his daughter before leaving the city and moving to the countryside to become a peasant's son-in-law. He left a newly laundered mosquito net and a sack of food at the door.

So Mother put her two-year-old daughter on her back and

climbed the long flight of stone steps above the ferry pier. She saw him standing beside the abandoned cable-car tracks above Heaven's Gate. There he told her he'd found a peasant girl, nothing special, but honest and decent. His meaning was clear: if Mother still had any affection for him, one word from her and he'd call off the marriage. But she said, 'That's good news. I'm happy you're going on with your life.' Then, after thanking him for the mosquito net and the food, she turned to leave. But he took her hand, asking her to come to the house on New People's Road with him.

Mother said no as she untied the strap holding the baby. 'You said you wanted to see your daughter. Well, here she is, look as long as you want. Take her home with you, in fact, then you won't have to ask me to see her again.' She handed him their daughter, turned, and walked off without looking back.

But the baby began to bawl as soon as he put her down on a cable-car tie, shrill, frightened cries. Mama, she called out as she crawled towards Mother. He stood there watching his daughter cry, without doing a thing. In that noisy place, with people all around, and all those ships' horns blaring on the river, Mother heard only her daughter's tiny cries, and rushed back for her.

He smiled as Mother angrily picked her daughter up.

'You see, she doesn't want me. She called out Mama, not Papa. I couldn't take her even if I wanted to,' he said teasingly. He lifted their daughter on to her back, wound the strap around her again, and put a brand-new blue brocade cap with felt lining on her little head. 'Take good care of her. She'll catch cold in this gusty wind,' he said.

'Don't worry,' Mother said. 'No wind can hurt her. Her fate is too coarse and too hard for her to die.'

That was the last time my true parents met. The forlorn sounds of my crying had sealed my fate once and for all. Once again Mother gave up the right to choose, although, in truth, she knew fate had given her no real choices. With me on her back, she walked down the steps to the ferry landing. Since it was the dry season, the river wasn't very wide; the sandy, rocky banks stretched all the way to the horizon. Her feet made deep imprints in the sand, some of which found its way into her shoes. With the going so difficult, she tightened the strap and bent forward, walking into a wind that blew sand in her face and hair. It was the briskest winter in memory, colder than the three years of killing famine, and more desperate than the winter her first husband died of hunger.

All the while, my natural father was standing at the top of the steps, his lanky body taking the full force of the cold wind. But as more and more people rushed past him to catch a bus or get to the ferry landing, he disappeared from view. He was just a young man who had lacked affection in his life, until he met Mother. From her he also earned gratitude for saving her children from starvation. He'd likely never felt important before, or needed; and so had fallen under the spell of love, from which he could not extricate himself.

Who can tell why people love and hate? Love is too personal to be understood by others. Take me, for example. Didn't I fall secretly and inexplicably in love with a man? A love that was illicit and, in the eyes of others, dirty and shameful.

But even I, who never gave a damn about following rules, could not understand my parents' adulterous relationship. When the three of us – Mother, my natural father, and I – were sitting together in the teahouse, it seemed forced, awkward. By bringing me into the world, they had bestowed upon me a life of suffering, for which neither of them would take responsibility.

As we left Loquat Park and walked down the steep stone steps, a burst of fireworks lit up the dark sky, turning the trees and buildings around us into flickering silhouettes. Colourful shooting stars rained down on the city and on our heads, like strange flowers from heaven. The sky was still lit up as we walked to the cable-car station at the crossroads. The sound of exploding fireworks was deafening.

'I don't want you following me any more,' I said. 'I don't want to see you again.' I still couldn't swallow how they had imposed their arrangement on me, keeping me in the dark for all those years.

He never expected to hear something like that, and his face froze. I could see the grief in his eyes, like those passengers in the foreign film, when the realization hit them that they were doomed to go down with the ship.

But I didn't care. I wanted him to give me his word.

With a nod of his head, he agreed, but didn't look at me.

At the ticket window he said he'd see me to the ferry landing. But I said no, I'd go alone, and he knew better than to force the issue. I joined the crowd of boarding passengers, choosing a seat towards the rear and holding on to the blue fabric for dear life. The car's seats all faced upwards, and I could see him standing behind the railing at the ticket collector's booth. When the cable car started sliding slowly down the mountain, he waved. I wanted to wave back, but stopped myself. So as not to see him or let him see my face, I turned to look at the clutter of wooden shacks halfway up the mountain, where house lights blinked and sputtered, as if about to die out. The car reached the bottom in no time. The exit was directly opposite the city's main train station, which swarmed with people, a noisy, boiling cauldron of humanity.

Mother was still awake, waiting up for me. When she opened the door, she breathed a sigh of relief and went back to bed. Father's shoes were under the bed; he was facing the wall, and I was tempted to go to him. I thought of all those hard times we'd gone through together, Father and me, and how I'd longed to throw my arms around him, and feel his arms around me. At least I'd like to have a good look at him; I couldn't recall ever studying his face the way a daughter ought to.

The bed creaked as Mother rolled over. Father must have

been fast asleep. I went out into the hall to wash quietly, and when I returned from dumping the water in the courtyard, Mother was sitting up in bed. 'Get some sleep,' she said softly. I walked out of their room, passed through the hall and went up to the attic.

SIXTEEN

1

I was long in the habit of keeping a diary, writing down things I'd have no interest in reading the following day. In my eyes, keeping a diary is a hobby for the weak and a consolation for the lonely; but each time I put mine aside, I came back to it before long and picked up where I'd left off.

Up in the attic, I noted the meeting with my natural father in two lines: teahouse, restaurant, cinema, Loquat Park, cable car, ferry, home, bed.

This cryptic sort of entry came quite naturally, not because so many people had suffered, even died, as a result of 'reactionary' diary entries, but because I had decided my family mustn't know about this meeting. With our crowded living conditions, privacy was impossible. What would Father have thought if he'd known? What about my brothers and sisters? And what would Mother have thought if she'd known how I treated him?

Better to avoid the subject. Besides, I'd just as soon forget the details anyway.

When I saw Father the next morning, I didn't show any emotion or say anything to him, my fleeting impulse of the night before long gone. Sleep is such a strange process, like death and rebirth, filtering out pain and suffering and drying up all desire and emotion. I took the blue fabric downstairs and handed it to Mother, then went about my own business. With all my brothers and sisters home, we were stepping all over each other. Just about every family in the compound had relatives visiting, and the noise level was especially high. I could see that Mother was on edge, and it was some time before she and I had a chance to be alone in our room. 'I'll take you to Stonebridge Square when I've got a minute,' she said, 'and have a blouse made from that blue fabric.'

'He bought that for you.'

'You can't fool me, I know better.'

I ignored her and concentrated on peeling some garlic.

'Did he treat you all right?' When talking about my natural father, she invariably used 'he' or 'him'. She surely knew how he treated me, and was only asking to get me to acknowledge him as my father. At long last she had someone with whom she could talk about the man she'd loved. She looked at me with eager anticipation, waiting for my answer.

'So so,' I said with a sort of dismissive nonchalance. Why not? Between a father who supplied the sperm and one who raised me from childhood, I knew who was more important.

Mother tried to look busy for a while, then said she'd changed her mind about taking me to a tailor shop, since it would be too expensive and the quality probably not all that high. She snapped on the light, cleared the tabletop, and laid out the fabric, then sprayed water on it. After fetching the scissors, a tape measure, and some chalk, she found that the table was too small, so she moved the fabric over to the bed.

After taking my measurements, she asked if I preferred a blouse or a dust jacket to wear under my padded blouse. Summer had already passed, so before I had a chance to answer, she said she'd make me a dust jacket for the coming winter. She was back to her old self, a mother to whom my opinion was irrelevant.

She talked as she marked the material with chalk. 'You probably don't know,' she said, 'that he pledged in court to give eighteen yuan a month for child support, which he did every month up till your eighteenth birthday, without fail. Once Second Sister started teaching, he sent the money to her. But her fellow teachers were just as nosy as the people in this compound, always wanting to know where the money came from. So to avoid trouble, he began sending it to his mother – your paternal grandmother – and I crossed the river to pick it up. She's a good, decent woman. Every time I went there for the money, she had me stay for lunch. She said her son was born under an unlucky star, a man who was denied even his own daughter. And what city woman would want to marry a man as poor as he was? Which is why he had to marry into a peasant family.' Mother hadn't seen him during all those years, but she learned a thing or two about his life from my grandmother. It must have nearly driven her mad to be living so near to him, yet force herself to pretend he didn't even exist.

'He never asked to see you, because he knew that an illegitimate child was little more than a monster in the eyes of most people,' Mother said. 'This hypocritical society of ours wouldn't give you a moment's peace, nor be moved by your tears.'

When I didn't respond, she continued, 'Little Six, you have no idea how wretched a life he's lived. Yet those eighteen yuan every month not only kept you alive, they were a great help to the whole family.'

2

Then shouldn't my tuition be part of that? I thought but stopped short of saying.

I was not moved by Mother's words. As my natural father it was his duty to raise me. You used the money he gave you without ever telling me, I complained inwardly. I may have lived in this house with you, day and night, for all these years, but this isn't my family. I don't belong here, and I'll never trust any of you again.

Mother told me many things about my natural father: his peasant wife, his two sons – half-brothers I'd never met – my grandmother, and more. I certainly didn't like the idea of these people appearing uninvited into my life, which was chaotic enough already.

He had lived all this time in the factory workers' dormitory, going home once every week or two. He was a good father, and a good husband. Not only did he live a frugal life, he even brought garbage from the factory cafeteria home to feed the pigs. First he put it into plastic bags to keep it from spilling, then into buckets, and stood on the roadside trying to hitch a ride home; sometimes he waited for hours before a kind-hearted trucker picked him up, and sometimes all he got for his troubles were angry curses: 'Get lost, you prick, you and your filthy droppings!' On those days, he'd walk the seven miles home.

He did all the field work, from tilling the soil to seeding and fertilizing. His sons went out to forage hog-grass, which he and his wife chopped up and mixed in with the swill he brought home. The pigs gobbled it up, but grew slowly. At the end of the year, when they were fat enough to take to the slaughterhouse, the money earned from the sale would have to get the family through the coming year, including tuition and clothes for the two boys. Even late at night he could often be found by the pond washing vegetables to take to market the next morning and sell for some small change.

It wasn't until two years earlier that Mother had learned how hard his life had been, and she stopped going to pick up the child-support money from my grandmother. 'In earlier days, if he wore something halfway decent, he'd show it off proudly and ask me if he looked like a young tycoon. I'd laugh at his false vanity and remind him that the days of tycoons were long past,' Mother said sadly. 'But bad as things got, he never let a month go by without sending the eighteen yuan, which was nearly half his wages!'

'I don't believe you,' I said. 'I don't believe any of you.' What I meant was: No matter how good a man he may have been, you had no right to feel that much concern over somebody else's husband and father. You'd never find me doing that. I have room in my heart only for the father I've known all these years, the one who treats me better than you or anyone else in the family. At this point, I said bluntly, 'You should put him out of your thoughts altogether. Nothing about that man has a thing to do with our family.'

That caught Mother by surprise, and it took her a moment to respond. 'So you hate him, too, Little Six. I thought I was the only one you hated.'

She crumpled the sleeve she'd cut out of the cloth and sat down hard on the bed, shaking her head in frustration.

3

I went with Big Sister to the landing, where we stood on a stone ledge to wait for the ferry. 'I want to ask you something,' she said, 'and you have to answer me. Did Mama take you to see that Sun fellow?'

That caught me off guard.

'I knew it. Both of you away from home at the same time, then you come home with some nice new fabric – it had to be. For the better part of twenty years, she managed to stay away from him, but in the long run, she couldn't forget him.' She laughed smugly. 'Well, how's he doing?'

'I'm the one who wanted to see him,' I said casually. 'He's married and has children.'

'He must still hate me for what happened back then.'

'He didn't mention you.'

Big Sister had a basket strapped to her back. In it she had packed some things she wanted for herself. She always came home empty-handed and left with as much as she could carry. It's a wonder there was anything left after her visits. She adjusted the straps over her shoulders and stared at me. 'You don't need to speak up for him. Don't you ever forget that you grew up in this family. None of that living off one and supporting another. Without us you'd have been dead a long time ago. When you were two, you had a huge running sore on your belly, and the only reason you didn't die from it is that Father and Second Sister took care of you.'

Big Sister's eldest daughter was only six years younger than me, too big for me to hold; but I tried anyway, just to please Big Sister. She snatched her out of my arms, figuring I had bad intentions. Even at her young age, this niece of mine knew exactly where I stood in the family, and if she knocked over a broom or broke a bowl or something, she blamed me for it. Since her grandparents invariably believed her, I was the one who was punished.

'Don't give me that! Even your daughter knows she can step all over me,' I said, not caring about sparing her feelings. 'Don't forget that Mother sold her own blood to buy chickens to feed you after you had your baby.'

'That's what a family's all about. The old raise the young, then the young look after the old. Don't you know that?' She had raised her voice, but when she saw the glum look on my face, she stopped. I was never one intentionally to antagonize anyone, and when people lost their tempers with me, I normally just clammed up. It took a lot to get me to talk back.

The ferry set out from the opposite bank. The water had receded a bit, but only enough to expose a few stone steps; most of the sandy bank was still underwater.

She took the bag I was carrying for her, but told me to walk her down to the landing, where the passengers were disembarking; I could leave once she was on board, she said, then turned the conversation back to herself. As soon as she got home, she was going to demand her share of property from her second husband, even if it was only a cooking pot or a ricebowl. She'd made up her mind she was going to put up a fight this time.

I was sick of Big Sister's 'fights', and wanted to get her to change her mind. But she never gave me the chance. She said she was going to become an illegal resident in town. 'Don't you worry,' she said, taking my hand. 'You and I are in the

Hong Ying's real father's grave,
which has no tomb

Hong Ying's real father,
1986, shortly before
his death

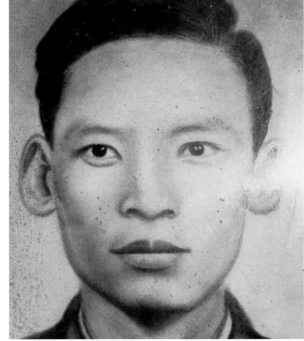

Red Guards' graveyard
in Chongqing, today

Hong Ying, aged
twenty-seven, at
the Chongqing
family house

Hong Ying at the Lu Xun Literature Academy, Beijing, 1989

Hong Ying in Tian'anmen Square, 1989

same boat in this family. We have to stick together. I won't tell your secrets to anybody, and you won't tell them mine. Right?'

4

I mulled over what Big Sister had said on the road home. While there were similarities in our situations, in reality they were quite different. But before I could think things through clearly, I was called out that night by Fourth Sister and taken to an open spot not far from Compound Six. When we got there I was surprised to find that everyone except my parents and Big Sister was there: all my brothers and sisters and their wives and husbands. Their faces were blurry in the murky light from nearby streetlamps, but I could see they were in an angry mood.

As I sat down on a low stool, it was like being back at school, when I'd been the lonely target of classroom attacks, like those Cultural Revolution criticism sessions where the masses stand up and hurl accusations at some poor miscreant, but I was surrounded by my family. What had I done?

Third Brother, the eldest son, was the first to speak, and it was clear that before she'd left, Big Sister had sold me out. She'd told them everything, including the questions I'd asked about the family, plus some of her own conjectures. What she'd said before boarding the ferry represented not just her views, but those of everyone else as well. I should have known she was one of those people who's never happy unless she's stirring things up: not until the Communist realm, her own life and this family were in a state of constant chaos, would she be content.

'Make your choice. Which family do you want?'

'You ate our food and wore our clothes, you even took food right out of our mouths. You can leave if you want, but if you do, we expect you to pay back for all those years in our house, including rent, medical expenses, and tuition.'

'We never did anything to hurt you, and you still had the guts to go and see that man. How we suffered because of you, carrying the shame all these years.'

'We raised you, and now that you're big enough to make a living on your own, you think you can just take off, is that it?'

Second Sister, who hadn't said anything up to this point, spoke up: 'Let's hear what she has to say.'

'What am I supposed to say?' I pretended I didn't know what was going on, which was how I'd dealt with the criticism at school. But this time my head really wasn't working. Even if every charge was unfounded, I didn't know how to say so.

'Does he want you to leave our home and go with him?'

'Say something!'

I tried to stand up, but Third Brother pushed me back down on the stool. They weren't going to let me go until this was cleared up. I watched some kids crossing the street with a ball.

I didn't like this family, but I didn't like other families either. I was a girl without a family. I didn't care who owed whom, I just wanted to be left alone. But I turned to face them. 'I'm not leaving this home,' I said with unmistakable clarity. 'And don't think you can drive me away. This is the only home I've got.'

That really knocked them for a loop. They didn't know what to say. They had expected me to bitch and moan about who owed whom around here, never entertaining the thought that I had no intention of breaking the bonds between me and the family. And I didn't bring up all the money my natural father had paid, even though they talked about money all the time. People are funny: they can't forget the wrongs they've suffered and can't remember the favours they've received. But I could agree that they had every right to blame me for some of their suffering, since they'd gone hungry during the famine because of me, and couldn't hold their heads up in front of our neighbours because they had a bastard sister at home. They had to slink around like dogs with their tails between their legs. So I preferred to acknowledge the fact that I owed the family an emotional debt I'd never be able to repay.

'OK.' Third Brother finally broke the ice. 'You are not to tell Mama what went on here tonight, or let Papa in on the fact that you know about your parentage. Got that?'

'I got it.' I nodded. 'Why would I want to hurt Papa?'

I felt like shouting, venting my spleen over how badly I'd been treated. But I didn't say anything more; I just sat there staring at them as they walked off mumbling threats. I'd always feared my brothers and sisters, as I'd feared my teachers. I wouldn't talk back to them, I'd let them do what they wanted, and I'd try to stay out of their way, preferring to hide in some corner where they couldn't see me.

After they left, taking their stools with them, I sat there alone; my head was spinning, and a rumbling in my ears sounded like metal bars crashing against each other.

Finally I got to my feet, picked up my stool, and walked slowly towards home. All of a sudden, I threw down the stool and started running, like a little girl, all the way to the steps on High School Avenue, and from there to the weed-covered playground. I ran and I ran, up to the very top of the hill, where it was darker and more deserted than anywhere. Finally, unable to run another step, I stopped and leaned up against a tree trunk to keep from collapsing. The sinister opening of an abandoned air-raid shelter looked out at me. Didn't everyone say that the Kuomintang had buried explosives all over the place? Then that meant that the entire city was a huge, ticking time bomb. Why couldn't it blow up at this very moment? Why couldn't the city just be wiped off the map?

SEVENTEEN

1

For several days after the grilling by my brothers and sisters I was too weak to go to school. I had a headache, a mild fever, and was weak all over. Mother was nicer to me than she'd been before. But I was in no mood to get along with anyone in my family. Their faces were like most of the houses on our street – crooked and twisted. They behaved as if nothing had happened. As for the neighbours, as always, they guffawed over vulgar comments, or fought over nothing, chasing one another up and down the street. But all this fell outside my life; their happiness and anger no longer meant a thing to me. I still had my chores to do around the house, I was ordered around by everyone, but I spent nearly all my free time closeted up in the attic, not wanting to see or be seen by anyone.

On this particular day I was carrying a basket of garbage to dump on the slope. On the way back I bumped into one of my schoolmates. 'Are you sick?' she asked me. 'How come you've not been coming to class?'

'Coming to class?' My voice was husky and raw.

'Yes, class.' Normally she wouldn't give me the time of day, and must have thought I was really sick to talk to me all of a sudden like this.

'Aren't you going to take the college-entrance exams?'

I just looked at her blankly. I'd forgotten all about the exams. She smiled and revealed a mouthful of crooked teeth. Then, as if it had just occurred to her, the smile disappeared and she said, 'Then you must not know that the history teacher is dead.'

'What did you say?' I was nearly shouting.

Startled by my reaction, she said, 'Don't take it so hard. He committed suicide.'

<h1 style="text-align:center">2</h1>

I threw down my basket and took off towards school.

Those were the most bizarre days of my life. So much had happened, in such rapid succession, that I was in a fog most of the time, my reasoning power dulled. The history teacher was already fading from my consciousness, even though only a few days had passed; my frenzied obsession with him of such a short time ago seemed to be nothing but a prurient dream. At that moment, the image of the history teacher choking the life out of himself suddenly materialized, bringing an immediate end to my self-pitying melancholy, and throwing me into confusion.

I headed towards school, but not to get any confirmation of the news. I believed that what my schoolmate said was true, and as I thought back to all that the history teacher had said to me, I should have guessed that this would have happened sooner or later. He had been wanting to take his own life for a long time.

He took a rope into the kitchen, not wanting his daughter to see him when she awoke from her nap, since a hanging corpse is a fright to behold: tongue lolling out of a twisted mouth, eyes rolled back into the head, an erect penis, the contents of the bladder and bowels emptied. He didn't want her tender heart to be scarred by what she saw. He pushed open the kitchen door, calmly tossed the fateful rope over a low beam, climbed on to a stool, and tied a noose in the rope. Then he pulled it taut, stuck his neck into the noose, and kicked the stool out from under him. With a jerk, he hung suspended in the air.

At that moment his body twitched violently and his legs began to jerk and flail. His fingers dug into the noose, but that was an involuntary movement. The rope swayed slightly from the weight of his body, the beam creaked briefly, and his hands fell to his sides as he turned limp and still, for ever.

I saw it all, how still you were, and not a word of explanation to anyone. Not to me, of course, since I meant little to you. In a world that brought you no end of disasters, I was an ordinary student who passed briefly through your life and counted for nothing.

That's right, counted for nothing. You didn't even want to see me one last time. But even if you had come to see me in my muddled state of mind, in shock over suddenly discovering the secret of my birth, I wouldn't have been any help to you. I'd have wanted to wait until I'd recovered from the shock, knowing that I'd see you soon, in class at least.

Recalling the time we spent together, I must have overlooked the moment when our eyes met and our spirits fused, when I could reach out and establish a true bond between us. If there had been such a moment, I'd have been in a much calmer mood now.

I admit it, I'm to blame, too. If only I'd thought of you more, I might have been able to save you; at the very least, I could have consoled you a bit before you died. But I didn't have time for you.

On the other hand, what good would it have done to meet again? What I wanted from you was compassion, a healing caress, and what you wanted from me was physical stimulation to ease your suffering. You didn't need love, at least not the burdensome love I offered you. It was you who said you were a bastard. You led me on from the very beginning, tricked me into having sex with you, because all you ever wanted was some easily obtained carnal gratification from your student.

You and I are selfish people who never loved each other; as in that family of mine, it was now everyone for himself.

I stopped in the doorway of that familiar office. The desks were as cluttered as they'd always been with newspapers and students' exercise books. There should have been teachers at their desks at that hour, and class monitors handing in exercise books; but the office was deserted, even though the hallways and stairs creaked from time to time.

I went up to the history teacher's desk; even without the teaglass, exercise books, textbooks, chalk box, and other odds and ends, it was still the same desk. His chair was as clean and neat as it had been when he was alive. I sat down in it.

His desk drawer was unlocked. Nothing but some blank sheets of paper. No pens or textbooks, just some neatly stacked paper, which I leafed through. There were none of his poetic writings, and certainly no letter for me. It took a special person to leave this world without a word to anyone. Apparently, he'd cleaned out his drawer beforehand.

I recalled something he'd said when he was justifying his concern for politics: 'Newspapers are the bridges to my inner thoughts.' So if I wanted to understand why he committed suicide, maybe newspapers offered the clue. Later I did go to the library, where I discovered that, in the days before he killed himself, newspapers were reporting large-scale suppression campaigns in places like Suzhou and Shanghai against 'individuals involved in beating, smashing, and looting during the Cultural Revolution'. Death penalties had been handed down for Organizers of Armed Violence. Way back on 5 September, *People's Daily* had carried a speech by the Chief Justice of the Supreme Court, calling for swift punishment of Cultural Revolution Murderers, Arsonists, Rapists, and Looters. Then in early October, newspapers around the country ran stories and editorials arguing that the four modernizations could be achieved only in the context of socialist democracy, with a sound legal system; that is, a nation governed by the rule of law.

The goal was to govern, of course, and any law would do.

Under this barrage of propaganda, his resolve to hang on crumbled. Was it the fear of prison or a guilty conscience that did him in? Had disillusionment claimed him, or was it something more profound? I didn't know, and didn't have any way of finding out. He, on the other hand, was now beyond worrying about this or anything.

I despised him. He'd tricked me, cheated me. Why grieve over a selfish man who thought he'd seen through society, life and history, then had chosen the stupidest method possible to resist their pressures? His knowledge and experience had helped explain the problems I faced, but had not provided the strength for him to endure what he faced.

But maybe I was being unfair to his memory. He and his family had been targeted by the Communist Party for so many years that they were scarcely able to breathe. Perhaps, after all, only his activities as a Rebel during the Cultural Revolution presented an opportunity to control his own destiny, yet that had led to disastrous consequences and even greater despair. The deaths of his younger brother and his mother, that is, the deadening realization that he had destroyed his family and himself, was a trick of fate that proved to be more than he could bear.

I thought back to the time we were talking about Yu Luoke, the young man who was executed because he had dared to speak the truth, and he had rudely stopped me in mid-conversation. His eyes appeared bright, but fear was hidden in them. At the time, I didn't think I deserved to be yelled at that way, and nursed a grievance over it.

He was morbidly pessimistic where his fate was concerned, but unfortunately, that sort of morbidity appealed to me. From there it was just a short step to interpreting the commiseration of a fellow pessimist as love, thus creating a pure and uplifting emotion to deliver me from the vulgar hopelessness of my slum environment. For a few precious days I thought I'd succeeded, but now I knew I'd failed miserably.

I felt as if I had become both people sitting across the desk from one another. I was talking, and I was listening, adding a comment from time to time to encourage the other me to keep talking. The office was frightening as hell when no one was talking; at those times a millennial dusk seemed to settle upon this lonely world.

His thermos was on the floor in its usual spot beside his desk. The clamour of students leaving class filtered in through the window, while a spirited game of basketball was underway outside, with players running around in pursuit of the elusive ball. Life went on as always, one day on the heels of the other, and no one sensed that anything was missing just because a particular person was gone; in fact, another history teacher had already taken over his classes. It was as if I were the only one who felt a depletion of life, even though the sky was still blue, the trees as green as ever.

He wanted to leave, and he chose the way he went. So be it. He had the right to determine his ultimate fate, didn't he?

I nodded to myself, and in that instant, a sound rose slowly from my heart, as if it were being plucked like strings on a harp; it was the music that had played on his gramophone that day when we made love in his bungalow.

Out beyond the window, the river flowed on and on; dappled rays of sunshine lay across my naked body. With his face pressed against my breast, he sucked on my nipple, biting it gently, the pain crying out for more. My eyes were filled with shame and desire, as if I were begging him not to stop, not to let go. He laid his hand between my thighs and once again his burning finger probed that wet, hot, starved spot; in a matter of seconds, my vagina opened for him.

Our two bodies formed a single entity, and even if we'd been surrounded by an audience of reproachful people, I wouldn't have wanted him to withdraw from me. I'd forgotten the name of the musical piece, but its sad beauty allowed me to see the twin peaks of joy and despair that rose above the wasteland of this world.

By then it occurred to me that he hadn't left a note, not

only out of concern for how it would affect me and my reputation, but also because he knew that he wasn't all that important to me, nor I to him, and that if I'd once been madly in love with him, it was his duty to set me straight with a silent farewell.

That evening I went alone to the riverbank, where I tore up every diary entry that hinted at him, and tossed them into the river, to be swallowed up and swept away.

Popular local belief has it that the souls of the hanged become evil ghosts, much like hungry ghosts, and are denied transmigration, reincarnation, and entry into Paradise; it is also believed that all waterways lead to the underworld. And so he was a sufferer in life and would remain a sufferer in the afterlife; but if the river indeed flowed to the underworld, carrying to him these pages that he'd never read, would he say again 'You'll understand one day'?

3

Within half a month, a man who had left my life long ago suddenly returned and another who had made a brief appearance departed, as if my life were a lawn for them to cross at will.

It was at this moment that I made up my mind to leave home.

I knew I suffered from escapism, the disease of weaklings, but as I gazed at the clutter of compounds halfway up the mountain, and the slow spread of lamps being lit, I knew that only by escaping could I ever find peace.

The ferry was tied up on the opposite bank, reluctant to head this way. I huddled in an inconspicuous corner as the crowd of people waiting for the ferry swelled, not knowing where I was going, how I'd get by, or, for that matter, what I was searching for. My only goal was to get away.

In my backpack were some books and a few changes of clothes. I kept telling myself that I had to concentrate only on getting to the other side of the river, a thought that had a calming effect. I overheard a couple next to me talking.

'Have you heard? A couple of labour-reform inmates tried to escape.'

'It wouldn't be the first time. But before these two could get very far, they were chased into the cadre-family living quarters, where they picked up a firewood axe and turned it on people to make good their escape.'

'That's not what happened. They went there to kill the warden, and even used the axe on his children.'

'Were they caught?' a bystander asked.

'What do you think? Their skull-pots were smashed before they knew what hit them.'

'Maybe the wardens will start treating the inmates a little better.'

'They can't back off now. If anything, they should tighten the screws even more. "Treating the enemy with leniency means cruelty to the people." ' A political slogan flowed naturally from the man's mouth.

The mooring hawsers were secured to the iron bollards and a sailor blew his whistle. As soon as the arriving passengers had disembarked, we boarded the ferry. The couple grabbed a seat without missing a beat in their conversation, but now their voices were drowned out by the sound of the engine.

We rocked from side to side as the murky waves from a passing steamship hit the sides of our boat and sent screeching passengers jumping away from water that washed over the deck. I stood at the railing, since the cabin was already crowded, and more people kept squeezing in. It should have been the low-water season, but the river was swollen, engulfing the muddy banks up to the foot of the mountain. Water was spilling over the stone steps I'd taken down to the pontoon quay, and the river didn't appear to be receding at all; people commented that they'd never seen it so wild before. The stilts supporting squat houses along the riverbank were partially submerged.

The anchor was raised, the sailor blew his whistle again just before jumping on to the fantail and hauling in the hawsers.

Once the ferry was clear of the pontoon, it turned 180 degrees and headed for the opposite bank, its light illuminating the surface as we sliced through the water like scissors, leaving a white wake; water beyond the circle of light undulated in the murky darkness.

4

Mother always said that three was my lucky number. In the Sichuan dialect, the words for 'three' and 'hill' sound the same. I was born in the year of the tiger, so living near mountains brings me good luck; but once a tiger is out on the plains it is at the mercy of its enemies. Mother also said that fortune-tellers were unanimous in proclaiming my 'eight natal numbers' to be unpropitious, too loaded down with the Yin element, and that I was in for hard times if I moved away from the mountains. Maybe she was just trying to scare me, who knows.

But I've always liked the number three and its multiples. I'm convinced there's an arcane connection between me and this number. Three sixes are eighteen – as in my eighteenth birthday – which is an obvious code, but one I've been unable to decipher.

Which brings me back to the same old question: why, when I was a girl of three, had Mother chosen Manjusri to be my guardian bodhisattva? Could she have known that I would suffer not only over a need to know things, but by the inability to deliver myself from that which I learned?

Mother knew me better than any person alive, and might have been worried.

That first night I slept on a bench in the crowded steamship waiting room at Heaven's Gate, using my backpack as a pillow. Passengers weighted down with luggage walked past as I curled up; the dreams started as soon as I closed my eyes: the river was frozen solid, so I started walking. But when I reached mid-river, the ice began to melt and crack noisily. There wasn't another soul anywhere in that sea of white. Then the bodies of drowned dogs and cats began floating to the surface, and I hurriedly opened my eyes to get out of the scene. I wasn't worried that the bodies of people drowned in the river over the years would start to appear, but fearful that my family would track me down.

It was already very late. If they hadn't noticed my absence today, they'd surely discover it tomorrow or the next day. How would they take it? Mother would curse me up one side and down the other. Her disappointment would be greater than anyone else's. Father, who seldom showed his emotions, would feel that I'd hurt them in some unpardonable way, and that he had raised me in vain. Fourth Sister and Dehua would gloat over how our parents had fed and clothed a heartless little brat like me and over the fact that they'd no longer have to share the attic with anyone, no longer be denied the right to live like man and wife. Who knows, maybe their screwed-up marriage might actually take a turn for the better, as I left them with the space they badly needed. Third Brother, the eldest son and self-proclaimed head of the household, would rant and rave, accusing me of betraying my own family, then he'd take everything of mine out and throw it into the river; he might even go to find my natural father and demand my return. My natural father, the person who had to share responsibility for my birth, and whom I had no intention of ever seeing again. My demand that he promise to stop following me had already bruised his fatherly pride, and now he couldn't follow me even if he wanted to.

Go on, you people, raise all the hell you want. See if I care.

Maybe my small-mindedness was keeping me from thinking good thoughts about any of them. But whether they rejoiced or grieved over my departure, before long they'd be used to not having me around.

Enough, I said to myself. Stop worrying about them. It's time to start looking for a roof over my head. Around nightfall, as I was passing by the recycling station on my way to the ferry landing at Alley Cat Stream, I spotted the nymphomaniac standing on the stone bridge. Even in the dark, I could see she was naked from the waist up, exposing her breasts without a thought for the people around her. Her face was as filthy as her hands and arms, but her eyes weren't cloudy, like most crazies. Gusts of wind off the river billowed her long baggy trousers. Wasn't she cold? On impulse, I walked up closer to say something. But she just bared her teeth and giggled at me.

I didn't laugh back. I wasn't in a laughing mood.

Unable to sleep on the bench, I sat up and looked around.

The floor was littered with scraps of paper and gobs of phlegm, the benches and other available spots occupied by out-of-town refugees who begged on the streets by day and slept here by night. A beggar whose snot-streaked, slobber-covered grey beard was as long as his matted hair stood in the doorway. 'Help a poor man out, I beg you,' he was saying. Though he was probably in his forties, he called all the men uncle and all the women auntie, and even fell to his knees to grovel at their feet.

The sight of that beggar gave me the shivers. Was I looking at my own future? Suddenly I was afraid. But that soon passed. I'll survive, I assured myself. I'd go with anyone, man or woman, who wanted me, for I had learned the art of seduction. That may not have been something to be proud of, but I had to admit it took courage.

If he or she treated me well, that would be my good fortune. If not, well, tough luck. It's not as if I hadn't had my share of tough luck already. All that counted was that I'd left my hillside home on the other bank and severed ties with my past. The way I looked at it, no price was too steep for a new life.

My head felt as if it would explode from so much mental gymnastics, sending it flying right off my shoulders. So I concentrated on a fly buzzing around me, and in no time, my mind turned blank. A moment later, I slumped over on the bench, fast asleep.

EIGHTEEN

1

The weather turned cold as autumn deepened with each passing day, and my health deteriorated. Long used to sleeping badly, now I was also bothered by a poor appetite and frequent nausea. The mere sight of greasy food at roadside stalls made me dizzy and sick to my stomach. I didn't feel like eating even when I was hungry, since I had so much trouble keeping food down. About all I could manage was half a steamed bun with lots of plain water. In two months I was skin and bones.

Knowing I needed help if I was going to survive, I went to see a doctor, an old man who felt my pulse, then gave me a half-hearted check-up and asked when I'd had my last period. His white smock flashed before my eyes. I just shook my head.

'How long?' His face underwent an immediate change; now he was looking at me with contempt in his eyes; his white-topped head was tilted back so far it seemed ready to snap off.

I lowered my head and counted backwards. More than a month. No, that's not right, it's been over two months. 'About two months,' I sputtered. The thought had never crossed my mind. I was nervous and I was frightened. Sweat beaded my forehead.

'You're only eighteen?' he asked as he read my card, shaking his head. He was about to write something, but had second thoughts. He put down his pen and uttered the fateful word.

How I made it out of that examining room I'll never know. After walking through the gate and down a few steps, I stood motionless by the side of the road. 'Pre-marital pregnancy!' I'd learned in school, even as a little girl, that this was the most shameless sin of all, scarier than death itself, and I seriously considered jumping headlong in front of an approaching bus. A car pulled up in front of the clinic to deliver a patient, and I didn't move. I didn't recognize myself in the reflection of the window, so I walked up to get a better look in the mirror: my face had a pale-grey cast, my hair was a mess and considerably thinner than before, and my sunken eyes seemed too big for my face. I don't know if it was a symptom of my pregnancy or something else, but there were spots on my cheeks. Only old people were supposed to have those. I couldn't bear to look any more, so I turned away.

No, I couldn't die, I must live on. I had no right to end my life now, not after surviving everything the world had thrown at me up to this point. Besides, I'd just begun to form an idea of what kind of life I wanted to lead from now on.

I'd been with the history teacher only once, and I was pregnant. One time was all it took for me to be with child.

That must have been how it was when Mother got pregnant with me. Sleep with a man once and you're pregnant. That's how it was with the Triadman, and how it was with my father. Apparently I'd inherited her phenomenal fertility, but was it really a genetic thing, or was it common to poor women everywhere, a natural compensation for their impoverished existence? Are hungry women naturally endowed with hungry wombs? Mother's first thought was of abortion, but she hadn't carried it through.

What was I thinking? I wanted to get rid of this child?

Just putting it into words like that gave me a scare. It was his child, maybe a son, I hoped so, one that would look just like him, an ordinary appearance, nothing special, but without the neurotic temperament of an artist, someone uninterested in being a poet or a painter. The last thing in the world I wanted

251

was for him to be contaminated by his father's karma. Better he grow up as a very ordinary man; the more ordinary he was, the more likely he'd live a satisfying, happy life.

But here I was, a woman lacking even the most basic qualifications for survival, let alone security and happiness; how could I guarantee the health and well-being of the child in my belly?

Who was I trying to kid? If I was ever to break out of the cycle of poverty, I had to single-mindedly remove every burden that might hold me back. But if I decided to go ahead and have the child, I'd need to find it a convenient father, start a family in a hurry and try my best to make ends meet; of course, all my plans and hard work to break free would have gone for naught. My life would be ruined, and all because of this child.

Not only that, it would be another fatherless child, and all the love in the world wouldn't make his life any less fragmented. Society would be as cruel to him as it has been to me, so I could predict his future simply by looking at my own life. And there'd come a day when I'd have to tell him about his father, including our relationship, without his having to ask. When that day arrived, he would hate the world and all the people in it, just as I did. What had this child done to deserve a life of suffering that had been too much for me to endure?

Once I'd made up my mind, I suddenly understood that what I'd sought from the history teacher all along was neither a lover nor a husband, but the father I'd been denied all my life, a father as close as a lover, yet old enough to comfort and console me, intelligent enough to give me direction, and close enough to share my most intimate emotions, to treasure me, and to take pity on me sometimes. That's why the difference in our ages had never been an issue. Boys my age simply never interested me.

But all three of them had let me down. My natural father had paid dearly for my sake, yet had brought me nothing but shame. The father who raised me had done so with care and determination, in spite of the humiliation he suffered, but had never tried to get close to my heart. And the history teacher had failed to provide a deeper understanding of my life than I could have provided, and had simply left me, treating our relationship as an eminently forgettable affair.

This world, which had provided me with no true fathers, was incapable of putting forth a single plausible reason to bring this child into its realm. It would be far kinder to rescue him from the miseries that lay ahead before he even took his first breath.

2

I rose early the next morning and registered as an outpatient at the Municipal Gynaecological Hospital. The cobblestone road leading off the main street curved its way up the steep slope to the hospital; it was little more than a tiny lane, lined with food stalls and fruit stands on both sides, so narrow that motorbikes and stretchers vied with pedestrians for passage.

A light rain began to fall, which brought out the hand-kerchiefs and newspapers for head covers and sent people scurrying for shelter when the drizzle turned into a down-pour. But some people, unperturbed by the rain, strolled down the street as if nothing were wrong. Jostled by the crowd of women in the queue, I held my registration card and gazed out beyond the gate, where rain clouds had turned the street dark and gloomy. Proprietors of food stalls had lit flickering candles; the heat rising from a stove cast a blurry light on the people's faces.

I walked up to a desk alongside the wall and began filling in my registration card with a ballpoint pen secured with a string. I made up a name on the spot, and, of course, didn't dare enter my real age of eighteen. If any eighteen year old was seeking an abortion, either the family or the neighbourhood monitor would be notified, and the man responsible for getting her pregnant would be sent to jail for statutory rape. No, I had to say I was twenty-five, which didn't matter, since my face was haggard enough for a ghost, let alone a girl of marriageable age. Any sign of youth had long since vanished from my eyes.

The address and work unit were both false. In fact, the entire card was a pack of lies; the only thing real was me, that and the foetus in my belly.

After I sat down on a bench outside the examining room, I saw how prudent my caution in filling out the form had been. Lucky for me I'd gone to see that old doctor of Chinese medicine; I'd learned a lesson from that humiliating experience that served me well now.

A curtain – once white, but now a dirty grey with age – hung in front of the consultation-room door, which was thrown open. Women streamed in and out through the curtain, while their menfolk sat on waiting-room benches or paced up and down the hallway, puffing on cigarettes. Each time the curtain was drawn back, those of us in the waiting room could, if we wanted to, get a good look at the consultation room. Three examining tables were in continuous use by women who lay on their backs, naked from the waist down, their legs spread open; there were no screens to block our view, probably because they got in the way.

I blushed bright red at the sight, and forced myself to stare at my knees as I fidgeted on the bench.

It was nearly eleven o'clock when my turn came. A doctor who looked as if she was in her forties peeled off her surgical gloves and tossed them into the trash bin next to one of the examining tables. She asked what I was there for, to which I answered matter-of-factly that I hadn't had my period for more than two months and thought I might be pregnant. She told me to take off my pants. After a quick look, she said I was probably pregnant, but couldn't say for sure without a urine test.

'Can the procedure be done today?' I asked her.

'Sure.' She wrote something on my chart and said impatiently, 'Come back after you finish in the lab.'

I knew that if I asked another question, she'd give me hell.

I returned to the consultation room after paying the fee and receiving the results of my test, where I was given approval to have the procedure that afternoon, to my great relief. I'd barely stepped into the waiting room when a young woman in a perm jumped off the bench and confronted me. 'Did they ask for a certificate?' she asked.

'No.'

'Lucky girl. You look innocent enough, and that bitch of a doctor must have been in a good mood.' Her eyebrows had been pencilled in, I noticed. Pretty girls like her, who used make-up, were in for a rough time here. She said she had to produce a certificate of 'permission' from her work unit or a wedding certificate every time, and it was getting harder and harder to find a work unit willing to give her the permission slip she needed. She said her boyfriend refused to use a condom, and she'd already had three abortions.

After the talkative young woman finally left, I stood by the wall trying to look as if I were waiting for someone, but actually studying family-planning posters on birth control and sexually transmitted diseases. I was no longer the bashful little girl looking at illustrations in *Human Anatomy*.

The rain had stopped, but the sky was still dark and overcast. Three couples were ahead of me when I got to the surgery, which was in a separate, two-storey building; these women all had their men along with them. A wooden sign at the entrance of the corridor said 'Male Comrades Not Allowed', but it was a stricture more honoured in the breach than in the observance. I took a seat as far away from the others as possible, but could feel their eyes on me, as if I were some kind of freak. It hadn't occurred to me that men were required at this stage in the process. A couple of minutes later, a young moon-faced girl in short hair walked in, accompanied by a slightly older girl who handed the permission slip to the nurse on duty, a trainee no more than eighteen or nineteen, but old enough to have learned how to be rude. When the moon-faced girl asked how long before it was her turn, the nurse narrowed her eyes and bellowed, 'Get over there and sit down! This is a fine time to be worried. Why weren't you worried when you got yourself knocked up?' Having another woman along hadn't helped her a bit.

What about me? What would I say if she asked why I didn't bring a man with me? Other women could drag some male relative along with them and get away with it, but not me. I decided to say I'd been sent here for some training, and had to leave my husband behind. Actually, no one cared whether you wanted your child or not; for the sake of population reduction, the more abortions the better. But at the same time, they couldn't afford to give up time-honoured moral standards, and had to humiliate publicly sex outside of marriage. That way they made sure you understood that you were taking advantage of government policy and be-smirching Chinese-style Communist morality.

A scream like that of a slaughtered pig tore into the room. You'd have thought they were butchering people alive in there, and I was so scared I nearly wet my pants. It was all I could do to keep from running.

'First comes the pleasure, then the pain, so stop shouting!' This was the standard belittling comment you heard.

'If you want to cry, do it on your man's shoulder. Spoiled little tramps like you make me sick!'

That was the doctor talking as she scraped the foetus from the womb: no anaesthetics and no pain-killers. The men waiting outside were bundles of nerves; love suddenly lost all its poetic qualities. When the tear-streaked woman stumbled out of the operating room, her man ran up to steady her. That single gesture brought all the happiness a man could supply to a woman. Several weeping women were on the benches in the arms of their men.

My palms were sweaty. Maybe, I thought, there was a better way to die than this. But just then a nurse came to the door and called out, 'Yang Ling.'

No one answered. She tried again, and this time I realized that was the name I'd given myself that morning. I jumped to my feet. 'Are you deaf? This way,' she said as I followed her into the room, where she told me to take off my shoes and slip into some sandals that were behind the door. They were old and suspiciously dirty, and I paused for a moment before doing as she said.

A woman lay on her stomach on a bench alongside the wall to the left; she'd just come off the operating table, and was naked from the waist down. Two women – nurses or doctors, it was impossible to tell – were sitting at a desk filling in medical charts and jotting down the fees received for hospital sanitary pads, which they said were cleaner and safer than those sold on the outside.

'Take off your trousers and lie down on that table!' the woman counting the money said to me sharply.

I shivered as I took off my trousers, but when it came to my underpants, my fingers turned numb and I couldn't get them off. 'Be quick about it, and don't pull that bashful act in here!' I removed my underpants and looked at the woman, who didn't even deign to look my way.

After lying down on the operating table, I sensed how large the room was. The paint was peeling off the ceiling and walls; it had obviously been a long time since they were last painted. Three windows, like those in the high school, were cracked, and there were no curtains to block the view from the hospital grounds, which were devoid of trees. Not a sliver of sky was visible to me, not even the dark clouds. A fluorescent light hanging from the ceiling in the middle of the room was so bright it hurt my eyes. There were two operating tables in the room; the other one wasn't being used at the time. The paint on both was also peeling, creating rust spots here and there. The hospital was reported to have been built in the 1930s,

257

during the war with Japan, so it must have served several generations of women already.

'Ever had one of these before?' a doctor in a surgical mask asked as she sat down on a stool and dumped an armful of instruments wrapped in grey cloth on my stomach. The cloth was the same dirty-grey colour as a piece she laid across my lower torso.

'No,' I said.

'Open your legs wider, as far as they'll go.'

Every one of her impatient commands increased my anxieties and fears as I lay there staring at the ceiling and clutching the sides of the cold table. She opened the cloth bundle that lay on my stomach, raising a clatter as the instruments banged against each other. I didn't have the courage to look at all those forceps, scalpels and surgical scissors. The thought suddenly struck me that it wasn't too late to climb down from the operating table, that I could still keep the child, no matter what it cost me down the line; I wanted this child, just as I had wanted its father that day, and I would give myself to him, body and soul, the way I'd given myself to his father. Tears wet the hair on my temples. The doctor shifted her position, and from where I lay I could see a shallow white enamel pan under a table in which lay several bloody hunks of flesh shaped like pigs' kidneys. So that's where my child would end up. Now was the time to hop down from the table and get out of that room. There was still time. Holding on to this child would be the same as holding on to his father, the same as bringing his father back to life. But just as my legs moved, something cold and sharp was rammed up my vagina, and a piercing scream tore from my body. My hair was wet with tears. After the scream died out, I clenched my teeth and held on to the table with all my might.

Mother once told me that, when she was on the verge of collapsing under the weight of stones she was carrying, she would recite Chairman Mao's exhortation, 'Be resolute and fear no sacrifice, we remove all obstacles and achieve final victory.' If that didn't work, she sought protection from the Buddha. One way or the other, she'd tough it out. But I'd never got used to invoking Chairman Mao and was unversed in the ways of Buddha, so all I could do was clench my teeth even tighter and hold on to the table for dear life. The doctor, who didn't even have a nurse to help her, tossed the used instruments into a basket, then took something else from the cloth bundle on my stomach and stuck it inside me, drilling it up into my womb. Pain, swelling, and paralysis all mixed together made it feel as if all my organs were being ripped from my body, chopped into tiny pieces, then crammed back into me; no amount of howling and shrieking could make this tearing of flesh go away.

Once this became clear to me, I didn't scream any more. My teeth seemed fused together, but not another sound escaped from my throat. The fluorescent light above me kept shrinking, until it was only a tiny, swirling dot that came crashing down on me like a white-hot ball, finally turning the room into total darkness.

The next time I opened my eyes, the doctor was standing in front of me. She had taken off her surgical mask, and I could see that she was quite pretty. She had a mole on her chin and was probably no more than thirty or so. When she took off her surgical gown, she was probably somebody's loving wife and mother. She said nothing, and I couldn't tell what she was thinking. My skin was wet and clammy from head to toe and I'd bitten my lip. My hands, free of the table, were still clenched into fists. The room felt cold, with draughts chilling me from all sides.

I slid down off the table and slipped into the sandals. I couldn't bear to look at the child whose life I had just taken, and was struck by a premonition that I would never have children, not even if I could. No other child could mean as much to me as this one, who had lived inside me a mere two months. A child born to a woman like me must suffer more than its mother and face extreme hardships as he grew up.

Walking very slowly, and without anyone's help, I managed to make my way over to the bench, where I lay down and curled up, holding my hands over my private parts.

A nurse went to the door and shouted for the next patient, adding for the benefit of all the women who were waiting, 'This one over here didn't shout and scream. The rest of you could learn a thing or two from her.'

'Probably a mental case,' said an older nurse who was sitting at the desk. 'Go on, tell her to hurry up and get dressed. If she wants to pretend she's dying, she can do it outside.'

'Let her lie there until I fill out the form. She can leave then.'

After a short while, maybe three or four minutes, I sensed that I was holding a sheet of paper in my hand, so I forced myself to sit up on the bench and read it. 'Depth of uterus: 10. Chorion: Positive. Loss of blood: Abundant. Foetus: Positive.' That's as far as I got before I ripped it to shreds. Staring straight ahead, I got up, sending the torn pieces of paper fluttering to the floor. I didn't say a word as I put on my pants and my socks, changed into my cloth shoes, and, without waiting to see their reaction to my behaviour, walked slowly out of the operating room, supporting myself against the wall.

3

With warm water flowing through my hair and down to the soles of my feet, I ran the bar of soap all over my body, looking up from time to time at the water-level indicator to see how much remained. Each woman in the public bath was assigned a stall behind a wooden half-length door and an overhead cement ledge where clothes were put to keep them dry.

Owing, I suppose, to their unique constitution, Chinese women require a month of post-partum recuperation, a period of time spent almost entirely in bed, where they are served a highly nutritious diet. A miscarriage, natural or induced, is treated much the same: the woman wraps her head or wears a hat for a month, for a draught can lead to migraines later on. During this month, she brushes her teeth and rinses her mouth with warm water, and eats nothing raw or cold, to avoid the onset of tooth and gum problems. If she moves heavy objects, she'll likely suffer from backaches and sore limbs. She must wait a full month before taking a bath.

But I couldn't afford to abide by those rules, and within a few days I was out on the street, heading straight for the public baths.

It was the first time in my life I'd spent money to take a shower, and it was as satisfying to me as having nutritious food served to me every day by a loved one. I couldn't find the words to describe my peace of mind as the water ran down my body, which looked beautiful to me, even though I was skin and bones. I hadn't touched myself for a long time, especially my belly, which never had a chance to swell outwards, and now that there was nothing in there, I was gripped by the sense of its emptiness.

They said that the men bathed in a large communal pool. Women were assigned one of the twenty shower stalls. The attendant, a fat woman in a T-shirt and shorts, tramped up and down the slippery, steamy corridor in her galoshes. If she caught someone taking too long, she ordered her to step outside to get dressed, since there was always a long line of women waiting their turn. Bathers were not permitted to adjust the water temperature; that was her job. The bathers' legs, some nicely shaped, some not, were exposed beneath the wooden doors.

During those days, I ran over to the public baths any time I had the money and stood in the queue with a change of clothes. The water running over my body seemed to wash away all the bad memories and carry them down the drain all the way to the Yangtze.

4

The following summer, on impulse, I decided to take the college entrance exams. I wasn't prepared, but what the hell. I couldn't help but fail, and only answered about half of the questions on the last two papers. It was hopeless; my blood lines had ensured that I'd never set foot in a college class-room.

After failing the college exam, I was accepted into a vocational school for a two-year programme for the training of assistant accountants, which, in China, was only slightly better paid than blue-collar labour. The school was in a small town north of the Jialing River. Should I go or not? Now that I'd tasted freedom, I didn't like the idea of tying myself down to a 'vocation', but after two years of schooling, I'd have a job with a monthly salary of thirty yuan and, for the moment at least, a bit of security.

I went ahead and registered, two weeks after school had started.

The two years passed quickly. Once, just before Chinese New Year, I received a letter from home. Inside there was some money for fares. Mother included a note, the first letter she'd ever written to me: 'Little Six, come home for New Year.' That's all it said, and even then, the handwriting was atrocious and 'home' was miswritten. I kept the money, but didn't go home and didn't answer her letter.

After graduation, I received a job assignment. I shared a room with two other girls, where I slept on a narrow cot. I spent as much time away from work as possible, taking temporary assignments or leave to run errands; finally, I applied for sick leave to go home and regain my health. Then I took off and roamed the country, travelling alone to the north, where I went as far as Shenyang and Dandong, near the Korean border, and to the south, visiting Hainan Island and Guangxi, all the way to the border with Vietnam. I followed the Yangtze east, stopping at each city along the way, going where my feet carried me and roaming, as a way of life.

Second Sister and I corresponded infrequently. In one letter she wrote that Dehua was dead. After awakening one night with abdominal pains and a high fever, he'd been taken to South Bank Hospital, where he was operated on for appendicitis. But when they opened him up, they found he was suffering from advanced peritonitis, and the surgery sealed his doom. He died in agony.

I dreaded getting letters from Second Sister, since they never contained anything but bad news. She told me that Big Sister had moved back to the city, where she was living with the tall fellow I'd seen her with. Before returning, she and her husband had got into a terrible fight that had led to knife play. Her daughter, frightened nearly out of her wits, tried to stop the fight and received a cut in the face for her troubles. After crying piteously for days over this, Big Sister had a nervous breakdown. Then her husband took her to court, accusing her of causing the disturbance that had led to his accidentally disfiguring their daughter. She was taken into custody and spent two months in a detention centre. By the time she got out, she was back to her old self. Third Brother had a baby daughter; Fifth Brother had married a country girl.

'Auntie Zhang died two days ago, thanks to her bullying husband,' Second Sister wrote. 'You remember her, don't you? That former prostitute.'

Of course I remembered her. Second Sister never asked what I was doing, and seldom mentioned Mother or Father. She didn't need to. I didn't want to know anything about them when I was awake, but in my dreams I was always going back to Compound Six, to that house on the narrow lane in Alley Cat Stream.

The threshold connecting the hall with the courtyard had probably rotted away by now. The courtyard was blanketed with moss, while laundry still hung under the eaves on both sides to dry. The overcast sky was visible from the courtyard, but the roof over the large kitchen had collapsed, leaving two gaping holes above the stoves and the smoke-blackened niche that had once housed the stone Kitchen God. All the stoves, now under a pile of broken tiles and bricks and cement, were useless. The good thing was that the compound now had running water, so there was no longer any need to fetch water with buckets. Nearly all the neighbours looked new and different. Anyone who could manage it had moved out. Those who couldn't stayed put, watching their children grow to adulthood, get married and have children of their own. The original inhabitants and those poor souls who weren't allotted better accommodation still numbered thirteen families.

My family began cooking on a brazier in the hall. Baldy Cheng, who lived directly opposite us, was watering the soil in a clay pot as he sat there chanting and emanating his *qi* energy to the few shoots of garlic inside. He told Father that flowers would bloom on the garlic, which would bring him longevity.

There were still two beds in the attic, but the curtain between them was gone. One of the beds was covered by a grass mat and didn't appear to be in use. On the other bed, which was covered by a clean sheet, Father had spread out his medicine bottles and his transistor radio. He preferred peace and quiet over the bustle of a noisy compound, so it was only natural for him to move into the attic. A teacup rested on the little table, which had been moved up next to the bed. There were no tobacco leaves anywhere in sight. Had Father given up the habit after smoking for decades?

Fourth Sister had remarried and moved in with her in-laws. Her new husband was also a construction worker.

The doors of all the houses on the side lanes of Alley Cat Stream remained open during the daytime, and whenever someone had guests, neighbours would crowd around the door to enjoy the break in their daily routine. The only reason people closed their door was to keep the gossipy neighbours from seeing that they had something good to eat for a change; when the meal was over, the door was opened.

On rainy days, wooden tubs and buckets were moved into the courtyard to catch the rainwater, which would be used for laundry, to clean furniture, and, finally, to wash dirty smelly shoes and rubber sandals. Running water was still expensive.

The river was the same, so were the boats, the rolling hills and the people, whose pale faces had a mildewy cast. A new generation of labourers took over from the old, and life didn't change one bit.

I heard a voice inside me say: You must turn your back on all that. I spent my days with my face buried in books, all kinds of books, or writing poems and stories; I sent the decent ones off to be published, supporting myself on the little money they earned, and put the 'improper' ones away where no one else could read them. Most of what I wrote wasn't worth saving, and I just threw it away.

For a while I indulged myself in cheap cigarettes and poor-quality drink. In the mid-1980s, underground poets and novelists began showing up in cities all over the south, staying in one place for a while then moving on. I hung out with them, trying anything that was new, from writing styles to lifestyles. I carried condoms in my purse or my trouser pocket. Even if I didn't use them, by keeping them with me, I felt the presence of sex wherever I went. In my eyes, love was nothing but a mirage, marriage and child-bearing a joke. I was determined not to take the road most other women take. I guzzled alcohol as if it were water, and even though I was seldom intoxicated, I often pretended to be drunk out of my mind as I methodically drank others, sometimes a whole tableful of men, under the table.

I met most of my girlfriends at slow-dance parties, where we would cut each other's hair in outrageous styles not permitted in hairdressers' shops. We dressed simply, like the boys, and in the summer often wore skirts without anything underneath, going from one party to the next, at the homes of friends as well as people we'd never met. We'd bolt the door, close the curtains, and turn out the lights, for convenience, and safety as well. I was lucky I was never arrested. The police turned up from time to time, but only a few people were ever caught and taken in. Most of us escaped out of windows or back doors. And before long, we'd run into this or that person in some other city anyway.

Western pop music was all the rage in China's underground avant-garde scene of the 1980s. We'd choose a dance partner, throw our arms around him, and sway to the rhythms of some country song, losing sight of time and breaking free for the moment from our cares and outside pressures. At moments like that, I could even fantasize that happiness was in my grasp at last.

Then a disco song would take over, and I'd shove my partner away to writhe and squirm to the music with such violence that I'd nearly stamp holes in the floor with the heels of my shoes; it was almost as if the key to continuing my vagrant lifestyle were dancing up a frenzy until I wore myself out. My face quickly lost its youthful colour and lustre, and while my fleeting pleasures could make me laugh, I couldn't shed a tear for anyone, not even myself.

One night I drank more than I'd ever drunk before. The alcohol seemed to burn through my insides. Feeling closed in by the small, crowded room – the music wasn't bad, but the smoky air was beginning to get to me – I elbowed my way through the crowd of entwined dancing couples and went outside, followed by one of my girlfriends, who was concerned about my condition.

Under the dim lights the deserted street was a mess. I wanted to be alone, for I was disgusted by people, myself included. I ran off and ditched my girlfriend.

As I was walking down a lane, a nightsoil cart passed nearby, followed by the crisp bells of a water-spraying truck. I'd only walked down a couple of steps, supporting myself against a wall, when I suddenly began retching violently.

Drink came gushing out of my mouth, carrying with it sour bits of food. When the vomiting finally stopped and I could catch my breath, I took a piece of paper out of my pocket to wipe my mouth. But I saw it was a mimeographed poem from an underground magazine:

> Before the disaster struck, we all were children,
> Only later did we learn how to speak about it –
> the clamour gasping, like fish bones in the throat.
>
> The knocker trembles at our hammerings,
> we are searching the rubble for those lost ears,
> and howling our thanks, with no one left to hear.
>
> Only after it passed did we feel the terror:
> From wounds that did not bleed, lines emerge
> for yet another scene of escape, acted out
>
> under flashing lights. If we knew how we survived,
> by what chance, we would stop shouting, and return
> willingly to that moment when the disaster struck.

I still had the dry heaves, but was feeling much better. The poem seemed to have been written just for me, for all the times I'd managed to escape from disaster. I saw that the poet was someone named Zhao, and I wondered if maybe fate would somehow bring us together, if I would meet him, or someone like him, who had the capacity to understand what was in my heart. I could become a devoted friend to someone like that, maybe even fall in love with him; the flame of love would have a second chance to burn in my heart. And then again, maybe my own writing could eventually satisfy the hunger that had existed in my heart since the day I was born.

NINETEEN

1

I'd been away for years, and now that it was time to travel even further, I decided to go home for a visit; it was the beginning of 1989.

My nerves held up fine until I'd nearly reached the gate of Compound Six. What sort of reception was I going to get? Father was sitting by a small stove in the hall, bundled up in several coats and jackets and keeping his hands warm by tucking them into his sleeves. He was facing the front door, and even though by then he couldn't see a thing, he sensed my presence. I said: Papa. He smiled.

Mother came out of our room. Her back stooped more than ever, she had aged considerably since I last saw her. 'What did you come home for? I'm surprised you even remembered you had a home.' Her words grated on my ears, but the look on her face told me she was not just surprised to see me, but happy as well.

I laid down my canvas suitcase and took a look around. Everything was just as I had imagined it, including my parents, except older and more decrepit; nothing new or unusual, and no sense of warmth. I'd only come home to put a full stop on the chapter of my life at the place where I'd spent most of it. To what degree that included my parents I didn't know.

I'd stay only till the day after tomorrow or, possibly, tomorrow.

It was pitch black outside by the time dinner was over. Looking out the window, no matter how I craned my neck, it was too dark to see even the outline of the bare malus tree. When I undressed and went to bed, Mother was bowing reverentially to a Buddhist icon on top of the five-drawer bureau and chanting softly. No bigger than a water mug, the porcelain statue stood in front of a little incense burner. A more devout believer than ever, Mother had invited the Buddha into the house.

She climbed into bed and lay so close to me that I instinctively moved away from her. She pulled the quilt over to cover herself. A wooden plank set up above the bed, next to the wall, was piled high with summer clothes and several cloth-wrapped bundles. Not much of a bed, if you ask me, since you could easily bang your head if you weren't careful. 'Isn't there room in the trunks under the bed or in the bureau to put all that stuff?' I just had to ask.

'That shows how little you know,' she said. 'I wrapped those things up so I could get out of here in a hurry.'

Before I had a chance to ask why she'd have to get out in the first place, she told me she was prepared in case a fire broke out. First she'd lead Father outside, then come back for the bundles.

She's only sixty-two, I said to myself as I listened to her laboured breathing, but her mind seems much older.

My eyelids were getting heavy. How strange, I thought, to feel so sleepy here at home, when I normally couldn't sleep at all without sleeping pills.

Mother turned off the lamp. She said she hadn't received this month's pension. A number of shipyards were unable to pay their workers, and retired workers were lucky if they got half their pension. She'd gone there several times, despite the cold weather, but returned empty-handed. At the shipyard gate, several hundred pensioners staged a sit-down strike, but it was so cold she was worried it might affect her weak heart, so she didn't join. The strikers demanded their pensions or they'd stage a sit-down strike at Heaven's Gate Dock itself.

'They're all getting on in years, and it wouldn't take many days in this weather before they'd be at death's door.' Mother seemed to be mumbling to herself in the dark. 'Just going to the market at Stonebridge wears me out these days.'

I knew exactly what this was all about. 'I'm sleepy,' I said. 'I'll give you some money tomorrow.'

Mother appeared to have more to say, but she held back. I knew that her talk was a not-so-subtle reminder that I had a responsibility to take care of my family. Not a word about my life, no questions about what I was doing. As always, she didn't give a damn about me. But what would I tell her if she did ask? If she knew that her youngest daughter made a living from writing poetry and fiction, she'd neither believe it nor be able to understand it. I was fast approaching twenty-seven, but she didn't ask if I had a man in my life, let alone if I was getting married. She probably knew she was better off not asking this particular daughter anything about her life.

2

I woke up the next morning with the pungent smell of cheap incense in my nostrils – prayers to the Buddha. White smoke curled up out of the incense burner. Father, an early riser, groped his way downstairs and stopped in front of me. Out of breath, he was holding a bowl of dark-coloured medicine. He couldn't see me, but he knew I was standing in the doorway.

Mother returned from the market, taking some turnips, a few ounces of pork, and a bunch of onions out of her basket and laying them on the bamboo table just this side of our door. I went over to help her peel the onions and handed her some money. She counted it carefully, then handed back two of the bills. I took them without a protest. I told her I'd send more when I had it.

'At least one rooster in this brood knows how to crow,' she said. 'I always knew you'd be the filial one in this family.'

'I'm leaving first thing tomorrow morning,' I said, bringing her up short.

The smile on her face vanished. 'If you'd told me last night, I'd have bought more food this morning,' she said. 'Why didn't you say so earlier?'

Father picked up the fan lying beside the stove and began fanning the fire inside. Mother went over and grabbed it out of his hand. 'There's nothing wrong with that fire, what are you doing? Having a blind old fool around just makes my life harder!'

Angry with me, she was taking it out on Father. It felt good being grown-up, if for no other reason than Mother could no longer blow up at me any time she felt like it.

The atmosphere in the house was stultifying all that afternoon and early evening. Fifth Brother came home at dinnertime. He'd lost a lot of weight and looked about half his original size. All he said when he saw me was, 'Ah, you're back.' Even he had become little more than a stranger, and it could only be worse with my other brothers and sisters. My decision to leave the next day was the right one. I couldn't wait for the sun to go down and bring this day to an end.

Mother washed her feet, but didn't come to bed. The wall clock said twelve o'clock, the entire compound was asleep, and she was still rummaging through the trunks and the bureau looking for something. Whatever it was, she couldn't find it, and I figured her memory was just about gone.

Seeing how worried she seemed as I lay under the covers, I said, 'Maybe what you're looking for is in one of the bundles over my head.' With an exasperated slap of her own forehead, she climbed on to the bed and took down one of the bundles.

Too reluctant and too sleepy to look at her, I closed my eyes.

But I opened them again when she called to me, and I saw she was holding a harmonica in a blue baby's cap. I'd seen them both before. She handed them to me. 'You'll never see him again.' There was an indefinably gloating lilt to her voice when she said that, as if she knew she'd hit me where it hurt.

'How come?' I knew who she was talking about.

'He died of lung cancer. He asked to see you and me once more before he died, so his senile old mother went looking for Second Sister. She finally found her, but Second Sister never told me. Even if she had, you weren't here.' Mother was very sure of herself. 'And even if you had been, you wouldn't have gone.'

'I wasn't here,' I mumbled. Three years earlier, on the 20th of April 1986, when my natural father breathed his last, where was I, his twenty-four-year-old daughter? Probably hanging out with friends, drinking and laughing and throwing myself into the arms of some guy who thought he was in love with me, who knows? I couldn't recall, although something seemed to be pounding inside my head. I sat up and said drily, 'I'd have gone if he was dying.'

I couldn't see her face, though it was very close, but I had the feeling she was sneering. Then her hand reached up to touch her face. She wasn't crying, was she?

Second Sister hadn't mentioned this in any of her letters, and I knew she'd never say anything to me about it. My natural father's mother, my grandmother, had come looking for Mother because her son wanted to see me before he died. She'd been told, 'I don't want you in my house, and don't go looking for my little sister. She wants nothing to do with you.'

Second Sister would have guarded this secret the same way she'd guarded the other one: every month for all those years, the eighteen yuan for child support had been sent to her.

Later on, after Mother learned that my father had died, she had no unpleasant words for Second Sister, for, laden with guilt, she had taken the humble role in front of her other children, keeping the heartache and grief to herself.

She told me she'd experienced a strange feeling, and for several nights in a row had dreamed that my natural father was weeping like a baby and scolding her for not coming to see him. He'd never been like this in her dreams before, and she knew then that he was gone.

No hospital would admit him, since his lung cancer was in the final stages, and the plastics factory where he worked couldn't afford to pay his medical expenses. His family carried him on a stretcher from one hospital to another, until finally a small rural clinic with a few beds was generous enough to let him die there. His wife stayed at his side for a while, but it was too much for her. She didn't even accompany him to the crematorium, probably because she knew the position she occupied in his heart.

'He died with your and my names on his lips, and he begged his mother to come looking for us.' Mother paused for a moment, then told me he'd always denied himself good food, even something as small as an egg, and this had played a role in his sickness, since his constitution was frail and he worked with asbestos. My grandmother had grasped Mother's hand and wept. 'He was only forty-nine years old when he died,' she'd said, 'while a grey-haired old woman like me goes on living. Where's the justice in that?'

3

Maybe that was when Mother invited the Buddha into the house. She and Father began sleeping separately, and it's possible that she woke up every night crying. But she started taking better care of Father, who was ten years older than she. First thing every morning she went up to the attic to take care of his chamber pot and make him a cup of tea. She threw away his pipe to get him to stop smoking, because of his bronchitis. When he was sick, she took his meals up to the attic and fed him, then slept next to him to keep an eye on him, in case he choked on phlegm. She wanted to leave this world after Father, even if there was no one to take care of her, because if she died first and left him alone in his blindness, how would be survive?

She didn't love Father, but she cared for him in ways she'd never cared for my natural father. There was no one to whom she could reveal her loneliness and what was in her heart, no one except the Buddha. She had no one at all to talk to. Even now her voice was so low I could barely hear her. Father may have been blind, but his hearing was keen enough to hear Mother's voice through the thin boarding; she figured she'd hurt him enough for one life already.

I shivered when the icy harmonica touched my skin, which had finally warmed up inside the quilt. Am I too callous? Cold-blooded even? I reached out to pick up the little dark-blue cap, with its satiny cover and felt lining, both of which had been gnawed on by mice or moths. I closed my eyes and tried to imagine the scene back when my natural father took this cap out of his pocket and put it on my head. 'She'll catch cold in this gusty wind,' he'd said to Mother. We met for the first and only time when I was eighteen, and scenes of how he ingratiated himself, trying to win me over, returned.

At the time I hadn't paid much attention to what he said to me while we stood together on the city's highest point, in Loquat Park, but now I remembered how he enunciated every word.

He said: You aren't to divulge your background to anyone, especially the man you marry. He and his parents would hold you in contempt if you did, and you'd suffer enormously from then on.

He said he'd seen people take advantage of me when he was following me, and hated himself for not being able to come to my aid.

You should forgive me for not fulfilling my obligations as a father, he said. Forgive me and your mother. Treat her better, at least for the suffering she endured because of you.

Now that I think back, it was a magnificent night, with fireworks exploding all around. At the time I thought it was some sort of holiday, and I wondered what this city had to celebrate. By my calculations, I realized now that it must have been National Day. What could have been going on in my life at the time that could make me forget something like National Day? Just to make sure, I went to the library and found out that the Twenty-Third of the Eighth Month, that year, by the lunar calendar, the day my mother and natural father noted as my birthday, had indeed fallen on the 1st of October, the thirty-first anniversary of the founding of the People's Republic. That night, in the Great Hall of the People, the nation's leaders hosted a grand banquet for visiting dignitaries that included Cambodia's Prince Norodom Sihanouk and his wife, and Comrade Hoang Van Hoan, the exiled head of the pro-China faction of the Vietnamese Communist Party. It was still like the imperial court receiving homage from its vassal states.

I flipped backwards through the bound newspaper volumes. The paper, yellowed by age, tended to disintegrate under my trembling fingers as I approached 21 September 1962, the day of my birth. It was a Friday, the Twenty-Third Day of the Eighth Lunar Month, the year of the tiger. The major headline of the day involved nationwide demonstrations in condemnation of the aggression by the American Imperialists, and a celebration over the shooting down of a US U-2 spy plane in the service of Chiang Kai-shek. Chairman Mao personally received the Air Force heroes. There were other panegyrics as well: an improved strain of tobacco had been developed in Yunnan; Jiangxi Province reported a bumper harvest in tobacco; my own Sichuan Province provided more than 25,000 draught oxen to areas where there were shortages; the mid-season crop of rice in Guangxi exceeded all predictions; and so on. In fact, the news kept getting better, the lives of the people richer, the closer I came to the years of famine. Newspapers like this were invaluable. The best way to understand your own country and its history is to look back through its newspapers.

It was getting light outside; the cigarette factory blew off a howling load of steam. I couldn't sleep, so I got out of bed. Mother took a neatly folded blue floral jacket from one of the cloth bundles. 'Try it on,' she said. It was the fabric my natural father had bought for me nine years earlier. Mother had turned it into a jacket to wear over a padded coat.

I stood by the bed and put it on, carefully doing it up, one cloth button at a time, Mother watching my every move. At that moment, if she'd said, 'Stay a few more days, Little Six,' I'd have changed my plans. But she didn't, and I was more determined than ever to leave that morning.

I told Mother to get back in bed. When she did as I said, I lay down beside her in my clothes, then turned out the light.

Her eyes were closed, her breathing deep and rhythmic, but I knew she wasn't asleep.

At cockcrow, blasts from ships' horns came from the river into homes halfway up the hill, sounding like someone at a voice rehearsal, singing something over and over until they got it right. I got out of bed and put on my shoes. 'Little Six,' Mother said softly, 'I've always known this isn't where you want to be, that you're not one of us. Leave if you want to. I won't try to stop you, I owe you too much. I'll rest easy if some day you stop blaming me for everything.' She took something wrapped in a handkerchief out from under the pillow and handed it to me.

There was a wad of currency inside, all small notes, some new, some crumpled, and some dirty. 'That's five hundred yuan he secretly saved up over the years. Just before he died, he told your grandmother to make sure you got this for your dowry.' She saw me frown. 'Take it!' she said tersely, apparently not wanting to hear any explanation of why I didn't plan to get married. She wouldn't have listened even if I'd tried.

The morning fog swallowed up tier upon tier of Chongqing's hillside houses.

Suitcase in hand, I walked down to the river's edge, where the fog suddenly cleared, as if to allow me to board the ferry to the other side, where I climbed the stone steps all the way to Heaven's Gate Dock, Mother's first glimpse of the city after sailing downriver from her village home forty-six years earlier. Now the river was silent, as if muted.

So after I'd reached adulthood, and he was no longer required to send eighteen yuan every month for child support, even after he'd seen me fly out of his life, he'd still put money aside for me every month. Denied the opportunity to shadow me, he must have felt incredibly empty. I was the centre of his emotional life right up till the day he died. And me? I couldn't even bring myself to call him Father. Despising such senti-mentality, I'd tossed him aside without a second thought, unwilling even to turn back for one last look.

All of a sudden, tears filled my eyes; I tried to force them back, but they flowed unchecked, and I was racked with such pain that I fell against the wall and slumped to the stone steps.

4

In February 1989, I took a train to Beijing to study at the Lu Xun Literature Academy for Writers. In March, a number of small and some not-so-small gatherings were held on uni-versity campuses; students were debating the direction China should take now that 'socialism' in this country had been proven unbearably hypocritical. In April, Beijing students took to the streets to protest against corruption by national leaders and their children, and to demand democracy and freedom of speech. Slogans and songs rose and fell amid banners and placards; excited crowds filled the streets.

I joined the demonstrators as they laid wreaths in honour of a recently deceased leader of the reform faction of the Communist Party.

My thoughts drifted back to when I left Chongqing. I'd made a special trip to visit my natural father's grave, located on a remote weed-covered slope. His ashes were buried under a pile of rocks. No marker, just a little mound on a lonely mountainside amid dry pumpkin vines and cornstalks, near a gully planted with potatoes and sorghum.

By all appearances, his village wife and children had wanted to forget him too. All that time he'd squirrelled away eighteen yuan every month for his illegitimate daughter. Who wouldn't begrudge the loss of that much money? His heart had never belonged to that family, even though he'd worked hard to fulfil his obligations as husband and father.

Would my two half-brothers ever ask about their older sister? Very likely we'd never meet, not for as long as I lived.

The wide highway and both footpaths were wall-to-wall with people; even the trees and tops of walls were crowded. The demonstration made its way across the overpass and proceeded along Chang'an Avenue, where it was joined by university professors, journalists, and newspaper editors. One of their banners read 'We Shall Lie No More'. To me it was the most meaningful slogan in the entire demonstration.

All those people, voices in unison, with a clear blue sky over Tian'anmen Square, a sanctified place I'd dreamed of even as a little girl, with millions of people fervently devoting themselves to the struggle for the right to speak the truth and to respect the value of all human beings. They demanded a change in the cyclical repetition of fate for generation upon generation of sufferers. The marchers entered Tian'anmen Square. My heart beat faster when the stirring strains of 'The Internationale' filled the air.

I saw a little girl beside the Yangtze River in that mountain city of south China, running as fast as she could through the gloomy rain. That was me at five. I was thinking as I ran that, even though I didn't know exactly where I was, as long as I kept following the river downstream, sooner or later I'd find the shipyard where Mother worked as a porter. I'd tell her that Fifth Brother had been run over by a cable car and beg her to hurry back home to save him. The rain was falling more heavily, turning the riverbank into a muddy swamp. I tripped and fell into the mud, clambered back to my feet, and started running again.

Just then the sound of a harmonica, alien yet familiar, came on the air from across the wave-swept river, and it was as clear as when I first heard it inside Mother's womb. A smile spread across my water-drenched face.

Acknowledgements

Toby Eady, you have made me appear in myself and in my writing and treat my old self as a new friend
Irene Andreae, you stand by me whenever I am in need
Alexandra Pringle, Victoria Hobbs and Jessica Woolard, for showing me what patience looks like
Yindi, you let me go home in my mother's language
Henry Zhao, because of you, the black of my wound has finally faded
Hua, Ming, Jiang and Lin, you protected me and consoled me when the Massacre struck on Tian'anmen Square, we can now look back together in puzzlement at how we survived
I owe you what I am.